Praise for *Entrepreneurial Leader*

"'Visionary, articulate and always *pro bono publico*' describe Bill Donaldson, who made a perfect partner for me. He also knew when to be cautious. 'Dick, let's sleep on this' was one of his favorite sayings. He was usually right! Bill deservedly will be remembered as the father of public ownership for Wall Street firms, which led to incredible growth for the industry. I especially recommend this book to Millennials who want to be entrepreneurs."

—Richard Jenrette (1929-2018), former Chairman and CEO, The Equitable, and Cofounder, Donaldson, Lufkin & Jenrette

"The term *change agent* may be used too often, but it is a true description of Bill Donaldson's professional life. The new model investment bank DLJ shook up Wall Street; tradition-encrusted Yale University got a pioneering new management school; and a new chairman returned the SEC to its non-partisan roots. Quite a life story!"

—Paul A. Volcker, Chairman of the Volcker Alliance and former Chairman of the Federal Reserve Board of Governors

"Bill Donaldson has been a gifted leader in the diverse fields of finance, academia, and government. I've followed his career with admiration and benefitted personally from his pioneering work as founding dean of the Yale School of Management, where I earned my own management degree."

—Indra K. Nooyi, Chairman and CEO, PepsiCo

"Bill Donaldson's life is an example of what is great in America—he was a military volunteer, a person supremely well-educated at Yale and Harvard, an entrepreneur, a government servant, the founder of a major management school, a chairman and CEO of the New York Stock Exchange, and a businessman. The range of his life, and the lessons he learned, make a fascinating book."

—Stephen A. Schwarzman, Chairman, CEO, and Founder, Blackstone

"When health insurance giant Aetna was failing, his fellow directors turned to Bill Donaldson. He stepped up and created a vision for one of the greatest turnarounds in business. Bill's story and his insights are good reading."

—John W. Rowe MD, Richmond Professor of Health Policy,
Columbia University, and former CEO, Aetna

"Bill Donaldson has been an inspirational leader in the public and private sectors alike. Possessed of a quiet strength and an uncommon humility, he has consistently led by example, with equal doses of smarts and guts. When the SEC was listing in the wake of the Enron collapse, he readily agreed to take the helm and proceeded to right the ship as adroitly and as quickly as anyone could have, in his typical roll-up-your-sleeves, no-nonsense fashion. I'm so pleased Bill is sharing his story and his leadership insights in this book. Would that our country had more leaders like Bill Donaldson."

—Stephen M. Cutler, Partner, Simpson Thacher & Bartlett LLP,
and former Director of Enforcement, SEC

"Bill Donaldson's achievements are breathtaking. We encountered him as students at the Yale School of Management when he was the founding dean, and he has been a tremendous inspiration to us and so many others. Bill's life embodies the power of great leadership to transcend and transform."

—Roger Brown, President, Berklee College of Music; and Linda Mason,
Chairman and Founder, Bright Horizons Family Solutions

A Lifetime *of* Adventures
in Business, Education *and* Government

ENTREPRENEURIAL LEADER

WILLIAM H. DONALDSON

with

KARL WEBER

GREENLEAF
BOOK GROUP PRESS

Published by Greenleaf Book Group Press
Austin, Texas
www.gbgpress.com

Distributed by Greenleaf Book Group

For ordering information or special discounts for bulk purchases, please contact Greenleaf Book Group at PO Box 91869, Austin, TX 78709, 512.891.6100.

Design and composition by Greenleaf Book Group
Cover design by Greenleaf Book Group
Cover author photograph by Tony Rinaldo Photography

Publisher's Cataloging-in-Publication data is available.

Print ISBN: 978-1-62634-576-8

eBook ISBN: 978-1-62634-577-5

Part of the Tree Neutral® program, which offsets the number of trees consumed in the production and printing of this book by taking proactive steps, such as planting trees in direct proportion to the number of trees used: www.treeneutral.com

Printed in the United States of America on acid-free paper

18 19 20 21 22 23   10 9 8 7 6 5 4 3 2 1

First Edition

With gratitude and love, this book is dedicated to:

My wife Jane   *My very "best darling"*

My children Kim, Matt, and Adam   *The lights of my life*

My grandchildren Lars, Willy, and Henrik   *The next gen*

CONTENTS

Preface

An autobiography or a memoir should be the easiest of art forms to produce. After all, what could be simpler or more interesting than writing about yourself? Most serious-minded people, however, do not want to create something boring, unrevealing, or self-important. Successful people do not want a chronicle of their lives to be a flop. So the pressure is on to be compelling and enlightening about people, events, and self while being fair, honest, and at least somewhat discreet.

I suppose most people who've lived an eventful life ultimately find themselves looking backward, reflecting on the momentous changes they've witnessed, the memorable people they've encountered, and the challenges they've confronted—and they begin to think about what difference it has made.

That has finally happened to me—perhaps a bit later in my case than in many others, simply because I have remained professionally active into my mid-eighties, so that it's only recently that I've begun to ponder it all. It has been an enjoyable and varied life, one that has afforded me a range of exciting opportunities in all three sectors of our economy—corporate, government, and nonprofit. Glancing back on the story gave me the impetus to write this book.

But I didn't want to write a book simply to record what happened. Still less did I want to settle old scores, grind some personal political ax, or burnish my own reputation. Instead, my goal is to offer some insights into the lessons of my life and work—insights that others active in the intersecting worlds of business, education, and government and their impact on the larger society might find interesting and useful.

I've become convinced that entrepreneurial leadership, and the management methods, structures, and incentives that go along with it, are profoundly relevant to the success of every sort of organization. Consequently, I find I have tried to apply the concept of entrepreneurial leadership to every major challenge in my professional life. As a result, I've often experienced significant success, while occasionally suffering failure, frustration, even heartbreak, when I either failed to live up to the mission or, in a few cases, pushed up against the limits of what entrepreneurial leadership can do.

It all began in 1959, when, with a pair of talented friends and partners named Dan Lufkin and Dick Jenrette, I helped launch the first major new Wall Street investment firm in decades—Donaldson, Lufkin & Jenrette (DLJ)—which revolutionized the profession of investment research, grew into one of the most respected firms in finance and the place where it seemed most everyone in the industry wanted to work, and then defied the rules of the New York Stock Exchange to become the first company of its kind to become a listed public company on that exchange.

Pursuing a lifelong ambition, I then took a leap into public service, joining Henry Kissinger's State Department as an undersecretary of state. After that, I served as transition advisor to New York Governor-elect Hugh Carey and later as a special assistant and counsel to Vice President Nelson Rockefeller.

In 1975, I became the founding dean and a tenured professor at the new Yale School of Management, helping to launch an innovative professional school that addressed the complex management needs of a world in which business, government, and the nonprofit sector are intimately entwined. I tested the waters for a gubernatorial candidacy in New York before deciding, as the filing deadline loomed, that the inevitable fundraising and stump speeches part of politics wasn't for me.

I served as chairman and chief executive of the New York Stock Exchange, shepherding that venerable institution through one of the most tumultuous times in its history, and sought to prepare it for a new era of global competition among marketplaces.

At an age when many men and women are decreasing their professional involvements, I was asked to spearhead a turnaround at Aetna, the giant insurance company, which was facing significant business and management turmoil. As CEO, I helped reorganize the business and recruited an outstanding team to transform Aetna from an industry laggard into one of the nation's most respected companies.

And then, when the financial world suffered a massive loss of public confidence in the wake of the Enron and WorldCom scandals, President George W. Bush asked me, at the age of 72, to take over as chairman of the SEC, the national agency charged with investor protection and regulation of the securities markets. Assisted by a group of remarkable colleagues, including a key senior leadership team recruited externally, I helped to reform the agency and restore a sense of integrity to the financial industry—battling political opponents and self-serving industry insiders all the way.

As you can imagine, it all amounts to a stimulating series of adventures—most of them gratifying and successful, a few of them frustrating setbacks—with more than a handful of dramatic episodes and a cast of characters that includes many of our era's most notable leaders, from the era of Dwight D. Eisenhower to that of Barack Obama. I suppose this is why friends, family, and colleagues have long been urging me to tell the whole story in a book—which has emerged as the volume you hold in your hands.

It has been gratifying, as I have worked on gathering the threads of my experience and recounting the story as fully as possible, to have the opportunity to reflect on my own motivations and to examine the origins of my deep-seated instinct to tackle all manner of professional and personal challenges.

I've been thinking about the part that entrepreneurial leadership has played in my life for a long time. Back in 1975, while serving as dean at the new graduate school of management at Yale University, I had the opportunity to teach a class in entrepreneurial leadership. I recently dug out my old class outline and was pleasantly surprised to find that much of it remains topical and relevant today. I invited a number of notable entrepreneurial leaders to address the students, from Fred Smith, the founder of Federal Express, to Robert McNamara, the Ford Motor Company president who went on to head the Department of Defense and the World Bank. Along with the students, I learned a great deal from the observations and experiences of these leaders.

This book is based on the main concepts I presented to those students, updated for today's audiences and illustrated with stories and experiences from my own life and work as well as from the careers of leaders I've known and admired. I'll describe both the successes and the failures I've experienced— because I've learned that both success and failure can be deeply revealing of a person's character and of important truths about the world and about the challenges of leadership.

Having lived through my share of ups and downs in a career of more than sixty years, today I'm more certain than ever that entrepreneurial leadership as I envision it is the key to the potential revitalization of the institutions and organizations of our great nation. Perhaps some of the observations I'll share in this book can help stimulate the quest for such revitalization. At the same time, I hope to offer some insight and inspiration both to current leaders and to a rising generation of young people who are searching for ways to apply their own entrepreneurial instincts to the profound challenges of today. If my book finds its way into their hands—and perhaps motivates a few of these leaders of tomorrow to strike out in new and exciting ways, launching the prosperity-building businesses, the world-transforming nonprofits, and the innovative public initiatives that will help to revitalize our society—I'll consider it truly successful.

William H. Donaldson
New York City
October 2018

CHAPTER I

Earthquake on Wall Street: When DLJ Went Public

It was late afternoon on May 20, 1969, when Dan Lufkin, Dick Jenrette, and I met to sign off on the papers that we and our advisors had just completed. It was a momentous occasion for us. After months of plotting among the three of us, our underwriters, and several teams of lawyers, these papers would begin the process of enabling our hoped-for initial public offering (IPO) of equity in Donaldson, Lufkin & Jenrette (DLJ), the investment firm we'd jointly founded some ten years earlier.

Going public is a big event in the life of any corporation. The IPOs of famous businesses like Google and Facebook garner headlines around the world, create the financial basis for future growth, and excite millions with the possibility of untold wealth to be gained from owning part of a great, growing enterprise. But this IPO was no ordinary story of business success. Launching it would be a controversial decision that flew in the face of practices that had lasted generations.

DLJ was a member firm of the New York Stock Exchange (NYSE)—and such firms were forbidden by the rules of the

Exchange to access public equity capital through a stock offering. Technically, the rules stated that the Exchange's board of
governors had to approve any new partner or shareholder in
a member firm. But this in effect meant that public ownership
was impossible—after all, how could the board of governors
rule on the eligibility and appropriateness of, say, ten thousand
individuals buying shares of a member company?

This rule reflected the long-standing culture of Wall Street.
Many felt the NYSE had long been run as a kind of private
club, with a strict though unwritten code of conduct that was
even more important than the written rules. And because
the Exchange was viewed as having a sacred public trust as
gatekeepers of the world of high finance, the leaders of the
Exchange believed it was their responsibility to ensure that
dishonest operators were kept as far away as possible. History
shows, of course, that the powers that be had often failed in
this responsibility. Scams and deceptions have been a part of
stock market lore and legend for as long as the market itself
has existed.

Still, the members of the board of governors took their role
as gatekeepers seriously. And they believed that keeping member firms privately owned was the best way—perhaps the *only*
way—to prevent criminals and other unscrupulous types from
taking over the firms and owning seats on the Exchange.

Admittedly, there were also some more self-serving motives
behind the long-standing rule against public ownership of
Exchange member firms. There was the fear that some of the
big financial institutions, who were major customers of the
stock exchange member firms, would buy seats on the Exchange
if they could and therefore would no longer need the services
of long-standing member firms to buy and sell shares of stock
for them. Combine this sort of self-protective instinct (what
my partner Dick Jenrette called, with a smile, the Exchange's

"enlightened protectionism") with the high-minded rationale that you are "guarding the integrity of the markets," and you have a powerful combination of reasons for the Exchange to cling to its rule against its members going public.

But by 1969, there were plenty of signs that the rule was on its last legs. And now the three of us—the young innovators who'd founded DLJ with the avowed intention of shaking up the old ways of Wall Street—were poised to knock it down.

Why now? And why us? There were many reasons.

The most compelling reason was the spreading atmosphere of fear and even chaos on Wall Street. During the previous year, there had been extreme volatility in the U.S. equity markets compounded by record-breaking volume on the NYSE. The trading frenzy that resulted had led to something called "the paperwork crisis"—an expression that seems almost incomprehensible from today's vantage point, in a world where vast quantities of financial information are stored and shared via pixels that span the globe in nanoseconds. In the late 1960s, back offices charged with processing trades had become so backlogged that the Exchange had actually been forced to close for a number of hours each week to allow the documentation to catch up with the volume of transactions. Partly as a result of these problems, the prolonged bull market of the 1960s had turned bearish, and dozens of brokerage firms actually shut their doors as investors fled the market.

What did the paperwork crisis have to do with our going public? The problems plaguing financial firms, remarkably enough, were fundamentally due to lack of capital. Nearly all the firms on Wall Street at that time were partnerships; their ownership was split up among the leading employees, and most of that equity was divided and distributed at the end of every year—"cutting up the melon," as the saying goes. (Only a few of the most far-seeing partnerships—Goldman Sachs, for example—would retain a slice of the capital every year for investment.) This meant that most Wall Street firms simply didn't have the cash they needed to modernize and automate their processing systems—or, if they did, the partners who controlled the capital didn't care to invest it in that way. Underinvestment by the NYSE and its member firms led directly to the paperwork crisis—and demonstrated the fact that Wall Street was desperately short of capital. One big reason was lack of access to the public equity markets—the markets that channeled capital from investors to the great industrial firms of the day, from General Motors and Procter & Gamble to Westinghouse and IBM.

The paperwork crisis wasn't the only sign that Wall Street's way of financing itself was hopelessly outdated. Another was the rise of the so-called block placement business. This was the practice of asking investment firms to buy and hold large amounts of stock that an institutional client wanted to sell, but which the market couldn't profitably absorb all at once. Buying and holding, say, a million shares of stock pending the arrival of favorable market conditions took a lot of capital, far more than could be mustered by a traditional Wall Street partnership, where capital was effectively liquidated by distribution among the partners at the end of every year.

For a speech I delivered back in 1969, as the shortage of capital on Wall Street became more and more acute, I pulled together a couple of statistics that illustrated the nature of the capital crisis. First, I compared the growth in capital of the hundred biggest stock exchange member firms to the growth in stock transactions by the country's major institutional investors—pension funds, insurance funds, mutual funds, and endowments—which themselves were undergoing explosive growth. I noted that, over the previous ten years, the volume of transactions had grown 2.5 times as fast as the capital possessed by the biggest Wall Street firms.

In other words, the business was growing much faster than the companies that were supposed to conduct that business. No wonder those companies weren't keeping up!

Second, I calculated the average age of the owners of that Wall Street capital. The data revealed that about 60 percent of the capital on Wall Street was owned by partners or officers over 60 years of age—and 75 percent was owned by people over 55 years of age.

It didn't take a genius to note that older people weren't likely to want to invest a lot of their capital in the long-term growth needs of their firms. These men (and at the time they were virtually all men) were thinking about retirement, not about building businesses for the coming decades.

Statistics like these made it clear why there was a desperate capital shortage on Wall Street. The problem was, in part, a generational one. And that's why the three of us running DLJ were determined to do something about it. Dick Jenrette, Dan Lufkin, and I represented a new wave on Wall Street. I was just 38 years old at the time, and Dick and Dan were close to me in age. We sensed it was time to act—to put the financial industry on a sound footing for the final years of the twentieth century—even if that meant challenging some rules and shaking up the status quo.

We weren't the first people to point out that Wall Street needed access to more capital. Back in 1964, a commission had studied the issue on behalf of the Exchange and reached similar conclusions—but nothing had been done. (Blame the traditional Wall Street culture and the conservative practices of those who ran the Exchange.) Now it was time to force the issue. Shattering the rules of the stock exchange by going public wouldn't be the first time DLJ had flown against convention. In fact, DLJ was widely recognized on Wall Street as a firm that had repeatedly questioned the status quo.

When we'd opened our doors back in 1959—three guys in our late twenties supported by funds we'd raised from a bunch of college friends and others willing to take a flier on us—we'd been the first new firm founded on Wall Street in decades. We proceeded to revolutionize the field of investment research by developing detailed, in-depth analysis in the form of lengthy reports on companies we believed in, based on extensive shoe-leather reporting, customer and supplier interviews, and other investigative techniques like those an independent consulting firm might employ rather than merely reprinting financial statements provided by the firms themselves. We were among the first to direct investor attention away from the "Nifty Fifty" giant firms that had dominated the world of investing in the 1950s and toward the often smaller, innovative companies that would fuel economic growth in the decade of the 1960s and beyond.

DLJ pioneered in recognizing and servicing the rapidly expanding world of institutional investors—pension funds, college endowments, insurance companies, and others who were desperate for innovative but soundly researched ideas about where to invest their increasingly vast financial holdings. And we instituted managerial methods that were unusual in those days, especially for Wall Street: recruiting new employees not just by seeking people with business and financial experience, but also by seeking out the brightest young graduates from the leading business schools the way the greatest industrial corporations did; basing a team member's annual compensation on 360-degree feedback from clients, supervisors, peers, colleagues, and direct reports rather than on cronyism or favoritism; giving women prominent and responsible positions in research and investment management; and even making "having fun" one of our published corporate goals.

So we at DLJ were comfortable playing the role of iconoclasts. We'd been doing it for a decade.

We also had our own, specific reasons for wanting to pursue a public share offering. We needed capital to enhance our ability to strengthen our brokerage execution operations as well as to invest in new businesses. We were great believers in diversification. We'd already moved from our original perch as an investment research firm and brokerage house into such allied fields as investment management, private equity investments, real estate, and venture capital, all building on our expertise at in-depth analysis. We'd even bought the famous Lou Harris polling firm as a way of bolstering our research capabilities. Now we had still other plans for diversification—but they all required capital.

Going public was something I'd long believed in. In fact, a decade earlier, when Dick, Dan, and I had launched the firm, I'd predicted that someday we'd want to become a publicly traded firm, and that eventually this would be the norm on Wall Street. After all, financial firms like ours made money recommending and selling shares of other businesses and touting the virtues of a public market for corporate ownership; why would we believe in the value of public ownership for everyone *except* ourselves? Our belief in public ownership and our quiet assumption that someday we would follow this path was one of the reasons we'd always published an annual report about our operations, results, and business strategies, even when we were privately held and therefore were not required to do so by any rule or regulation. Issuing this report was a way of expanding the public reach of our ideas and our activities. It also was one of the factors shaping our business strategy: We always sought to manage the firm with an emphasis on increasing its overall long-term value rather than on paying high salaries or bonuses to the top executives (including the three founders).

DLJ, in a sense, had always thought and behaved like our image of a well-run public company. Now we were finally ready to make that image a reality.

* * *

The decision process and the complicated preparations for the move had been under way for over a year, with all the deliberation and debate among our small leadership group that might be expected in contemplation of such a precedent-shattering decision.

We picked First Boston as our underwriter. This was a prominent investment bank that was a top-flight underwriter of new securities. What's more, First Boston was itself publicly traded, and therefore, under the existing rules, could not be a member of the NYSE. The folks at First Boston would have loved to get a seat on the Exchange themselves, and so they were sympathetic to our quest. Together we selected the prominent law firm of Sullivan & Cromwell to represent us. All three firms worked on our IPO plans in the utmost secrecy, keeping the information as closely held as possible. Within DLJ, we three partners of course were privy to the plans, but only a small handful of others knew about them. It was much the same at First Boston and Sullivan & Cromwell. Given the fact that plenty of powerful people on Wall Street would be shocked and appalled—and feel personally threatened—by our move, we knew it was essential to keep the details absolutely secret until we were ready to reveal them at the right time. Any advance leaks could have made it easier for the opposition to marshal its counterattack and possibly derail our effort.

Among other crucial decisions, we agreed that no one at DLJ would sell shares we owned in the public offering. Our goal in going public was *not* to allow any of us to cash in on the value of the company. Rather, it was to raise the new capital we needed to promote the growth of our firm and enable it to meet the rapidly expanding demands of our customers and the markets. We made the decision to forgo selling any shares in order to clarify our long-term commitment to DLJ in the minds of the public. No one would be able to point to one of us selling his shares and say, "Look, the guys at DLJ are bailing out—that's the whole reason they went public in the first place!"

On May 20, 1969, the decision had been made and the legal and other preparations were completed: The SEC paperwork had been filled out, the official announcements for the press had been drafted, and the prospectus had been written. These documents reflected the facts that DLJ had enjoyed an unbroken track record of increasing revenues and rising profits, and that we boasted a stellar 50 percent rate of return on capital invested—a financial state of health of which we were justly proud.

Now we faced the issue of timing. We wanted to file our papers as quickly as possible to preclude any leaks. But by coincidence, the very next day would mark the first meeting of the newly constituted board of governors of the NYSE—including Dan Lufkin's initial attendance as a newly appointed member of that board.

As I've already mentioned, in those days, the stock exchange was run like an old boys' club. A succession of floor brokers had served as chairmen of the Exchange. Bernard J. Lasker, universally known as Bunny, was the latest one of those guys— a real old-fashioned floor broker. The son of a sponge-and-chamois importer on Beaver Street in lower Manhattan, Bunny had started his financial career as a runner (a stock market messenger boy) for Hirsch, Lilienthal at the age of 17. By 1968, he'd risen to become senior partner of his own firm, Lasker, Stone & Stern, and the following year he'd been elected chairman of the NYSE board of governors. He'd also become a close friend of many Republican politicians, including Richard Nixon, who had recently been elevated to the White House. I'll never forget being with Bunny and Nixon at a dinner party a few years earlier, when Bunny asked his friend, "Dick, if you become president one day, will you still take my phone calls?"

"Of course, Bunny, of course," was Nixon's answer.

A couple of years later, Bunny would do yeoman service during a catastrophic stock price collapse, shuttling between New York and Washington to find ways to stabilize the markets and reassure investors. During the insider trading scandal of the 1980s, his name briefly became a byword when one of the accused traders allegedly used the code phrase "Your bunny has a good nose" as a way of passing on a stock tip—though Bunny himself was never accused of any wrongdoing.

Dan Lufkin and Bunny Lasker were thick as thieves, and in 1969 Bunny arranged for Lufkin to get a seat on the board— which was quite an honor for DLJ. And Dan's first meeting of the board was scheduled for May 21. What should we do? Should we hold off on making our move until a week or two later? Or should we bite the bullet and make our plans known immediately to forestall any leaks?

We agonized over the decision. Finally, the three of us decided that the time pressure was simply too intense. We had to act. We agreed that Dan would use the next day's board meeting to announce our plan to go public to the leaders of the Exchange—and, inevitably, to the world.

It was an awkward position for Dan, to say the least— especially since he had been gradually drifting away from his leadership role at DLJ. Dan had been increasingly interested in pursuing independent investment deals and supporting his personal interest in the environment. He would soon become the first commissioner of the Department of Environmental Protection in the history of the state of Connecticut—a move that many saw as a possible stepping-stone to elective office. But now, with DLJ making this momentous move, we'd prevailed upon Dan to come back into the fold, at least temporarily—for which, in retrospect, I have to say I admire him. We needed Dan with us during this important time. Now he was being pushed into the position of having to break the news on our behalf at a meeting of the stock exchange's powerful board.

The rest of our plans fell into place accordingly. We agreed that I would take on the task of informing Gustave (Gus) Levy, the senior partner at Goldman Sachs and the retiring chairman of the Exchange, about our filing with the SEC. I would schedule a meeting with Gus for four o'clock, right after the close of NYSE trading, to coincide with the start of the board of governors' meeting. We also agreed that I would then make a second stop to meet with Bob Haack, the relatively new president and CEO of the NYSE, to present him personally with copies of our filing papers and explain our decision. Meanwhile, in Washington, D.C., our attorneys would be ready with the signed paperwork and would officially submit it at the offices of the SEC itself at precisely the same moment—4:00 p.m. The sequence of actions was planned like a precision military operation where the reaction of the players was very unpredictable.

With our plans made, Dick, Dan, and I shook hands and went to our respective homes for a restless night's sleep.

The next morning, I called Gus Levy's office and asked him whether I could stop by to see him after the closing bell, "on an important matter." "Sure," Gus replied in his New Orleans accent, sounding a trifle puzzled. Even then, Gus was a legend on Wall Street, a famously gruff, intimidating figure who was the master of every trading or underwriting opportunity and impatient of anyone who wasn't as meticulous as he was. Gus and I had served together on several outside boards and committees, and his firm, Goldman Sachs, was a major competitor in the block placement business in which DLJ was eager to grow. I also called Bob Haack and asked to see him briefly that afternoon during the first break in the board of governors' meeting, which I knew Bob would be attending.

At the appointed time, Gus greeted me cordially, and after a few moments of small talk, I handed him a set of documents.

"What are these?" Gus asked.

I took a deep breath. "These papers outline our plans to sell stock in DLJ to the public. Copies are being filed with the SEC as we speak. And at this very moment, Dan Lufkin is presenting the same plans to Bunny Lasker and the new board of the NYSE."

For several moments, Gus was uncharacteristically silent. Then he exploded. "Bill, you can't do that! It's against the rules of the New York Stock Exchange!"

I had to keep my composure. Did Gus really think we'd overlooked that fact? It was all we'd thought about for months on end. "We realize that," I replied. "But you know we've been talking for a while about the fact that Wall Street firms *have* to find a way to get access to more capital. And going public is the only way to do it." I went on to give a brief outline of our arguments as to why we believed this change was imperative. My hope was that the board of governors would consider these arguments and agree to alter their opposition to public ownership.

I knew, of course, that Gus and his successor, Bunny Lasker, would feel they had every right to urge the board to block our plan, and perhaps to threaten us with expulsion from the Exchange if we persisted in pursuing it. So I went on to explain, in as low-key and respectful a manner as possible, that we had considered what we would do if the board proved intractable. "If the board refuses to change its rule—which is its right—we'll reluctantly be forced to resign from the Exchange. We'd rather not do that, Gus. Without a seat on the Exchange, we'll no longer have direct access to the NYSE market. But we believe we can carry on our business in the same way that some other nonmember firms have done, by trading in the over-the-counter market." (Years later, this would come to be known as the Nasdaq market, and the advent of electronic trading would make it into a formidable alternative to traditional exchange trading.)

This threat to quit the Exchange was sincere. It was a course of action we were willing to take, but our real objective was to force the NYSE's hand—to push them to make the rule change that would allow us to remain members of the Exchange. In fact, our draft, "red herring" prospectus—which was required by the SEC's rules to state any business risk our company faced that could affect our future prospects—frankly stated that, if we were forced to drop our membership on the Exchange, it would put at risk some 70 percent of our revenues. That would have been a grim prospect. Although we had a fallback plan in the event the Exchange dug in its heels, it certainly wasn't one we were eager to put into effect.

I left Gus in a state of understandable agitation and headed for Bob Haack's office.

Meanwhile, Bunny Lasker was calling the new board of governors to order. I'm sure Dan Lufkin's palms were at least a bit sweaty as he asked for permission to address the board before the formal agenda began. There was silence as he approached the elaborate podium in that famous boardroom, holding copies of the same papers I had given Gus Levy a few minutes before. Everyone assumed, I'm sure, that Dan wanted to make some kind of polite, formal statement about how pleased he was to be joining the board and thanking his fellow members for the honor.

Instead, he repeated words very much like those I had used with Gus Levy. "These papers spell out our plans to sell stock in DLJ to the public. Copies are being filed with the SEC as we speak. And at this very moment, Bill Donaldson is informing Gus Levy [the departing board chairman] about these same plans."

The response was a long moment of stunned silence from the assembled governors—broken suddenly by a shout of "Judas Iscariot!" It was the voice of Felix Rohatyn, a well-known senior partner of Lazard Frères and himself a relatively new board member. The board erupted. Everyone began to speak at once, and the room filled with a babbling mixture of disbelief, disdain, and anger—and a few quiet voices expressing support.

Some fifteen minutes later, I was in the office of Bob Haack, president of the Exchange, for the meeting we'd timed to coincide with the first break in the board meeting. Bob himself had raced from the meeting to see me, having realized what the purpose of the appointment was. Bob was apoplectic. "What the hell are you guys doing?" he demanded. He ranted for several minutes about the irresponsibility and inappropriateness of our plans and about the headaches we were creating for him and the board. "Do you have *any* idea about the issues I'm dealing with? The paperwork crisis. Companies folding. The market getting shut down. All this talk about getting rid of fixed commission rates. And you guys pick *this* time to pull this stunt!"

Among other reasons, Bob was upset, I think, because we'd preempted his own efforts at more gradual, long-term change. It was an open secret that Don Regan of Merrill Lynch, the biggest and most prominent retail investment firm on the street, had already been on Bob's back about allowing public ownership of stock exchange member firms. In fact, it was widely understood that Regan desperately wanted Merrill Lynch to be the first member company to go public. Now DLJ, a relatively small young firm, had stolen Don Regan's thunder—and Bob Haack would have to deal with the fallout. No wonder he was exasperated.

I tried to explain our position as best I could, although Bob wasn't in a very receptive mood. I told him that I would be glad to continue the discussion at his convenience, but that now I had to get back to my office to handle the press.

We had prepared and distributed a press package, embargoed until after 4:00 p.m., which contained the same explanation and reasoning that we had presented to the SEC and the NYSE leadership. Those were the days before the Internet, Twitter, Facebook, and even cable news—all of which today would jump on a story like this within seconds. But when I returned to my office, I found a call waiting from a prominent reporter for *The New York Times*. "What's this all about, Mr. Donaldson?" he asked. "It seems to say here that you're going public. But that's not allowed by the rules of the Exchange, correct?"

"That's true," I replied. "But I assume you've read the notes we've provided to you—the same very carefully written papers we sent to others in the press as well as to the SEC and the NYSE—"

The reporter interrupted. "Look, Mr. Donaldson. I have not had a moment to read your 'very carefully written papers,' and I've got a deadline in thirty minutes. So if you want the news in the paper tomorrow, please tell me what you are doing—and just cut to the chase."

Which I proceeded to do. Such were the circumstances that surrounded our announcement.

The reaction was mixed. The evening of our announcement, Dan Lufkin attended the traditional dinner at which new members of the NYSE board of governors are honored. But Dan was chagrined to find himself shunned rather than feted—during the pre-dinner cocktail hour, most of his fellow governors literally turned their backs on him. The ice wasn't broken until Gus Levy himself approached Dan. "I want to tell you something," he said. "I don't agree with what you fellows are doing. But I admire your courage in speaking out at the meeting today and in coming to this dinner tonight. It's the stand-up thing to do." Dan greatly appreciated Gus's gesture.

The opposition to our move came from companies and individuals who were very comfortable with the old, clubby Wall Street. Felix Rohatyn, for example—the distinguished banker who'd accused Dan Lufkin of being a traitor—would have liked to help his company Lazard Frères maintain its leading position on merger and acquisition deals among stock exchange member firms. Opening up the membership to a vast infusion of capital from the public would make it possible for many other companies to begin competing for that business. It's not surprising that Rohatyn was less than thrilled.

On the other hand, Merrill Lynch's Don Regan was supportive: "It's about time somebody did this," was the gist of his public position on the issue. (Rumor had it that he quietly began hinting to people that DLJ had acted as his stalking horse, deliberately paving the way for Merrill Lynch to go public soon afterward. This wasn't true, of course; we acted purely on our own, not as anyone else's trial balloon.) Other retail-oriented investment firms like Dean Witter joined Merrill in supporting the idea; like us, they relished the opportunities for expansion and growth that public capital could bring.

The press found the story fascinating, as they generally do when someone shakes up the status quo. Dan, Dick, and I appeared on the cover of *BusinessWeek* under a sketch that made it appear as though the facade of the NYSE headquarters was collapsing due to an earthquake. In November, at the annual Financial Follies dinner presented by the New York Financial Writers' Association, we were depicted in a skit by three writers dressed up in Little Lord Fauntleroy outfits. The three naughty lads sang a song with the lyrics:

> We are the kids who made Haack sweat!
> We said we're going public,
> And we don't give a damn!

If they won't let us have our way,
Then we'll take it on the lam!

In the end, it appears that Dick, Dan, and I were right in our belief that the time was ripe for the shift to public ownership. The paperwork crisis and the other dilemmas facing Wall Street demanded action; DLJ just happened to be the catalyst that made it happen. On July 17, the NYSE board of governors announced that they'd decided to approve, in principle, the concept of public ownership of stock exchange member firms.

Nonetheless, the actual process of conducting our IPO took much longer. In its role as arbiter of the markets and overseers of stock offerings, the SEC took almost eleven months to prepare the regulations and particularly the accounting rules that would apply to our IPO. Their position was that this lengthy period of evaluation was necessary because we would surely be only the first of many investment firms to seek public ownership. The eleven-month delay gave us ample opportunity to explain our reasoning to the financial world and to the general public, which gradually came to accept and ultimately to welcome our initiative.

It was a tough period on the Street. During all this time, the NYSE market was under selling pressure. That pressure affected our IPO. We sold 800,000 shares at $15 on the day our prospectus was approved. Our record of positive revenue and earnings growth remained intact. However, our history of earnings growth had been adjusted downward to reflect the new SEC accounting rules devised for our case, including a painful one that required us to flow the valuations for our sizable portfolio of nonmarketable investments through our profit and loss statement (P&L) on a quarterly basis. That adjustment made it appear as though we'd actually lost money for the first time in our most recent reporting period. By the following year, market conditions had improved to the point where our long-term record of revenue and earnings growth remained uninterrupted.

Looking back, that cover of *Business Week* was inaccurate in one important way. It symbolically depicted DLJ as causing an earthquake on Wall Street that might destroy the financial industry. In reality, we believed that our challenge to the old rule would, in the long run, put Wall Street on a stronger, more secure footing. And so it proved. Soon after DLJ went public, other member firms followed suit, with Merrill Lynch (of course), Bache & Company, and Reynolds & Company being among the first.

In fact, my old partner Dick Jenrette has said that, if these and a number of other leading firms hadn't gone public and infused Wall Street with significant capital in the early 1970s, it's possible the market itself might not have survived the crash of 1974. There's no way to prove it one way or the other, of course, but I suspect he may be right.

* * *

From today's long-term perspective, I find it most interesting to reflect on how taking DLJ public embodied the entrepreneurial approach to life's challenges that has shaped my whole career.

I think it's unfortunate that the word "entrepreneur" has become somewhat devalued by overuse. Many people today seem to assume that an entrepreneur is someone who takes a fanciful business concept—the latest digital technology, some new marketing scheme, the current online fad—and tries to ride it to instant riches, often in the absence of any solid business plan, any track record of revenue and earnings, or any underlying social benefit. If one of these "moon shot" projects fails, the entrepreneur launches another and then another, always hoping that a bonanza will eventually fall into his lap.

In my view, this image is deeply misguided. Instead, I believe entrepreneurial leadership is about the application of creative thinking and prudent risk-taking to build innovative, long-lasting organizations in any sector of the economy, including the private sector, the not-for-profit arena, academia, and government. Entrepreneurial leaders use their management skills and strategic insights to meet significant human needs and contribute to the well-being of society. They also hope to generate sustainable income for themselves, their employees, and other stakeholders of the organizations they launch, but this is distinctly a secondary goal. Defined in this way, entrepreneurial leadership is a noble calling and the ultimate source of much of America's greatness.

As one of the cofounders of DLJ, I wasn't thinking such lofty thoughts when we hatched our plan to go public. But in retrospect I can see how that plan epitomized the spirit of entrepreneurial leadership I've come to believe in. In bringing change to the outmoded rules of Wall Street, my partners and I had recognized an unmet need, developed an innovative strategy to meet that need, and employed our best tactical, organizational, communication, and leadership skills to carry out that strategy. The short-term result: an immediate competitive advantage for DLJ and a greatly increased capacity for our firm to serve the expanding needs of our customers. The long-term result: a more sustainable economic structure for Wall Street and a stream of technological and business innovations that would revitalize and transform the financial services industry in the decades to come, making it better able to help fuel the vast economic growth enjoyed by the United States and other advanced capitalist nations during the 1960s, 1970s, and beyond.

This, to me, is entrepreneurial leadership at its best—leadership practiced in the spirit of innovation and with the goal of building long-lasting, value-creating institutions. It's the same spirit I later tried to bring to organizations in other arenas, from the world of higher education to the U.S. government.

How did I manage to get myself into a position where, while still a young man in my thirties, I was able to help shake up the venerable culture of Wall Street and build a company that others in the finance world either envied, imitated, or feared? That's a story that begins in the depths of the Great Depression in one of the old industrial cities hardest hit by the worst financial collapse in history—an unlikely time and place, you might think, for a kid to get bitten by the entrepreneurial bug. But that's exactly what happened.

CHAPTER 2

Entrepreneurial Stirrings:
From Buffalo Boyhood to Yale Days

I was born in 1931 in Buffalo, New York—a time and place that, at first glance, might not seem to provide the most plausible environment for a young person to imbibe the spirit of entrepreneurial leadership. It was the depths of the Great Depression, an economic calamity that devastated what had once been one of America's most vibrant, rapidly growing cities.

Located at the crossroads of the Great Lakes and the Erie Canal, Buffalo had taken advantage of its location to become a hub of steel production, auto parts manufacturing, grain transport, and other major industries. As long ago as the 1880s, hydroelectric power generated by nearby Niagara Falls had made Buffalo the first major U.S. city with widespread electric lighting, earning it the nickname "The City of Light." By the end of the 1920s, Buffalo had a population of 573,000, making it the thirteenth largest city in the United States. But the stock market crash of 1929 and the years of economic downturn that followed threw thousands of Buffalonians out of work.

The federal government fought back. The Works Progress

Administration (WPA) and other New Deal programs poured money into Buffalo. Millions were invested in public housing, an upgraded sewer system, airport expansion, and the building of public amenities like Memorial Auditorium, Kleinhans Music Hall, a modernized Buffalo Zoo, a new federal office building, and a new stadium. These public projects employed thousands and helped stave off poverty for many in the region. But private industry declined sharply. The auto industry, centered in Detroit, at the opposite end of Lake Erie, was decimated by the Depression, and the carmakers' purchases of parts and supplies from Buffalo manufacturers declined sharply. Smaller automakers like Pierce-Arrow, actually based in Buffalo, shut their doors altogether.

These troubles impacted my family in a personal way. My father, Eames Donaldson, was a Yale-educated engineer who had helped start a machine-tool manufacturing company called Metal Mold Castings, which garnered most of its business from the auto industry. So when sales of cars plummeted, Dad's business went belly-up.

My dad was forced to fall back on a series of not-very-lucrative jobs to support my mother, my brother, and me. He spent many years setting aside cash from every paycheck to pay back the investors in his castings business who had trusted in him. Dad didn't make a big deal out of that behavior, even though it cost our family a lot of the comforts of life that we might have otherwise enjoyed. It also cost us as a family, as his jobs forced him to spend much of his time away from home. But my father's actions probably added to my sense of self-reliance and resilience. It also symbolized the integrity and sense of personal responsibility that he took for granted—along with most Americans in those days. Or at least that's how I remember it.

The same message of personal integrity and responsibility was reinforced for me one time when, as a grade-school kid, I succumbed to temptation and sneaked out of the local Kresge's five-and-dime store with a couple of cheap wallets stuck inside my shirt. I didn't need or want the wallets. I guess I just wanted to experience the thrill of seeing whether I could get away with it. When Dad found out about my escapade, he made me accompany him to the store, confess my shoplifting to the manager, apologize, and turn over my ill-gotten gains. It was excruciatingly embarrassing. It also cured me forever of any notion that rules of moral right and wrong could be broken without deep personal regret and humiliation.

In retrospect, I'm awfully glad I learned that lesson before launching a career that began in finance. Our nation might be better off if everyone in the financial industry—and elsewhere—had a similar childhood experience, no matter where they started their careers.

My mother, Guida, came from an interesting immigrant family. Her father, Henry Marx, was one of thirteen children who left Germany in the 1880s to escape persecution and settled in Toledo, Ohio. Although it was never discussed openly in the family, it is likely that they were Jewish and converted to Christianity when they arrived in the United States. Each of the thirteen became a professional—doctor, politician, educator, or businessperson—including the women. Only two had children: Henry and his brother Irwin. Both of these men became successful businessmen, ultimately taking over the G. A. Gray Company, a tool-and-die enterprise in Cincinnati, Ohio.

Guida's mother was significantly younger than her father, and she tragically died soon after Guida's birth in 1900. Guida was raised by an adoring father and her Aunt Werna. Although women rarely went to college in the early 1900s, Guida graduated from Smith, a fact she seldom discussed.

Guida Marx and Eames Donaldson married after college and settled in Buffalo. My mother was an extrovert—charming, lovely, often mischievous, gregarious, surrounded by friends, beloved by shopkeepers, and dedicated to her two sons. I was more like my mother. My brother, Ted, was like my father—serious, studious, always first in his class. My mother would read for hours on end to Ted, who early in life had serious eyesight problems that he later overcame.

Along with her effervescence, my mother also had a dark side—a tendency to lapse into periods of serious depression. A modern psychologist would probably say she suffered from bipolar disorder. Once when Ted and I were in grade school, and again later when we were in high school, she was institutionalized for a while, and we boys were tended to by close relatives. Her absence was barely discussed, as was the custom back then, but I imagine it also increased my self-reliance and resilience.

My dad died of a heart attack at 62, while, ironically, my mother, although racked with emphysema from a lifetime of smoking, lived to be 86.

Ted graduated from Yale with high honors as an engineer, served in the Navy, and attended the renowned Chrysler Institute. Unlike me with my multiple careers, Ted spent his entire career successfully at Chrysler. Most of that time, he was based in Detroit, but he was on assignment in England for a decade, where he also raised four sons—John, Steven, Geoff, and Peter. Though he never worked in finance, he was a lifelong avid investor.

My dad's business troubles, aggravated by the market crash of 1929, also taught me an unspoken lesson about the risks inherent in launching a company. I can imagine that being a father who'd lost everything due to a business failure might have caused him to react by advising his son to avoid entrepreneurship—to stick to the apparent security of a corporate career or a civil service job. But that was never his counsel. I always had the feeling that I was born to be someone who conceives,

builds, and nurtures an organization rather than simply joining one. In short, an entrepreneurial leader—although back in
the 1930s, that wasn't as popular a term as it later became.
My boyhood dream, to the extent that I had one, wasn't about
getting rich or being a glamorous wheeler-dealer, two of the
images of the "entrepreneur" that became widespread during
the greed-is-good era of the 1980s. I was more focused on being
my own man, running my own show (often with partners), and
making things happen—a traditional American ambition one
can trace back to the pioneers.

My father encouraged me to think in terms of self-reliance.
For example, in my early teenage years, like many kids, I was
impatient to learn to drive and get a set of wheels, with the freedom that would imply. I even hatched a scheme that I floated
with my dad to travel to Canada—just across the border from
Buffalo—where I'd heard it was possible to get a driver's license
at the age of 14. But my dad simply said, "Where are you going
to get a car from? I hope you're not looking at me! If you want
a car, you'll have to work to pay for it."

That was typical of his attitude. Dad was always challenging me to find my own way to accomplish whatever I wanted.
As a result, I always assumed I would spend my adult years
doing something independent and creative. I never pictured
myself getting a lifetime job with one of the giant companies
that dominated the American economic landscape in those
days. I was always thinking about things I could do on my own
or with a couple of partners.

At the same time, my dad instilled in me a healthy respect
for the dangers involved in any kind of speculation. Years later,
in 1959, when I told him that my friends Dan Lufkin, Dick Jenrette, and I were planning to start a New York City investment
firm while still in our twenties, Dad was dubious about the idea.
He didn't try to discourage me—but he clearly doubted that

three young men had much chance of competing successfully against the grand old firms of Wall Street. I can't blame him for that—practically everyone on Wall Street felt the same way.

Perhaps, adding up all these influences, the path I ended up taking is not too surprising. I became an entrepreneur, spending more than six decades of my life in founding or dramatically reshaping a series of organizations, some in the for-profit business arena, others in the worlds of academia and public service. At the same time, I rejected the commonplace definition of an entrepreneur as primarily a risk-taker—someone who gambles on one money-making concept after another, always in search of the big bonanza that will generate vast and instantaneous riches. Instead, I always focused on doing everything I could to *reduce* the level of risk involved in the organizations I was associated with, and on shaping management systems, corporate cultures, and ethical models that would stand the test of time, producing lasting value for employees, clients, stakeholders, and society at large.

That, to me, is what entrepreneurial leadership is really all about. But it took me many years of education, experience, and reflection to arrive at that understanding. As a kid in Buffalo, all I really knew was that I wanted to do something interesting, challenging, and fun in my life, and in the process to be as successful and productive as possible.

During the early 1940s—the formative years when I was between 9 and 14 years old—the Second World War was an overwhelming presence in my life and in the lives of everyone I knew. My older brother Ted joined the Navy after high school. Like most of the male role models I knew and looked up to at that time, he considered military service a natural choice to make. Other people around me, male and female, were working in the Buffalo companies that had geared up to provide goods and services for the war effort.

The sense that our entire society was caught up in the effort to achieve a great goal—to defeat Fascism and defend the freedom of our nation and of peoples around the world who were depending upon us—permeated my experience. I was happy and excited about supporting the cause through kids' activities like collecting old newspapers and scrap metal to provide raw materials for the U.S. war machine. I carefully followed the progress of our military through newspaper and radio reports and the newsreel footage shown in the local movie theaters, and I admired the staunch, quiet, self-sacrificing heroism of leaders like Dwight Eisenhower and others.

The war years instilled in me a lifelong appreciation for the importance of public service—a value that, as you'll see, would later play a major role in shaping many of the decisive choices in my career.

Meanwhile, I was also taking the first baby steps toward my future as an entrepreneur. Like a lot of kids, I tried my hand at starting several businesses in my home neighborhood—lemonade stands, newspaper delivery routes, and the like.

My most ambitious early business effort was an experiment in being a publishing executive. After someone gave me a secondhand typewriter as a gift, I got together with a couple of friends to create our own magazine—an eight-page compilation of jokes that we titled "Read 'Em and Grin." We cribbed the gags from comics, newspaper columns, and stories we heard from people around the neighborhood. Most of them were real groaners ("What did the hat say to the necktie? 'You hang around, I'll go on a head.'"). A few were borderline dirty ("It's all right to tell a girl that she has pretty ankles but don't compliment her too highly"). My buddies and I were too innocent to grasp the implications at the time.

Having gathered our contents and typed them up, we needed to figure out how to turn them into a commercial property. My dad helped by introducing us to a friend of his who ran a local printing business; he agreed to print several hundred copies for us as a favor. We also talked a few of the local businesses into buying ad space. Our first issue featured carefully typed ads for Elmwood Music Shop, Sigl's Delicatessen, Henning Mortensen ("caterer of high quality baked goods"), and S. S. Kresge Company—the same Kresge's I had once victimized during my short-lived career in crime.

Armed with bundles of folded and stapled pages, we four partners sold our humble publication door-to-door. Three of us were eager about our fledgling publishing business, but the fourth guy wasn't as committed. When he didn't sell his quota from our second edition, we paid him off with his unsold copies—my first lesson in how business partnerships can get tricky at times.

The disappointing sales of the second issue of "Read 'Em and Grin" short-circuited my career as a big-time media mogul. But I look back fondly on the episode as one of my first adventures in entrepreneurship.

From 1943 to 1949, I was a scholarship student at the Nichols School in Buffalo, a private all-boys school founded in 1892. Nichols wasn't a boarding school; all the students lived at home with their families. I worked and played hard during those high school years. I earned academic honors, including the prestigious Headmaster's Award for my high grades and extracurricular activities, and served as business manager of the yearbook while playing on the varsity football and hockey teams. (Hockey has always been the leading sport at Nichols, and my love for the sport has persisted ever since. Until well into my seventies I enjoyed getting out on the ice occasionally and knocking the puck around with my younger son, Adam.)

I kept busy during the summers, too. During the school break in 1948 (following my junior year), I worked at a warehouse unloading freight trains. And during the summer of 1949, after graduating from Nichols and before going away to college, I cofounded and comanaged a little company called United Enterprises. My partner was a fellow named Chet Dann, who would later be one of my roommates in college and a life-long friend. Basically, Chet and I hired college kids to do house painting and all sorts of odd jobs. We drummed up business by going around town, knocking on doors, and introducing our-selves. If no one was home, we'd leave behind a penny postcard pre-addressed to us, bearing the following message:

Announcing the formation of
"United Enterprises"
A group of Nichols Graduates are eager to do "any & all"
of your summer jobs. Give us a try! we'll do any dollar
job (such as washing your car) free, just to prove our worth.
Simply sign&drop this card in a mailbox or phone. Gr.4638
W.H.Donaldson and C.G. Dann

On the back, we listed "some of the jobs in which we are experienced," from lawn care and painting to window washing and car waxing.

In particular, we were looking for houses that needed paint-ing. We'd ring the doorbell and say, "We'll paint your house for a good price." Sometimes the homeowner wasn't interested, but sometimes he was, and we ended up getting quite a bit of work.

We were also flexible about the kinds of work we would tackle. One time we rang the doorbell of a disheveled-looking house, and told the woman who answered our ring, "Your house really needs painting."

She said, "Yeah, it does, but look at the steps up to the house. Those are much worse."

So I said, "We do stairs, too."

She said, "You do? How much would it cost?" We gave her a bid, and soon found ourselves taking on work as carpenters. Unfortunately, we didn't know what we were doing. We got the stairs half built, then realized we didn't know how to build risers for the stairs. Fortunately, there were some carpenters doing a job a few blocks away, so we found them and said, "Would you guys come back and help us? We're in real trouble on this thing." They finished the job for a cut of our fee—although the steps were different heights, not exactly the way they're supposed to be built.

They did the job, though. Many years later, when I revisited my old neighborhood, I saw those same stairs still in use on that house in Buffalo. I recognized them by the mismatched risers, which had remained unchanged for all that time.

We had a couple of good tennis players who were working for us, and that opened up a new line of business with families that played tennis—we gave tennis lessons to kids. We cut lawns, trimmed hedges, fixed broken drain gutters—you name it. By the end of August, we had fifty guys working for us. Essentially, anybody who needed a job in our part of Buffalo got a job with us.

I used my share of the profits to finally get the car I'd been wanting ever since I was 14—an old Model A Ford that needed plenty of repairs. I fixed it up myself with the help of the father of a friend.

The story of United Enterprises reveals how far I'd come in learning to think and act like an entrepreneur. It wasn't about making a lot of money, although of course the money came in very handy. It was about building something and being independent—running our own show and pursuing goals that we set for ourselves. And Chet and I were, I think, admirably creative, flexible, and opportunistic—recognizing the need to change and expand our business model when new opportunities for value creation came along.

Looking back, I think I had a pretty typical middle-class background for my time and place. My family never experienced the extreme hardships of true poverty; we were never homeless or hungry, and despite his business setbacks, my dad was always able to support us in decent fashion.

My parents didn't have a lot of money or any special social or business connections. But thanks mostly to the above-average grades I'd accumulated at the Nichols School, I did experience one meaningful advantage that would help set me on a path to success in life. That was the opportunity to go to Yale—one of the best universities in the country.

Like the other Ivy League universities, Yale was not the diverse, multicultural institution it has since become. Admissions officers placed a heavy premium on evidence of what they called "character," a qualification one historian has noted seemed to be "present almost congenitally among high-status Protestants."[1] Though I came from a Protestant family and was a "legacy," since my dad and brother had gone to Yale, I wasn't among the "high-status" crowd. But perhaps that benefited me. Like other members of Yale's middle-class cohort, I was aware of how fortunate I was to be a student there, and I made the most of the opportunity. During my subsequent four years at Yale (1949–1953), I worked hard on my studies, earning admission to the Torch Honor Society (one of just ten junior students to be selected) as well as a spot on the dean's list. I also played hockey on the freshman and varsity squads. Ultimately, I was selected for Skull and Bones, one of Yale's famous (some would say infamous) secret societies.

Not only did I learn a lot at Yale, but it gave me the chance to make meaningful personal friendships that have been important to me in my subsequent careers. Entering into the powerful network of Yale alumni was a benefit that some of my upper-crust classmates may have taken for granted, but for me it opened doors that might otherwise have remained closed.

Important friendships, for me, were with the Bush family, who were already a well-known American clan. Prescott Bush, the patriarch, had graduated from Yale in 1917 and gone on to become a prominent Wall Street executive and an advisor to both Republican and Democratic politicians, including President Harry Truman. In 1952, he was elected to the first of two terms as a U.S. senator from Connecticut.

My classmate Jonathan Bush, a son of Prescott's, is almost exactly my age (born less than a month before me) and remains a good friend of mine today. He is the younger brother of George H. W. Bush, sometimes called "Forty-One," because he served as the forty-first president of the United States. I had occasion to meet Forty-One and some of the other family members, including Jon's nephew George W. Bush, later to be known as "Forty-Three." The younger George had a reputation as a wild kid and was sometimes considered the black sheep of the family, at least in his youth. The two of us weren't close. But I suppose my status as a friend of the family didn't hurt my chances in 2002 when Forty-Three was considering naming me the chairman of the Securities and Exchange Commission. I got the job, and the political controversies I later became embroiled in may have led some observers to wonder whether President Bush had fully understood what he was in for when he appointed a fellow Yale graduate. But I'll save the details of that story for a later chapter.

The Bushes at Yale are well-known members of Skull and Bones, the senior society that meets in a little stone building known as "The Tomb" on the University's New Haven campus. At least ten members of the Bush family (some by marriage) have been Bonesmen, dating back to Prescott Bush. Many other Yale graduates with reputations in business, public service, the arts, and other fields have also been members, and in 1984 we even had a presidential election that pitted two Bonesmen against one another—George W. Bush (class of 1968) for the Republicans and John F. Kerry (class of 1966) for the Democrats.

All I will add here is that I think that Skull and Bones is a great organization, and even greater now that they've admitted women—an enlightened policy it took them just 150 years to adopt.

As I had during high school, during my Yale years I earned a bit of extra money and learned more about the world at various summer jobs. In the summer of 1950, after my sophomore year, I worked as trailer-truck driver doing delivery work in western New York for S. M. Flickinger, a Buffalo-based wholesale grocery company. The following summer, I worked as copublisher of a seasonal newspaper called *The Connecticut Shore*, which boasted a circulation of 3,000 from New Haven to Rhode Island.

The most fun I had at Yale was being business manager of the *Yale Daily News* during my senior year. That was a genuinely big deal. The *Yale Daily News* calls itself "the oldest college daily" in America (a claim that is sometimes disputed by partisans of the papers at Harvard, Columbia, and elsewhere but that appears to be vindicated by history). Countless staffers of the paper—reporters, editors, publishers, chairmen—have gone on to distinguished careers in a host of fields, especially journalism and politics. They include Sargent Shriver, first director of the Peace Corps; John Hersey, the Pulitzer Prize–winning author of *Hiroshima*; Calvin Trillin, the brilliant *New Yorker* humorist; and even Theo Epstein, general manager of the Chicago Cubs baseball team that won a long-awaited world championship in 2016.

Cartoonist Garry Trudeau's legendary comic strip *Doonesbury* made its debut in the *Yale Daily News* (under the title

Bull Tales) during Trudeau's years at Yale. And during my time at the college, one of the editors of the paper was a fellow named Bill Buckley (Yale '50), who soon made waves on the political and cultural scene with his 1951 book *God and Man at Yale*, which decried the influence of liberal secularism at our alma mater. Buckley later became the editor and publisher of *National Review* and for decades was arguably the most influential thinker and writer in the American conservative movement.

I loved being a part of this vibrant, colorful institution. Best of all, in the summer of 1952, I served as copublisher of *Seventy-Five: A Study of a Generation in Transition,* a book commemorating the seventy-fifth anniversary of the paper. Those of us who pulled the book together seized the opportunity to interview a bunch of Yale graduates who'd been successful in different spheres of activity. I got a chance to meet one of my predecessors at the *Yale Daily News* whom I found most inspiring—Henry Luce, who cofounded *Time* magazine with Briton Hadden, another Yale graduate who got his start in journalism at the *Yale Daily News.*

I visited Luce in his New York office, where I found him to be a serious, even somber sort of guy. But once he began talking about his early years, he brightened up. Luce recounted for me the story of how, after deciding to start *Time*, he and Hadden traveled around the country to raise the money to do it. (It was the same sort of quest that Dan Lufkin, Dick Jenrette, and I would go on years later when we decided to launch our investment firm.) Having heard that I was from Buffalo, Luce told me about how he and Hadden had visited my hometown to talk to Seymour Knox, a wealthy Buffalonian who'd been a classmate of theirs, and raised some money from him. Ultimately the Knox family made a fresh fortune by being among the earliest investors in Time Inc.

Luce also told me about how he and Hadden were working on the top-secret plans for *Time* in a little office they'd rented in a building on 42nd Street in New York, right across the street from the offices of the *Daily News*. They were working late one summer evening with a window wide open because of the heat when a gust of wind blew the papers out the window and onto the street below. The two of them had to rush downstairs and gather up their plans from the street before any of the reporters from the *News* spotted them and blew their cover.

I got a big kick out of hearing Luce's stories about his days as a youthful entrepreneur. I loved the idea that a couple of Yale grads not much older than myself could hatch a business plan that would ultimately grow into one of the world's great news corporations. It rekindled my fascination with the media industry—an interest that dates to my publishing of "Read 'Em and Grin" back in Buffalo. A few years later, after I earned a graduate business degree, I was offered a job at Time Inc. I was intrigued, though I ultimately chose a different opportunity. Even later, my interest in the world of media would lead me, some years down the line, to flirt seriously with the notion of becoming a New York City newspaper mogul—a story I'll tell more fully in the proper place in this book.

But the chief significance of my stint as copublisher of *Seventy-Five* and my meeting with Henry Luce was that it strengthened my determination to launch a business of my own one day—if not in media, then in some other industry. The only thing I didn't know was which business arena I would plant my stakes in.

CHAPTER 3

Learning to Lead:
From Quantico to Harvard

I was awakened by a blinding light shining in my eyes, along with the blasting noise of what sounded like a low-pitched bugle inches from my head. I sat up with an abrupt start. I was confused as to where I was and what was causing the increasing din of deafening noises—running feet and a harsh male voice screaming, "All right, you people, drop your cocks and grab your socks!"

Where was I, and who was ripping away the blanket that a few seconds ago had been covering my body?

As my dreams faded and the harsh reality intruded, I gradually realized where I was. I was in the lower half of a two-tiered metal bunk bed, one of dozens in a long row in one of several identical barracks at the U.S. Marine Corps Officer Candidates School (OCS) Command in Quantico, Virginia. The invisible hand that was completing the separation of me from my tightly held blanket belonged to an unfamiliar, hard-looking male face shouting, "On the deck, candidate! Out that door in five minutes sharp, without a wrinkle in your sheets and blankets!" The shouts and confusion surrounding us belonged to a scrum of some one hundred skivvy-clad men, their heads shaven, struggling to don ill-fitting starched green fatigues as they bent to hurriedly arrange their blankets and to stuff their feet into their new, rough-hewn combat boots, all while a bevy of angry-sounding drill instructors screamed at us to "Move! Move! Move!"

My feet reached for the ground. I struggled to avoid banging my head on the hard steel frame of the metal bunk bed and to disentangle myself from the mess of blankets and sheets being ripped from my body. I glanced at the radium dial on my wristwatch: 4:30 a.m. I did my best to arrange my blankets and sheets in some semblance of order and joined the other laggards staggering into the damp chill of predawn.

Outside on the vast parade field, I joined a mass of hundreds of other bewildered males all similarly clad and trying to respond in the dark to a chorus of shouted orders. Rising above the rest with a cry of "Fall in, you fucking idiots!" was the voice of the man who had ripped my covers off. It was Sergeant Hughes, who, the night before, at the end of a grueling day, had brusquely informed all of us assembled in our dingy barracks building that he was now our absolute boss; that we, the new candidates of Platoon F ("That's for 'fucking,' you fucking idiots!") had better put everything we were carrying—new-issued shoes, socks, underwear, metal dog tags, utility and dress uniforms, and so on—into the foot lockers at the end of each double-decker bed; and that lights would be turned off in ten minutes. "You *will* be in the sack by the time the lights go out!" he warned. "And, oh yes, fuckers, anybody that fails to secure their sheets and blankets properly will find them on the floor in the morning. Move out!"

All of this came flooding back into my mind as the sun slowly appeared on this cold and damp September morning.

Meanwhile, out of the mass of humans milling about seemingly without direction, rough platoon formations, each numbering forty men, were gradually taking shape. As further orders were barked out by the sergeants, hundreds of cold recruits were dimly beginning to learn what "falling in" meant, what "standing at attention" was supposed to look like, and how the wrath of our leaders would feel when their commands were not followed instantaneously and precisely.

After what seemed like hours but was in fact just a few minutes, we stood in our best version of a formation, shivering in the cold and furtively whispering to one another as we waited to see what would happen next. The less fortunate candidates among us—those who hadn't managed to hold themselves in an appropriately upright and attentive posture—were singled out and ordered to run around the perimeter of the field before being allowed to return to the ranks. More minutes passed.

Suddenly a small cavalcade of military jeeps and sedans, fender flags flapping in the breeze, approached and pulled up at the head of the platoon formations. A collection of Marine dignitaries emerged from the cars and began to climb the steps of a wooden dais at one end of the parade ground. Trumpets blared, and from somewhere behind us—I dared not turn my head to look—a military band broke the near-silence with a stirring rendition of the "Marines' Hymn," the famous melody by Jacques Offenbach often known by its opening lyrics: "From the halls of Montezuma / to the shores of Tripoli." We candidates stood a little straighter as an amplified voice from the platform shouted, "Attention, Marines! The commandant of the United States Marines!"

A tall Marine officer, with battle ribbons and metal insignias covering most of his upper body and a uniform that remained stiff and pressed in the breeze, strode to the microphone. This was Lemuel C. Shepherd Jr., the four-star general who, a year earlier, in 1952, had been named by President Harry S. Truman as the twentieth leader of the U.S. Marine Corps. The band fell silent, and the commandant began to speak.

His address was a formal greeting to us, the new class of Marine officer candidates. It began with comments on the "beautiful sunrise, the invigorating effect of early arising," then moved on to a respectful recitation of the battle-hardening experiences of the noncommissioned officers who now stood in front of each platoon and who would be our leaders and mentors for the next fourteen weeks. Then he followed with a brief recitation of the history of the U.S. Marine Corps, studded with the names of World War II battlefield locations—Tarawa, Iwo Jima, Corregidor—that were familiar to the great majority of us, the assembled recruits.

Most of us had grown up during the early 1940s and were stirred by the recitation of this modern history which we'd heard about as children and teenagers in a country embroiled in all-out war. Through daily newspaper stories, radio reports, and movie theater newsreels, we'd been exposed to frightening images of black-helmeted German storm troops goose-stepping through the Arc de Triomphe and khaki-clad Japanese fighters wending their way through insect-infested jungle trails. These, we'd learned, were the enemies who threatened our homeland and our way of life. As our older brothers marched off to war, we, the younger generation, had dutifully attended school, played sports, and begun to chase girls. Yet the nightmare dreams of foreign armies invading our tranquil cities, towns, and farms were never far from our thoughts.

As the early morning sun slowly illuminated the parade field, the commandant spoke about the war that had recently been raging on the Korean peninsula. He spoke of the heroism of those who had come before us in the Corps and of the handful of those in the platoons assembled this morning who had been selected from the battlefields of Korea to undergo the training that lay ahead for all of us—training that would culminate for all assembled ("if you make it through") in being commissioned as officers in the Marine Corps.

I thought about an older friend of mine who had come back to Yale while I was a senior there. He'd served in Korea as a Marine lieutenant and returned after being badly wounded. His vivid descriptions of the challenges and rewards of serving our country as a Marine had been one of the factors that had motivated me to enlist in the Corps.

The commandant ended his address with words of encouragement and respect for the course we had chosen, and with a crisp salute, he stepped down from the platform, followed by the gaggle of officers and enlisted men who'd shared the dais with him. As the band behind us resumed the Hymn, they walked in formation from the front row toward the rear platoons.

I was startled when the group suddenly stopped at my platoon, and the commandant, followed by several officers and highly decorated NCOs, proceeded to walk between our ranks only to stop suddenly at the candidate standing next to me.

I had noticed him the night before. Unlike most of us, he was no raw recruit. He was an older-looking guy who'd been assigned to the top bunk above me—a somewhat silent, seemingly very self-confident soldier who wore the same new uniform as the rest of us, with no markings or designation of rank. We'd exchanged a few words in the moments before lights out. "I just got back from Korea," he'd told me.

It was only later that I learned of my bunk mate's background. He was a former master sergeant named John W. Chinner, who had fought not only in Korea but in the waning months of World War II. More remarkable, as a member of the U.S. Marine Reserves, Chinner had received the Marine Corps' most respected combat award, the Navy Cross, surpassed only by the

Congressional Medal of Honor. With his platoon assigned the mission of seizing a strategic hill position in Korea, Chinner had braved grenades and automatic-weapons fire to kill several of the enemy, outflank three enemy bunkers, and single-handedly force the enemy troops to abandon their positions.

I knew nothing of this story as I stood at attention beside Candidate Chinner on that raw September morning. So I was stunned when the commandant paused in front of Chinner, saluted him, shook his hand, and without a word proceeded down the ranks. The accompanying officers followed him, with the NCOs close behind.

But the surprises weren't over.

Suddenly, one of the officers trailing the commandant, a tall staff sergeant around six-foot-one and bearing an ugly scar across his cheek, his uniform heavily bedecked with an array of colorful decorations, stepped in front of me. He faced me toe to toe, his nose less than an inch from mine. "We have been waiting for you, Donaldson!" he barked. Without another word, he turned and followed the commandant's party.

I'll never forget the shock that this brief encounter occasioned. How in the hell did this sergeant know who I was? How had he picked me out from among the hundreds of assembled candidates? Most important, what ominous meaning was implied by his words to me?

Over the months that followed, I got to know Sergeant Banacek—he of the multiple decorations and the fresh scar across his cheek. He was a classic Marine drill instructor, from his imposing physical appearance (the so-called "command presence" for which DIs strive) to the constant stream of profane and unrelenting gallows humor he directed toward us recruits. It was clear that he regarded us as pathetic excuses for men who would have to be incredibly lucky to make it through the rigors of Officer Candidates School. But the horrific, customized hazing I anticipated from him, involving God-knows-what physical or psychological torment, never materialized.

It wasn't until weeks later, while we were out on maneuvers one day, that Sergeant Banacek explained the origin of the personalized greeting he'd given me that chilly September morning. It seemed that on the day of graduation and commissioning of the OCS class that had preceded mine, one of the newly minted second lieutenants, Merwin Haskel, had taken Banacek aside. After pledging him to secrecy, Haskell had informed Banacek that his college friend Bill Donaldson was scheduled to arrive at Quantico among the next batch of officer candidates. Would Banacek welcome me as only a Marine drill instructor could do?

He had done so—and instilled a healthy dose of fear in me in the process.

Whenever Merwin Haskel and I have met over the years since then, we've exchanged a ritualized greeting: "At attention, Candidate Donaldson!" "Yes sir, Lieutenant Haskel!"

As for my fellow candidate John Chinner, I noticed a couple of remarkable things about him during our time together at Quantico. As a recipient of the Navy Cross, he was treated with respect bordering on awe by virtually every Marine officer and NCO he encountered—exactly the opposite of the treatment accorded to the rest of us candidates. But equally noteworthy, he never behaved as though he expected such deference or deserved it; in fact, he followed the orders of officers who were younger and far less experienced than himself with the utmost humility.

This behavior from both sides says something profound about the Marine Corps model of leadership. Being around John Chinner and recognizing what he stood for taught me more about ideals like honor, service, and respect than any number of books or speeches.

This, then, was the introduction to my fourteen weeks at Quantico. They included rigorous classroom study of subjects ranging from weapons handling and basic combat to Marine Corps history, the Uniform Code of Military Justice, and moral and ethical leadership. They also included demanding physical training—hiking, running, swimming, shooting, close-order drill—all performed under conditions of intense psychological stress.

Looking back, it was an amazing learning experience—one that toughened me up, mentally, physically, and spiritually. The Marine Corps was able to take a diverse group of recruits—skinny kids and fat guys, football players from Oklahoma, farmers from Mississippi, street kids from Harlem, and Ivy League grads like me—and mold us into a military unit with remarkable *esprit de corps*, ready and able to work together and to follow our officers in a spirit of respect and self-reliance.

The Marines generate this sense of unity and teamwork through a host of strategies and symbolic actions, great and small. For example, whenever a unit is in the field, at chow time, the last man in line is always the highest-ranking officer—a gesture that embodies the principle that leadership is all about serving the team, making sure that your followers are taken care of before you think about yourself.

It would be wonderful if every would-be entrepreneur and organizational leader could experience a bit of the Marine Corps style of leadership.

I graduated from OCS in December 1953 and earned my commission as a second lieutenant. I will never forget that day—partly because I had gotten through my first Marine Corps experience and now had the gold bar that signified I was a Marine officer—but more vividly because I recall my fellow aspiring officer candidates who had failed to be commissioned being assigned to clean up the grounds while the rest of us were celebrating. That stark image of the difference between success and failure has stayed with me all these years later.

For the next several years, I served in the Corps as an infantry officer. I was a tactics instructor and a rifle platoon commander at Camp Pendleton in California, and I also served in Japan, which was part of what we called the Far Eastern theater. However, I never fought in Korea. Dwight D. Eisenhower, the military hero of World War II who had run for president in 1952 on his promise to end the war in Korea—and had earned the first vote I ever cast—had traveled to the war zone right after the election, begun negotiating a settlement, and signed an armistice in July 1953. So I was one of the lucky ones—thanks to an accident of timing, I never had to fire a shot against the enemy.

A most unusual posting came about in 1954 when a brigadier general named Colston Dyer called me into his office. Dyer was a pilot and an air wing commander who had flown fighter jets in World War II and helicopters in Korea. With the Marines now developing plans to create a unified force to conduct landing assaults via helicopter, they had chosen Dyer to lead what was being called the First Provisional Marine Air-Ground Task Force. "I'm going to Hawaii to head this unit," Dyer told me, "and I'm going to have both pilots and infantrymen under my command. I don't know much about infantry. How would you like to be my aide?"

I liked the sound of that. I ended up spending the last several months of my Marine service stationed with General Dyer at Kaneohe air base on the windward side of Oahu. It was a choice assignment—gorgeous scenery, amazing tropical weather, and a rich and varied social life. As for the work, it wasn't terribly onerous. I learned about helicopters, hobnobbed with senators, congressmen, and other luminaries who visited us to learn about the Marine Corps' most advanced new initiative, and helped put on shows to demonstrate that helicopter combat was the future of the Marines.

If there was any downside to the job, it was having to fly around Hawaii in a helicopter with General Dyer. He had been a very experienced pilot, but his piloting skills in a helicopter were somewhat untested, so when we'd fly from Kaneohe to Honolulu in the powerful air currents that are common there, the ride would often be too bumpy for comfort. I'd taken a couple of flying lessons while I was off duty at Quantico—just enough to discover that I wasn't going to be any good at it. So I just had to grit my teeth and hang on tight when the general and I took off in a high wind.

Otherwise, life as a young Marine in Hawaii was pretty good. One incident I remember vividly sums up the kinds of tasks I had to handle.

November 10 is celebrated every year as the birthday of the Marine Corps (that's the day in 1775 when the Corps was officially established). On that date in 1954, General Dyer and I spent the day attending festivities at various Marine Corps locations. Late in the afternoon, having returned from a celebration at Pearl Harbor, we drove back in a motorcade to a hangar at a Marine base where the troops and officers had been partying all day long. When we got out of our cars, the reception we got was extremely raucous—not because of the general, but because of the absolutely gorgeous young woman whom I'd invited to join me for the day. The Marines, who'd been drinking for several hours, were unrestrained in their expressions of admiration for my date. It was all anyone could do to get them to keep a respectful distance when we disembarked from the general's motorcade.

The climax of the evening was a traditional ceremony in which General Dyer was called upon to cut a grand birthday cake using his sword. With a flourish, the general removed his blade from the scabbard that I held at his side and made the first cut in the cake, drawing cheers from the crowd. Then he handed me the sword, and, for some reason—perhaps distracted by the persistent ogling that my lovely date was getting from my fellow Marines—I stuck the sword back in its scabbard without wiping it first.

The smile on the general's face said it all. "You're going to clean that sword tonight," he informed me. "And I don't want a single cake crumb in the scabbard when you're done."

So the festive day and my exotic date ended a little differently than I'd hoped—with me sitting at the kitchen table in the general's house, patiently sponging birthday cake frosting out of his ceremonial scabbard.

After departing from active duty with the Marine Corps in 1955, my first idea about a career possibility was to get into the helicopter business. Despite my nervousness about flying with General Dyer, I bought into the enthusiasm for helicopters that was so widespread in both military and civilian circles in the 1950s. I figured that one day soon, millions of people would have helicopters in their suburban garages.

Accordingly, armed with a supportive letter of introduction from General Dyer, I visited the offices of Sikorsky Aircraft in Bridgeport, Connecticut, a pioneer in the design, building, and sale of helicopters. They actually offered me a job, but it was in their manufacturing plant, which didn't strike me as interesting or suitable for me. So I turned it down. I also visited New York Airways, which had just inaugurated helicopter service from the roof of the Pan American building in midtown Manhattan to LaGuardia and Idlewild airports (the latter now known as John F. Kennedy International). They, too, offered me a job—as a ticket taker. I turned that one down too.

A bit frustrated, I decided to follow up on an introduction offered by a college friend of mine. "My dad runs an investment banking firm on Wall Street," he told me. "So he has connections to practically every kind of business. I know he could offer you some advice about getting into the helicopter industry."

I scheduled an appointment and called upon my friend's father in his handsome, wood-paneled office in downtown Manhattan. He listened to me with kindly curiosity, then asked, a bit bemused, "Why do you want to get into helicopters? Here on Wall Street, we work with all kinds of businesses. One day we might get involved with helicopters. But in the meantime, we're working on every other kind of company you can think of. That's a lot more interesting, if you ask me."

I was quite naive. "What do you do here, anyway?" I asked. I honestly had no idea what an investment banker did, and in fact the entire purpose of the financial sector was pretty much a blank slate to me.

He smiled and replied, "Well, if you're interested in learning about it, I could give you a job sitting at that desk over there" (and he pointed to a seat just a few steps outside his own office). "That would be the best way to find out exactly what we do." And that is the analytical process that led me to begin a career on Wall Street.

The man who offered me that job was George Herbert Walker Jr., then the senior partner of G. H. Walker & Co. The firm had been founded by his father, also named George Herbert Walker. He was the uncle of George H. W. Bush and the great-uncle of George W. Bush.

Why did the head of the firm make such a quick decision to hire a friend of his son's? I think he liked what he'd heard about my Yale background. And he liked the fact that I'd served in the Marines. It was a classic case of being at the right place at the right time—or maybe you could call it dumb luck. I strongly doubt that I would be quite so fortunate if I were entering the job market for the first time today. But at least I was smart

enough to recognize a good opportunity when it came my way.
I said yes.

I started work almost immediately, sitting at that desk just
a few steps away from Mr. Walker's office and serving as his
assistant. It was a job that gave me ample opportunities to listen, read memos and reports, prepare correspondence, attend
meetings, and otherwise immerse myself in the work of an old-
fashioned Wall Street financial firm.

I quickly got involved in a number of noteworthy transactions. For example, Mr. Walker's nephew, George H. W. Bush,
who had moved to Texas after graduating from Yale in 1948,
had recently formed a company called Zapata Oil with a small
group of fellow businesspeople. G. H. Walker & Co. served as
underwriters for Zapata, raising money for the company, and I
served as the junior man on that financing project.

I enjoyed what I was doing and I was picking up a good bit
of business knowledge. But I also felt strongly that I needed a
lot more systematic background and information before I could
call myself a real professional. So after about ten months on the
job, in 1956, I decided to go to Harvard Business School (HBS)
to get more training. I paid for the program through a combination of funds I'd saved during my years in the Marines and
from my salary at G. H. Walker, a GI Bill grant, and a financial
grant-in-aid from HBS itself.

The course of studies at HBS was very rigorous, including
classes on manufacturing, marketing, finance, human resources,
and administrative processes. Just as important was the diverse
set of acquaintances I made, many of whom became lifelong
friends, and the varied business backgrounds they brought to
the classroom.

I have a letter, dated September 24, 1956, that I wrote to
my boss, Mr. Walker, that briefly discusses my first few weeks
at Harvard: "Still too early to give much comment on program

here," I wrote. "Extremely intensive of course, with an equally interesting group of people. To illustrate: seated around me in class are a British economist of ten years' experience, a lieutenant colonel air force jet pilot, and Thomas Dewey's son." (Thomas Dewey had been the governor of New York from 1943 to 1955 and had run against FDR as the Republican candidate for president in 1944.) A substantial percentage of my HBS classmates were veterans. My roommate, for example, turned out to be a Navy lieutenant I'd met while being mustered out of the Marine Corps at Treasure Island in San Francisco.

My course of studies at HBS lasted for two academic years. In between, I went back to work at G. H. Walker for the summer, and they sent me out with one of their senior partners to the Sure-Seal wax refinery, a troubled Utah-based business in which they'd invested substantial money. I lived in a hotel in Salt Lake City for three months.

Salt Lake City wasn't in the same league as New York City or even Honolulu when it came to social life. The young women in town weren't interested in a guy who came from a non-Mormon background, and the only recreational facility I could find was a soda fountain in the lobby of my hotel. So I dedicated myself strictly to work. It was a fascinating experience—my first opportunity to delve deeply into the workings of a particular company. Within a few weeks, I felt I'd figured out what was wrong with the company, and I proposed a number of specific strategic and managerial changes to improve matters. I was operating in much the same way a business consultant would do—parachuting in, applying an outsider's analytical perspective, and offering advice to fix problems.

My recommendations must have worked, because when the summer ended, G. H. Walker proposed that I remain in Utah and take over Sure-Seal as its president. I was sorely tempted, especially after they offered me an almost unheard-of amount of money—an annual salary of $10,000! But after agonizing over the decision, I decided that I needed to stay the course and complete my business education at Harvard. I came back East, and I'm glad I did.

As a matter of fact, I loved my time at HBS. Then, as now, much of the classroom instruction was by the case method, in which an organizational dilemma is examined in detail and debated among the students. I found that the assignments tended to follow a consistent pattern. I would read a case study about the problem, complete with financial data and background information, and I'd usually conclude that a particular solution was the correct one. But then, when I discussed it with a few classmates in a study group, I'd hear about four other solutions, each of which had its merits. And then, when the entire class got together to analyze the case under the leadership of a professor, I'd learn about a number of other factors I'd never even considered.

Learning that way showed me that, in many cases, the deeper you delve into a problem, the *less* obvious the answers are. Oddly enough, I found this to be an empowering experience. Since nobody really knows the one perfect solution to the kinds of tough real-life challenges organizations face, it's important to have the courage to ask questions, to propose answers, to challenge assumptions, and to experiment—all of which are key elements of the entrepreneurial drive.

Rather than deferring to the expertise of engineers, financiers, or lawyers, you learn to question, challenge, and analyze everything. I discovered that "Why should we do things the way they've always been done?" is a question that can be asked in almost every situation—and one that should be used far more often than it is, not only in business but in government, in academia, in the nonprofit world, and in society at large.

I graduated from HBS with a master's degree in June 1958

and went back to G. H. Walker, where by now I'd been named the manager of the mergers and acquisitions department. Thanks to my training at HBS, I now understood much more about the broader business and economic context within which investment banking is practiced. I'd also had my feeling for the "big picture" of any business decision strongly enhanced—and the entrepreneurial instinct that I'd been nurturing since my Buffalo boyhood had been sharpened further. One of these days, I sensed, I would want to start a business of my own. But in the meantime, I was continuing to grow and learn in my perch at G. H. Walker.

During this period, one of the key pieces that would make my entrepreneurial future possible emerged in the form of Dan Lufkin.

A good friend of mine who had been in the same class with me at Yale and had also served in the Marines, Dan had graduated from HBS a year ahead of me. We'd remained in touch, and now we both had jobs working in the New York investment scene—me at G. H. Walker and Dan in the office of Jeremiah Milbank, a wealthy man and a philanthropist who was constantly searching for interesting investment opportunities. I had also started an investment club when I was at G. H. Walker, and while I was away at Harvard, I'd asked Dan to run it for me based on his "vast" one-year experience with Milbank.

Living in New York wasn't as costly then as it is today, but it was no bargain for a couple of young guys on a budget. So Dan and I ended up sharing an apartment on East End Avenue near 79th Street with two other guys. We had a great time, working hard, enjoying the scene, and swapping ideas about our possible futures. With savings from my Marine Corps salary, I'd bought a nice little Ford. In fact, I'd actually picked it up at the factory in Michigan and (much to my chagrin) ended up burning a hole in the seat cover when I dropped an ember from a celebratory cigar I was smoking while I drove it home to Buffalo. But I liked that car, and Dan and I used to drive in it together from our place on the Upper East Side down to Wall Street, where we both now worked.

It was during those early morning drives that Dan and I got to talking about the superficial company research that was then all that was available to the growing number of institutional investors. We noted the many good, fast-growing businesses that offered real financial opportunities. One of us said, "Somebody ought to start an investment firm that would bring those opportunities to light."

We looked at each other.

And that's where the next chapter of the story begins.

CHAPTER 4

A New Kind of Investment Firm: DLJ Impacts the Financial Industry

The entrepreneurial bug from way back in my Buffalo boyhood was still eating at me in June of 1958. Worse than ever, in fact. It was clear to me that my job at G. H. Walker was just a way station—an apprenticeship in which I could sharpen my understanding of how Wall Street and the world of business work. I was itching to start something of my own—a business I could build into something big, new, and lasting. So every day, while doing my best work for Walker, I had my eyes open for an opportunity I could seize on my own behalf. And my old friend Dan Lufkin shared the desire to start a business of his own.

It didn't take long for Dan and me to come up with the idea we both had been looking for.

We had begun to notice several interesting realities about the world of finance. One was the poor quality of the investment ideas that were in general circulation. There was very little in-depth, qualitative analysis of companies going on. Instead, the research that crossed our desks from ratings organizations like Standard & Poor's or brokerage firms like

Merrill Lynch was really just statistical analysis that regurgitated the numbers from company balance sheets—useful in its way, but very superficial.

Partly as a result of this apparent paucity of good investment ideas and analysis, the big investors—organizations with lots of funds to allocate, such as banks, pension funds, and endowments—were sinking practically all of their money into bonds and only the very bluest of blue-chip stocks. Those shares of giant companies that had benefited from the growth of the U.S. economy following World War II were widely known as "The Favorite Fifty" because that's where most of the investment money was going. The companies on this list, like U.S. Steel, Procter & Gamble, DuPont, and the "generals"—General Foods, General Mills, General Motors, and General Electric—were sound and safe businesses, but they weren't really great investment options. Their sales revenues and profits were continuing to grow, but slowly—quite a bit more slowly, in fact, than their share prices, which had been bid up and up by all those investors eager to find a home for their capital. That meant the stocks of the Favorite Fifty were selling at very high price-per-share to earnings-per-share multiples. In other words, those stocks cost a lot more than they were really worth.

At the same time, Dan and I could see that the sheer volume of investment money looking for stocks to buy was growing quickly. The mutual fund industry was just coming into being; companies like Putnam and Fidelity were beginning to pool vast sums from thousands, then millions, of individual investors, and all that money needed someplace to go. As the volume of money held by pension funds, insurance companies, endowments, and banks continued to grow, these institutions were becoming increasingly dissatisfied with the meager returns being offered by bonds and blue-chip stocks. As these big investors grew more and more aggressive, Dan and I realized there would be a market for an investment firm that could respond to their needs. But how?

We thought we had an answer. We noticed that the rapidly expanding postwar U.S. economy included a lot of interesting, often smaller companies that boasted high-quality products, loyal customers, and histories of uninterrupted growth. These companies, many with market caps under $50 million, were growing ten times as fast as the giant firms that made up the Dow Jones Industrials. Yet their shares were selling at price/earnings multiples that were far more reasonable—five to one or six to one rather than twenty to one. In other words, these small-company stocks were as underpriced as the Favorite Fifty were overpriced—which meant they represented a huge buying opportunity for the savvy investor. But how could we make these relatively little-known companies as attractive to conservative institutional investors as the giant firms whose names everyone knew? (As the old saying went, "No one ever got fired for buying IBM.")

An idea gradually began to take shape. At Harvard Business School, we'd analyzed lengthy case studies that detailed the strengths and weaknesses of companies from many industries. We'd also seen the kinds of analytical reports generated by great management consulting firms like McKinsey & Company. Reports like these brought you *inside* a company, enabling someone with little knowledge of a particular industry to make an informed judgment about the prospects of a firm. Yet few investors had ever seen such reports. With a handful of exceptions—for example, Smith Barney—few brokerage firms had even tried to delve that deeply into the stories of individual companies.

Dan and I sensed that a financial firm that developed detailed, accurate, high-quality research about promising smaller companies could have a powerful edge over the rest of Wall Street. If we could produce in-depth research reports that would give the rapidly growing pool of institutional investors the courage to invest in fast-growing small businesses, we could help those investors make very good returns, help those companies to continue expanding, and do well for ourselves in the process. The more we talked about this concept, the more we were convinced it represented a viable business opportunity.

The two of us also formed a solid nucleus for the prospective company. Dan and I had a lot in common, as well as our shared vision about the potential of a research-oriented investment firm. However, we felt we needed a third partner to complete our team. "The two of us get along well because we're so alike," I told Dan. "But the problem is that we're *too much* alike—both Yalies, both ex-Marines, both young and a little wet behind the ears. Why don't we recruit someone else who'll bring some additional strengths to the team?"

After some thought and discussion, we came up with the name of Dick Jenrette. Dick had been in the same class at HBS as Dan, a year ahead of me, but he was a couple of years older than us. He was a Southerner, a people-oriented person with a solid record of academic achievement and a reputation for high integrity. Dick was also on an upward career track at the highly respected firm of Brown Brothers Harriman, which meant he was practically set for life. Why would he want to cast his lot with the likes of Dan and me?

So we took Dick out for dinner one night. I don't remember where we went—I'm not even sure that we paid for his meal. But I do know that Dan and I did our level best to talk Dick into sharing our vision, describing the incredible opportunities we imagined in vivid terms.

Dick's response was exactly the one you might have expected: "No one has ever heard of the two of you, and yet you want to build a business by convincing some of the world's oldest and most conservative investors to follow your advice and invest in companies they've never heard of. You two must be crazy."

After dinner, Dan and I returned to our shared bachelor pad and agreed, "Well, *that's* not going to work!"

But the next morning, Dick Jenrette called us up and said, "I may be crazy too. But I've thought it over, and I'm with you."

At the time, we didn't ask Dick to explain his change of heart—we were too delighted and afraid that he'd reconsider. But Dick later said he was more convinced by our personalities than by the strength of our business concept. "Bill and Dan are just very attractive and popular and bouncy," he later told an interviewer. "They have very affectionate personalities, and I knew that they were winners. I knew we'd figure out something, *and* that they would be fun to work with . . . so I said, 'Let's go for it.'"[2]

Now we had a team of three partners to guide our business. At some point, of course, we had to figure out what to call the thing. People sometimes wonder how it got to be Donaldson, Lufkin & Jenrette, especially since that order is not alphabetical (in which case Jenrette would have come second). You might think that Dick would have had a beef about being relegated to third place, but in fact it was Dan Lufkin who raised the issue. It was one evening when we'd spent a few hours going over our plans for the business. In our car heading home that night, Dan spoke up. "I think we ought to call ourselves Lufkin, Donaldson & Jenrette," he declared. It was an awkward moment, since we'd already been using Donaldson, Lufkin & Jenrette as a working name on documents.

A brief, slightly embarrassing debate ensued, which was soon settled by Dick Jenrette. "I think it should be Donaldson, Lufkin & Jenrette," he announced, willingly accepting the final position for the sake of harmony among partners. Somehow this seemed to be the decisive word on the subject, and in that way Donaldson, Lufkin & Jenrette—or simply DLJ—was born. My entrepreneurial dream was becoming a reality.

* * *

While Dan, Dick, and I began putting together the pieces we would need to launch our new company, something important was happening on the social front. One of the big turning points in my life had occurred when, at a party my first night back in New York after leaving the Marine Corps, I happened to run into a lovely young woman named Evan Burger, whom I'd last encountered when I'd invited her to the junior prom at Yale. Unfortunately, my timing had been terrible—I'd extended the invitation just two weeks before the dance, which she took to mean she'd been my second or even my third choice. (Actually, I had just procrastinated.) Thoroughly insulted, Evan had turned me down, and I'd assumed I'd lost my chance at getting to know her forever. The assumption was reinforced while I was overseas, when I read in the paper that Evan Burger had gotten engaged.

So when I spotted Evan at that party (to which I'd escorted another girl), I was a bit startled—and still attracted, despite my belief that she was off-limits. I waited until I had a moment alone and sidled up to her.

"How's marriage treating you?" I asked.

Evan shrugged. "We didn't get married," she replied.

"Oh, really?" I responded. "Isn't that interesting."

Much to my delight, I discovered that Evan had managed to forgive me for my awkwardly orchestrated prom invitation, and that she would not be averse to seeing me. I managed to get her number before the party ended, and within a couple of days I gave her a call. I learned that Evan had graduated from Vassar and was working in a New York office as a secretary, and that she'd formed no other strong attachments since the end of her engagement. Evan and I began dating, and the two of us gradually became a serious item.

Evan and I got married in September 1960 at her family's home church in Hewlett, New York. (By then, DLJ had been up and running for some nine months.) We moved into an apartment on the Upper East Side of New York, where we lived for the next four years, before moving to a larger place on Park Avenue. We were living there when we adopted our daughter, Kimberly, in March 1967, and our son, Matthew, two years later.

When she wasn't tooling around the city on her bike, Evan threw herself into civic life. She ultimately became a significant force at the Spence-Chapin adoption agency. She was also a cofounder of the Yorkville Volunteer Center. With a small group of other philanthropic women, she started the New York Women's Foundation, which became a model for other such foundations around the country.

I was the first of the DLJ triumvirate to tie the knot. Dan Lufkin gave up his bachelor status just four months later, in January 1961.

Dick Jenrette is a different story, and an interesting one that says something about the times in which we lived. For many years, Dan and I thought of Dick as what people then called "a confirmed bachelor"—a guy who, for one reason or another, just never gets around to marrying. Occasionally Dick would double-date with Dan or me and whatever young women we were escorting at the time. But Dick's relationships with women never escalated to the point of reaching marriage.

Once in a great while, someone would wonder aloud (usually behind closed doors) whether the third cofounder of DLJ was possibly more interested in men than women. (The word "gay" wasn't then the almost universal term it has since become.) The question arose not just because Dick never married but also because, starting around 1966, he was very close to Bill Thompson—a wonderful guy with whom Dick shared many interests, such as renovating historic homes. Whenever this speculation reached me, I always responded the same way: "Absolutely not!" That's exactly what I believed to be true, though I suppose in retrospect I was a bit naive. I felt I was defending my friend against a charge that would have been considered quite scandalous at the time.

Dick ended up bearing the brunt of some criticism from outspoken gay activists in the 1990s, who felt that it would have been helpful to the cause if a prominent, successful, and highly respected business leader like him had "come out of the closet." But Dick chose to keep his sexual orientation a private matter—which was his right, of course. As far as I know, the only time Dick publicly discussed his relationship with Bill Thompson was at Bill's funeral in 2014, when he gave a moving eulogy for the friend with whom he'd spent forty-eight years.

We've come a long way since 1960. In today's world, millions of people who love others of the same sex are free to express their feelings publicly in a way that was scarcely imaginable when I was young. It's a change for the better, and I hope the last vestiges of prejudice based on sexual orientation are on their way to extinction.

* * *

Meanwhile, even as Dan, Dick, and I were forging connections while we worked for other firms, we were working away on our plans for launching DLJ. One of my early strategic suggestions was the idea that we should buy a seat on the New York Stock Exchange. There were a couple of reasons for this proposal. One was that being members of the Exchange, and subject to all the institutional rules and controls that implied, would give us credibility among potential clients—kind of a *Good Housekeeping* seal of approval that would make it easier for institutional investors to feel comfortable doing business with us.

At the same time, owning our own seat on the Exchange would make a huge difference in our cash flow. The seat would enable us to buy and sell shares of stock on behalf of our clients. That was a lucrative line of business to be in, especially in those days of fixed brokerage commissions, when institutional investors were paying as much per share for an order of one million shares of stock as a small investor would pay per share for an order of one hundred shares. So we saw our seat on the Exchange as a tool that would enable us to get paid more for our research (albeit indirectly) than we could earn by simply selling our reports or getting paid by the hour for our work the way a consulting firm might do. In today's business jargon, the seat offered us a way to "monetize" the services we'd provide and to realize and capture a share of the value created.

The only downside was that a seat on the Exchange would be expensive. A seat cost around $150,000, a pretty penny in 1960 dollars. And that wouldn't be the only start-up cost we would have to cover. So we set out to raise money from anybody and everybody we knew. We spent several months making phone calls, taking people out to lunch or for coffee, and visiting them in their offices and homes. Our targets included old classmates from college and business school, work acquaintances, and friends and relatives of the above. Many were skeptical, but enough were impressed by our ideas for the business (or at least by our enthusiasm and persistence) that they ponied up some cash for our project. Somehow we got it done. In the end, we raised something over $600,000, mostly in the form of loans, to get the company started.

When we formally announced the formation of Donaldson,

Lufkin & Jenrette, the initial response was pretty underwhelming. We were the first new firm founded on Wall Street in several decades, which many people considered a good indication that there was no need for us. We preferred the theory that the dearth of new organizations suggested a huge gap that we were well equipped to fill. Furthermore, our modest career histories and obvious youth made it easy for more seasoned veterans of the industry to dismiss us as a trio of newcomers who could scarcely be expected to have insights, ideas, and judgments that would have eluded the old pros.

In an interview years later, Dan Lufkin recalled visiting more than ten industry leaders on Wall Street—top executives from firms like Goldman Sachs and Lehman Brothers—and finding that not a single one considered our idea viable. Dan says that one fellow he knew from Lehman Brothers told him, "We're going to squash you like a fly on the wall."[3]

Even my dad back in Buffalo wasn't convinced that we knew what we were doing. "You guys haven't had much experience," he said doubtfully. Of course, his own business history may have colored his reaction. Having started a business and seen it blow up in the crash of 1929—and then having spent years of his life working hard to pay back the investors whose cash had been lost—had left him understandably shell-shocked and risk-averse.

My own takeaway from my dad's sad experience was different from his. Rather than shying away from taking business risks, I vowed we would work doubly hard to make sure we got every detail of our business plan right, so we could have a good shot at building a business that would last for the long haul and survive whatever ups and downs the economy might throw our way.

We did what we could to establish some credibility for our fledgling company. We published a small sixteen-page booklet titled *Common Stock and Common Sense* to explain our business philosophy. It made the case that investors seeking high growth from stocks in the coming decade should turn away from the Favorite Fifty in favor of the "Future Favorite Fifty"—smaller companies poised for exceptional growth whose stock prices had not already been bid up to the point of having unreasonable price/earnings ratios.

The booklet also analyzed four key characteristics we felt investors could use to identify the growth stocks of tomorrow. These included "a steadily improving record of sales (recognizing unit as well as dollar sales), per share earnings, and to a lesser extent, profit margins"; "a good record of new product or process development"; above-average management; and a field of operations "characterized by rapid development of new applications and new products within an expanding overall market." Along the way, the booklet dropped the names of many small companies, some of them little known, that offered enticing investment opportunities for the future, including American Photocopy (then the leader in the field of document imaging and reproduction), Papercraft (a Pittsburgh-based maker of gift wrap and related products), Beauty Counselors (a firm that distributed cosmetics through local salespeople, a bit like the better-known Avon), Haveg Industries (a wire and cable company that would soon be making products used in the Apollo space program), and Heli-Coil Corporation (a maker of wire thread inserts that give added strength to metal fasteners).

Common Stock and Common Sense was a selling piece—a kind of advertisement thinly disguised as a research report—but it offered a thoughtful framework for what we were going to do as well as some concrete ideas that investors could begin to put into practice immediately. We distributed copies as widely as we could, often while making courtesy calls on prospective institutional clients, and we got a very positive response.

Still, when we opened our door for the first time in December 1959, we didn't have any clients to our name. Our first office was a tiny little place at 51 Broad Street that we subleased from another firm. It was inhabited by six of us—we three partners; a receptionist in charge of answering the phone and taking messages; a secretary named Pat Derby whom Dick had recruited from Brown Brothers Harriman; and a trader friend of Dan's whom we'd hired to execute stock orders once our (nonexistent) clients began to provide them.

There was a flurry of excitement that morning when the first visitor appeared. We heard the sound of the elevator arriving at our floor, the iron gates opened, and a distinguished-looking gentleman in an expensive gray suit emerged. He was a prospective customer that Dan had visited, come to check out the new kids on Wall Street. It was a great moment, which swiftly gave way to dismay as we all realized how utterly unimpressive our offices looked—cheap metal desks, bare floors, and unshaded light bulbs dangling by wires from the ceiling.

Luckily, Dan rose to the occasion. He leaped up from his desk, rushed over to our visitor, draped an arm warmly over his shoulder, and pushed him back into the elevator, saying, "Let's go have a cup of coffee!" Dan conducted the rest of his sales pitch at a corner table in the nearby deli—a more attractive location than our spartan headquarters.

But the day wasn't over. Later than morning, the phone rang. It was an old HBS classmate of ours who was now helping to run the pension fund for General Tire and Rubber. "I read your booklet," he said, "and I like some of those investment ideas you offer." Before the call was through, he'd given us a 10,000-share order for American Photocopy. To us, that seemed like an enormous order. More important, the commission on the sale was around forty cents per share, netting DLJ a cool $4,000.

Not bad for our first day in business—and a harbinger of things to come. We ended up earning commissions of around $150,000 from that one account in our first year—one of half a dozen good-sized accounts that we attracted during that time span.

It wasn't long before a handsome stream of revenues and profits began to flow into DLJ. The institutional investors we'd counted on as our core clientele responded much as we'd hoped. They appreciated the analysis we provided about promising investment opportunities, and they liked our honestly aggressive business philosophy. When we began sending out regular research reports about the attractive companies we were discovering, clients would call to thank us and ask for more ideas. "If you like the work we're doing," we'd say, "send some of your other brokerage transactions our way. We'll execute trades for you, and the commissions we earn will pay for even more great research information." The quid pro quo made sense to people, and our business was up and running. We signed up a roster of clients, started expanding our team, and began building a reputation for DLJ as the hot new house on Wall Street.

In those early days, the three of us all worked on teaching ourselves how to do investment research. We all had some experience in picking stocks, and our business school education had taught us a lot about how to analyze and evaluate a company's strategy. Dick Jenrette even said that his experience as an investigator for the Counterintelligence Corps of the U.S. Army had sharpened his research instincts, showing him how to ask probing questions and dig deep beneath superficial perceptions. So we worked on mastering the art of stock analysis, learning a great deal from one another in the process.

The crucial element that DLJ brought to the research game was an investigative mind-set. We did much more than just read company reports and study balance sheets. When we were interested in a company, we would meet the CEO and some chief officers, which enabled us to gauge the strength of their leadership and the soundness of their strategic thinking. But we didn't stop there. We also talked to customers, competitors, distributors, suppliers, and others with on-the-ground knowledge of the company's strengths and weaknesses. We analyzed the quality of their products and services, and did old-fashioned gumshoe reporting to uncover the industry scuttlebutt about the company.

Sometimes our detective work punched giant holes in the public image that a company was striving to present. We heard great things about a dental-supply company based in Rochester, New York, that had developed a supposedly revolutionary new drill. But how could we determine whether or not the new gadget was truly poised to take the market by storm? Dan and I infiltrated a dentists' convention to ferret out the truth. We chatted up professionals who'd personally tested the new device and heard nothing but complaints. Needless to say, we passed up the opportunity to recommend that company to our clients.

Our goal was to find companies that we believed were poised to experience annual growth of 15 percent or more—companies capable of doubling their earnings in a five-year period. Over those first few years, we unearthed quite a few examples, drawn from a wide variety of business fields. Among the winners that DLJ recommended were American Greetings (a greeting card company run out of Cleveland by a team of three brothers), Dun & Bradstreet, Diebold, Alcon Laboratories (an ophthalmic drug company), McLean Shipping, A. C. Nielsen, Mead Johnson, and Hershey.

In each case, our thorough research and careful analysis yielded a report that explained the nature of the business in clear, simple terms that any intelligent investor could understand, detailing the company's products, markets, competitive situation, strategic positioning, strengths, and weaknesses. In short, we provided investors with all the data they needed to decide whether a particular company would be a good fit for their portfolios.

It was the kind of information and analysis that wasn't widely available at the time. And it paid off. A study of the fifty-one companies we recommended between 1960 and 1963 found that they outperformed the Dow Jones Industrial Average by more than 50 percent.

Along the way, we encountered plenty of curious business circumstances. One company we admired was American Photocopy, the firm whose shares had been the first ones a DLJ client had purchased through us. American Photocopy had parlayed an old imaging technology that used specially made coated paper into a thriving business, taking advantage of the fast-growing U.S. economy and the huge need it was generating for convenient ways to reproduce documents.

One day I was visiting a DLJ client named Bert Tripp, who was in charge of the endowment fund run by the University of Rochester. I was talking up American Photocopy as a great investment opportunity. After listening to me in silence for a while, Bert said, "Come with me." He led me out of his office, along hallways and down flights of stairs, until we arrived at a dark corner deep in the bowels of one of the university's biggest buildings. Bert took out a key and opened a locked door, flicked on a light switch, and said, "Look at this."

I saw something I'd never seen before—something very few people anywhere had ever seen. It was one of the first plain paper photocopiers ever made, developed for the fledgling Haloid Xerox Corporation by Chester Carlson and John Dessauer. Xerox had lent an advance prototype to the university for testing. And having used the machine, Bert knew full well that it would soon revolutionize the copying business and render American Photocopy's equipment obsolete.

This revelation forced us to quickly rethink our belief in American Photocopy as a high-growth investment opportunity. In fact, we urged the leaders of American Photocopy to consider buying the then-tiny Xerox company. "Xerox has the breakthrough technology," we told them, "but you have the sales force, the market contacts, and the reputation. Combine the two and you will be unbeatable." Sadly, they rejected the idea. Like many companies faced with an unforeseen challenge, they preferred to cling to the status quo rather than embrace a new product with the potential to cannibalize their existing business. Today, American Photocopy has been relegated to the dustbin of forgotten business history.

In the years that followed, we at DLJ became quite close to the executive team that was building the success of Xerox. We admired them greatly and, I think, we shared some of their business philosophy. In fact, DLJ in those days was close in spirit to many of the companies we researched and recommended. Like them, we were small, entrepreneurial, and highly ambitious. Like them, we thought we had a better idea than our big competitors, and we were determined to build a great company by providing a unique product to meet a need no one else had recognized. In the 1960s and 1970s, DLJ and many of those small companies would grow up together, changing the face of American business.

* * *

O. M. Scott, the producer of seeds and lawn-care products, best known today for Scott's Miracle-Gro fertilizer, was one of DLJ's early success stories. Yet it nearly became one of our biggest disasters, due to a simple but almost fatal oversight.

Dan Lufkin was our lead researcher on O. M. Scott. He studied the company's history, competitive position, and product line, and over time he became close to Paul Williams, the company's president. In the years since World War II, O. M. Scott had been growing like a weed (pardon the expression), taking full advantage of the burgeoning U.S. economy and the powerful demand for lawns and gardens among the millions of Americans who were starting families and buying homes in the rapidly expanding suburbs. What's more, the company believed there were huge growth opportunities still ahead, and our research suggested they were right. So O. M. Scott became the subject of one of our first research reports, in which we enthusiastically recommended their stock.

In the weeks following the publication of our report, O. M. Scott's stock started to go up—in fact, it quadrupled. Our clients who'd bought the shares were thrilled, and we were pretty pleased about the brilliance of our research. Until one Saturday when I walked into a hardware store that stocked Scott products.

Ever alert for fresh marketplace insights, I found the manager. "How are Scott sales?" I asked.

"Terrible," he replied. "The company got us to take on their whole line of stuff for the spring season, and we've hardly moved a single item."

This was troubling news, to say the least. "Whoa, that sounds bad," I said. "It must be tough for you to be on the hook for so much inventory that you can't move."

The manager smiled. "Oh, we're not worried about that," he said. "We buy Scott's products on consignment. We don't pay them a penny until the stuff sells. And if it doesn't sell, we can send it back to them, and we don't owe a thing. Here, take a look in the back." And he showed me a storage room behind a STAFF ONLY door, stacked high with bags of Scott products.

I left the hardware store, went to the first phone booth I could find (in those days before cell phones), and called

Dan, who was out in Ohio researching yet another company. "Dan," I said, "do you know those Scott sales to retailers are on consignment?"

"They're what?"

"On consignment. That means the millions in product sales they showed in their last financial statement aren't for real—not until the stuff is sold at retail. And from what I hear, a lot of it may not sell at all."

There was a long silence on the phone. "That's not good," Dan finally remarked.

In its aggressive push to build Scott sales ever higher, the company's management had pursued a risky financial strategy—one that DLJ's research had simply failed to uncover.

Now we were faced with a painful dilemma. Our clients had been buying Scott's stock on our recommendation—but it was clear that the company performance was due to take a tumble once its sales strategy inevitably collapsed. What should we do about it?

Dan, Dick, and I conferred. We quickly decided that we had to face up to the problem if DLJ was to retain its credibility among investors. We also did a fresh analysis of O. M. Scott's long-term prospects, taking into account the new information we'd received about their current finances. We concluded that the company was still a candidate for strong growth, once the short-term sales decline was factored in.

Based on all this, we wrote a letter to all our clients in which we explained exactly what had happened and took responsibility for our mistake. In effect we wrote: *We still believe in O. M. Scott for the long haul. But in the short term, it's going to be a disaster. If you want to hang on to the stock, that's fine. But if you don't have the stomach for some ups and downs, let us know. We'll help you find a market for your shares so you can exit the stock at a minimal loss.* And that's exactly what we did.

As you can imagine, our clients who'd bought Scott on our recommendation were not pleased that we'd missed an important part of the story. But they respected our honesty and our willingness to help remedy the damage we'd done. Virtually all of them remained clients of DLJ, grateful to realize that we'd stand by them through good times and bad. And many of them held on to their Scott stock, which turned out to be a good long-term buy, just as we'd thought.

Thankfully, missteps like the Scott fiasco didn't happen often. But when they did, we followed the same approach. For example, when trouble struck Permian Corporation, a Texas petroleum transportation company that we'd recommended, we alerted our customers, warned them that the company was heading into a tough patch, and offered to help those who wanted to sell their stock. But we also assured them that Permian's long-term prospects were still good, and many chose to rely on our judgment and stand pat.

Around the time of our Scott misadventure, we made the acquaintance of two famous figures of that period. One was Peter Drucker, perhaps the single most distinguished theorist of business management and leadership who ever lived. Drucker was an advisor to O. M. Scott, and when Dan happened to encounter him there, he invited Drucker to visit with us at DLJ. Drucker was a fascinating and brilliant man who ended up serving as an advisor to us for a number of years—though at times I found his professorial style a bit frustrating. When he lit up his pipe and began telling us stories from his illustrious consulting career, we always knew there would be a gem of wisdom at the end of each tale—but it seemed to take a long time to emerge. I suppose that's the kind of culture clash that can happen when a seasoned old guru tries to instruct a trio of impatient young entrepreneurs.

Something similar happened when a magazine asked Dan, Dick, and me to pose for a magazine cover shot by the world-famous portrait photographer Karsh of Ottawa. His iconic images of figures ranging from Churchill, Einstein, and Eisenhower to Ernest Hemingway, John F. Kennedy, and Martin Luther King Jr. have come to define an era. We were flattered to become Karsh's latest subjects, but it drove us a bit crazy to have to carve two hours out of a busy work day to pose for him. We kept taking breaks to make quick telephone calls, confer with our assistants, sign off on memos, and so on. Somehow the picture got made, but we later heard that Karsh complained to students in a photography class he was teaching about the three young businessmen who couldn't sit still for a picture.

* * *

Looking back on those exciting early years of DLJ, I'm proud of how much fresh thinking we brought to the world of finance—particularly the field of stock investing. Today, the idea of providing in-depth research on growth companies to investors is quite familiar (though the *quality* of the research provided is still often lacking). But when Dan, Dick, and I got started, it was almost unheard-of. As Justin Schack wrote in a 2001 retrospective article in *Institutional Investor* magazine, "DLJ effectively transformed a genteel Wall Street club, in which information consisted of whispered confidences, into a marketplace of ideas."

Timing was one key to our success. We started DLJ when we did because we could see that institutional investing was on the verge of exploding, and because those institutional investors were hungry for ideas about how to make their money grow faster. Sure enough, by 1969, institutional trading, which had accounted for just 30 percent of the volume on the New York Stock Exchange when we launched DLJ, had grown to 70 percent. Our research—and the research of other firms that soon began to imitate us—played a powerful role in helping to fuel that growth. And the boom in stock investing also provided much-needed capital to America's fast-growing businesses, spurring economic expansion, creating jobs, and generating greater prosperity for millions of people. The 1960s became known as "the go-go years" for U.S. business, and DLJ was one source of that energy.

The approach to research that DLJ pioneered also encouraged individuals to take a flier on stock investing. We helped people realize that picking great companies wasn't an arcane science only PhDs in mathematics could practice; instead, it was a matter of common sense, thoughtfully applied.

In one instance, a widow came to visit us at DLJ, saying that she'd done well managing her investments on her own, but that she now wanted some professional help in managing it. When we looked over her portfolio, it was quite impressive. So we asked her, "How did you pick this fine roster of companies?"

She replied, "I keep a chart of the advertisers in *Life* magazine. When I see the first ad, the company goes on my chart. If they survive a full year and are still advertising, I move them up the list. If they're still advertising at the end of the second year, I buy some of their stock. And if they're still advertising in the fourth year, I buy some more."

This wasn't a scientific system—but it had a certain logic behind it. Any company that could pay the expensive advertising rates of *Life* magazine for four years in a row had to be a solid company. So it wasn't just an accident that the widow's portfolio had done well. The story illustrates the fact that there's no magic behind stock analysis. It just takes observation and a bit of analytical discipline. That's the approach we championed at DLJ, and it's one that worked for millions of American investors.

At the same time that DLJ was introducing a new way of

thinking about stock investments, we were also developing a new style of corporate culture—one that felt particularly innovative in the traditional world of Wall Street.

One element of that unique culture was our belief in transparency. Publicly traded companies are required to publish an annual report covering their performance for the previous year and detailing their plans for the future. DLJ starting publishing an annual report publicly long before we were publicly held. Some wondered why we'd go to the trouble and expense of creating such a document, and others questioned why we would reveal our results and our strategic plans when we weren't required to do so. But we liked the idea of letting our employees, customers, and other stakeholders understand exactly what we were doing and why. It was our way of treating them as teammates and partners, and I think they appreciated it.

From the beginning, our annual report always listed DLJ's ten most important corporate objectives, starting with our absolute commitment to integrity in all our dealings. But the last objective on the list was the most surprising, and my personal favorite: "Have fun." Back then, very few companies, especially financial institutions, would have publicly declared fun as one of their business goals—it's more like the playful ethos associated today with Silicon Valley companies like Apple or Google. But we were young, ebullient, and enjoyed bringing a spirit of innovation and vitality to Wall Street. I think that attitude helped us attract some of the brightest and most creative people in business.

The spirit of fun also helps to explain why we developed the habit of giving team members at DLJ animal nicknames. Mine was The Eel, a title that traced back to the time when Dick Jenrette was planning to come to HBS to recruit students for jobs at Brown Brothers Harriman. I was a then a second-year student, and when I filled out Dick's pre-interview form, one of the questions was, "If you were an animal, what animal would you be?"—one of the offbeat questions interviewers sometimes like to ask as a way of probing a candidate's personality. I answered, "By the way, for you to brood on, I've decided I want to be an eel." Somehow the name stuck—despite the fact that, tongue in cheek, I'd chosen one of the worst animals you could imagine for him to contemplate. My mother always hated hearing me called The Eel, no matter how often I patiently explained to her, "Mom, it's my nickname!"

That started our animal-naming craze at DLJ. Dan Lufkin was The Fox, I suppose because of his clever, sometimes wily personality. And Dick Jenrette was The Bear, because of his relatively cautious, conservative style. (As you probably know, on Wall Street the optimistic bull and the pessimistic bear are always supposed to be battling for control of the market.) We went on giving animal names to new members of the firm for quite a while. For example, John Castle, one of the recruits we hired from HBS, was dubbed The Doberman Pinscher because of his killer instinct. We hired an investment strategist named John Corcoran, a "wise man" with round spectacles who, naturally, became known as The Owl.

Fun was also an important principle in our hiring practices. Of course we wanted to find the smartest people in the business, but no matter how smart they were, if we didn't like them personally, we wouldn't hire them. We also hired a lot more women than did other Wall Street companies—not just as secretaries or receptionists, but in responsible decision-making positions with real growth opportunities. Remember, this was the *Mad Men* era, when sexism was rampant in American business. We took advantage of the fact that most companies didn't recognize and reward the talents of women by hiring many of the smartest women coming out of colleges and making them associates at DLJ. They usually started out as research assistants, and many later graduated to become analysts and portfolio managers. In time, a number went on to head great companies of their own, on Wall Street and elsewhere.

Even when DLJ was still a small, fledgling company, we made a point of recruiting candidates from the best business schools—Harvard, Wharton, Stanford. We were sending a signal that we intended to make DLJ one of the best-run, most professional firms on Wall Street. As it happened, we ended up attracting many of the best minds of the new generation. Eight out of the first ten we hired were either Baker Scholars at Harvard Business School or Phi Beta Kappas in college, which put them somewhere in the top 3 percent of graduates. And simply visiting the campuses of those great universities planted the importance of DLJ in people's minds. Dick Jenrette recalls many great, cordial interviews with those young B-school graduates. When we had to turn down some, we always tried to do it with class and dignity, saying, "We wish we could hire you." Many of the candidates that we didn't hire ended up running great firms elsewhere in business, and some became tremendous clients of DLJ.

The way we managed our business internally was also unusual. Unlike other Wall Street firms, we did not have individual accounts tied to particular account managers who were paid commissions on trades made. Instead, we organized DLJ so that everyone was considered to be working on all our accounts, and commissions on trades went into the company coffers rather than into any individual's paycheck. We were a true team, which was unique on Wall Street at the time.

What's more, we did away with the traditional distinction between salespeople, who had personal contact with the clients, and internal employees like research analysts, who remained hidden inside the firm. Everyone at DLJ was expected to make connections with our clients whenever appropriate. And why not? We were proud of the insights and knowledge that our people generated, and we knew that investors would benefit from being able to learn from them firsthand. So rather than creating a cadre of salesmen with great social skills but little real investment knowledge, we opened our doors so that clients could talk to our investment experts and ask them tough, probing questions.

We further enhanced the value of our unique DLJ team by developing an unusual system for determining compensation. As I've said, we eliminated the traditional commission-based pay approach, which created incentives for companies to encourage needless trading by clients (in order to jack up brokerage commissions). Instead, we decided to base an individual's compensation on the collective judgment of the entire DLJ community—including our clients. It was one of the first examples of what has come to be known as the 360-degree evaluation system. Everyone at DLJ had a chance to offer a thoughtful judgment about the effectiveness and contributions of their colleagues, without regard to hierarchy or power: The receptionist had her say about each of us partners, for example, and her opinion carried some weight in determining our income. And of course we solicited input from DLJ customers, whose opinions were most important of all.

I won't say everybody was thrilled by the results of this system, but nobody could argue with the judgment rendered by such a large and diverse group. Most people agreed that our 360-degree system was more fair and meaningful than having one's bonus decided by an individual manager or even a small committee of executives who might have unspoken bias or favoritism.

But the most important component of DLJ's corporate culture was our insistence on absolute integrity. We made it abundantly clear that every action, every decision, every policy we carried out must be based on doing the right thing—for our clients, and for everyone affected. We would bend over backward to avoid conflicts of interest, or even the appearance of conflicts, and we made a point of avoiding entanglements with people whose ethical standards were suspect.

This strict integrity standard sometimes cost us money. On occasion, a somewhat shady character who'd already made a lot of money on the Street would approach us with a business proposition—sometimes a very tempting one. We always politely refused. As a result, DLJ had a remarkably clean ethical and legal record, free of SEC investigations, serious customer complaints, and even untoward rumors. This produced a self-reinforcing effect: Because DLJ got a reputation as one of the "cleanest" houses on Wall Street, people with strong moral codes were attracted to us, both as clients and as employees.

Combine that sterling reputation for honesty with the other features of DLJ's culture—our sense of fun, our openness to high-quality people from varied backgrounds and to women at the professional levels, our belief in transparency, our avoidance of rigid hierarchy, and above all the excitement of building a great new business based on innovative, entrepreneurial thinking—and it's no wonder that DLJ soon became known as the firm where so many on Wall Street wanted to work.

Of all the great things we accomplished at DLJ, that may be the one of which I'm most proud.

CHAPTER 5

Tides of Change: Reinventing DLJ

Donaldson, Lufkin & Jenrette was launched and built its early success based on the quality of our innovative investment research. But we didn't stop there. During our first several years in business, we gradually expanded the number and variety of our service offerings, finding new ways to provide value to our clients and to help fuel the continued growth of the dynamic U.S. economy.

We had been in business only around six months when I said to Dan Lufkin and Dick Jenrette, "I think we've got to get started in Europe." During my time at G. H. Walker, I'd seen the power and influence of Scottish investors in the U.S. markets. The Scots had a long tradition of investing in the United States; in fact, the building of America's railroad infrastructure in the nineteenth century had largely been financed by Scottish investors. "I'm going to go to Scotland to introduce our firm."

Making connections in Britain was culturally very different than in the United States. If you wanted to do business with one of the great American banks—J. P. Morgan, for example—you had to start at the bottom, perhaps with one of the junior analysts, and work your way up through the ranks gradually, a process that might take years. In Scotland, they do just the reverse. You start by seeking an introduction to the senior partner, which can only be obtained through a mutual acquaintance. If the senior partner agrees to meet you and decides you are worth doing business with, he then connects you with some of the junior members of the firm, and business may begin to flow. In my case, one of my G. H. Walker connections gave me introductions to senior people at some of the big Scottish investment firms, so I set off to Edinburgh for my first prospecting visit.

Many of the Scottish investment companies have offices around Charlotte Square in Edinburgh, and I duly sought appointments to meet with their senior partners, moving from one building to the next over the course of several days of meetings. But the granddaddy of all the Scottish financial firms was Alliance Trust Company, and a visit there required an early morning "milk train" ride to the city of Dundee. It was an exciting moment when I was ushered into the presence of David McCurrach, universally recognized as the most distinguished investor in Scotland. He served Alliance Trust as its manager, director, and chairman for forty years, finally retiring in 1980. We had a most productive meeting, in which I learned about Alliance's approach to investing and was able to explain to him the kind of research DLJ intended to do. Alliance began channeling some of its U.S. investments through DLJ, and we enjoyed doing business together for many years thereafter.

My respect for this great exemplar of the Scottish financial tradition had an influence on one of DLJ's most important business diversification projects. Having helped our many institutional clients to build successful portfolios through our research reports and strategic investment advice, we became increasingly interested in having a hand in directly managing investment funds for our customers. After all, since we'd proven our ability to help mutual funds, pension funds, endowment funds, and other institutions earn better returns on their money, why not offer to manage those funds directly ourselves? We'd relieve the institutions of the necessity of maintaining a department to tackle this task, we'd earn an appropriate fee for the service we'd provide, and everyone would benefit.

There was only one problem with this plan. If DLJ began offering investment management services, we might be viewed as competing with some of our best customers, who were themselves in the investment management business. Perhaps they would fear we might try to poach some of their customers, or hold back our best investment ideas for our own use rather than sharing them as we'd always done.

We had no intention of permitting such conflicts of interest to arise, but communicating this convincingly to our customers would not necessarily be easy. As a symbolic gesture, we decided to give the investment management division a name of its own so as to downplay its connection with DLJ. Dick Jenrette has called this strategy "a fig leaf," adding, "You wouldn't think switching the name would make a difference, but it did. There was no longer an overt stigma attached to DLJ taking accounts away from our big institutional clients."

The name we chose for the new investment management division of DLJ was Alliance Capital, selected partly out of respect for the Alliance Trust Company in Scotland, but perhaps more importantly because we thought we could expand the division by acquiring other investment firms, thus forming an "alliance" of multiple businesses. There was never any difficulty with our friends and customers in Scotland over this matter of nomenclature, and DLJ's Alliance Capital division quickly became successful.

The ironic coda to this story is that, after DLJ was acquired by Credit Suisse many years later, the corporate attorneys for Credit Suisse got the idea of suing Alliance Trust Company in Scotland for "stealing" the Alliance brand from the DLJ division—precisely the opposite of what had really happened. The Credit Suisse lawyers had no idea about the real story behind the name. Thankfully, their plan to sue our innocent Scottish clients didn't go anywhere.

One of the first institutional clients we gained for our Alliance division was Litton Industries, a company with an interesting history. Back in 1953, a pair of businessmen named Tex Thornton and Roy Ash, both formerly executives at the Ford Motor Company, had bought Litton, then a little company that made microwave tubes. Thornton and Ash set about using acquisitions and mergers to transform it into a giant business that would be the first really successful conglomerate. By 1961, Litton had completed twenty-five mergers, mostly with technology companies, and operated a total of forty-eight plants in nine countries with sales of $245 million. By 1965, the company had over $900 million in annual sales derived from five thousand different products.

We got to know Litton when we researched them as a potential investment, and, in conversations with the company's top executives, we mentioned that DLJ was in the process of launching an investment management division. Litton decided to give us their pension fund to manage, an $8 million account at the time that was a key initial client for Alliance. It was followed by the Ford Motor Company and Whirlpool, and Alliance was off to a great start. By the early 1970s, Alliance had grown to be the largest nonbank manager of pension funds in the United States.

Alliance also promoted the concept of having multiple managers for a pension fund rather than putting all of those (often sizable) investment eggs in a single basket. Dick Jenrette talked about this in an interview in 2002, comparing it to the investment strategy used by a legendary silent film star and movie executive who had her own large portfolio to manage. "I had thought it was a good thing when Gloria Swanson pitted Brown Brothers against Morgan and Bank of New York; it got everybody on edge," Dick observed. "Years later, DLJ, through Alliance Capital, pioneered the idea, 'Don't let one bank manage your pension fund. Introduce a little competition to get it on the edge.'"[4]

This meant that, in some cases, Alliance had to split the management of a particular pension fund with one or more other organizations that could be viewed as our rivals. But we didn't mind the competition, and in most instances it benefited our clients by giving them access to a broader range of investment ideas and helping them build a more diversified, and therefore less risky, portfolio.

A further step in DLJ's growth was our acquisition of the pension management business owned by Moody's, the giant financial rating agency. Moody's owned a public pension fund business that was gigantic. However, the division wasn't generating any profits for Moody's. So over time, the leaders of the firm had come to feel that this business was a distraction from Moody's core mission of evaluating and rating the financial status of companies. We purchased this business and merged it with Alliance, significantly expanding our money management business in one fell swoop.

Our next acquisition was a more counterintuitive one for a financial firm. One of the leading public polling organizations in the 1960s was Louis Harris and Associates. The company founder and president, Lou Harris, was politically connected and a friend of then-president John F. Kennedy, who was also a leading Harris client. However, Lou wasn't sure how to manage his privately held firm with an eye to future growth and increased profitability. So when Lou visited DLJ and asked for our advice, he was surprised when we said, "We ought to acquire you."

A polling company and a financial firm might seem an odd fit, but there was a certain logic to the idea. Harris's expertise at uncovering and dissecting changes in public opinion had the potential to unearth trends that might be highly relevant to businesses of all kinds—and might suggest promising investment opportunities. We explained this concept to Lou, and it appealed to him, so the deal was done. Louis Harris and Associates became part of the growing family of DLJ businesses, and Lou and I became close friends. He introduced me to many of his political friends, and he invited me to join him at the Republican and Democratic Party national conventions, those quadrennial exercises in hoopla and propaganda that are such a colorful feature of the American political scene.

Unfortunately, we never figured out how to convert the value of the Harris polling approach into concrete research results with financial value to DLJ or its clients. Largely for cultural reasons, we never managed to fully integrate Harris's organization into DLJ, and so the intellectual and strategic synergies that might have existed never materialized.

DLJ ultimately sold the Harris operation to the Gannett newspaper chain in 1975. Today, under the name of Harris Interactive, it mainly conducts Internet-based market research for corporate clients.

There was one big acquisition that Dan, Dick, and I dreamed about that wasn't meant to be. In the early 1960s, we hatched the idea that DLJ should acquire American Express.

At that time, Amex was not yet the financial powerhouse it later became. The credit card business, its economic mainstay, was still in its infancy, and when Howard Clark became the company's CEO in 1960, one of his first acts was to reject an offer to sell the unprofitable Green Card operation to competitor Diners Club. Clark knew what he was doing. He targeted affluent business travelers with clever television ads built around the slogan "Don't leave home without it," and Amex began its ascent. By the time we made our minnow-swallowing-the-whale offer to purchase the company, Amex was feeling its oats, and Howard Clark brushed us off.

But in 1963, Amex was hit by the worst financial crisis in its history—the famous salad oil scandal. An Amex subsidiary had leased tanks full of oil that served as collateral for loans to the Allied Crude Vegetable Oil Refining Corporation—loans that Amex had guaranteed. When it was revealed that the tanks contained much less oil than claimed, Amex was stuck with $100 million in bad debt. To its credit, Amex didn't renounce the debt but paid it off as best as it could, earning praise for its integrity from most observers.

The crisis changed Clark's attitude toward the idea of having a financial partner. He began to talk seriously with us about an investment. Eventually, as Amex's financial fortunes continued to rise, he turned the tables on us and offered to acquire DLJ. We didn't want to cede control to any other company. But in 1973 we agreed to sell Amex a 25 percent stake in DLJ. The move was applauded by a number of our own employees. We hadn't allowed them to sell any shares in our public offering, but now they could benefit from the opportunity to finally gain some cash liquidity on the value of their DLJ shares.

So American Express was the big fish that got away from us. But nonetheless DLJ grew enormously, both through acquisitions and internal expansion, during the 1960s and early 1970s. As I mentioned back in Chapter 1, one of the reasons we decided to break with Wall Street tradition (and the rules of the New York Stock Exchange) by offering shares of our company for sale to the public was our need for additional capital to fuel even more growth. We'd certainly tapped a powerful and lucrative stream of expanding market demand. By the time we went public in 1970, our prospectus showed that we were earning a return on equity of more than 50 percent—a level of profitability that made us the envy of most companies on Wall Street and beyond.

Those were heady times for Dick, Dan, and me. Through a combination of innovative thinking, fortunate timing, and good luck, we'd caught a wave of enormous growth in the U.S. economy and the financial markets, and we'd been able to ride that wave to the pinnacle of our industry while we were still relatively young men.

I vividly recall an evening that sums up the atmosphere of the time. I had flown to Chicago for a celebratory gathering with some of the key players in one of our most successful deals, involving stock in Paramount Pictures. We were enjoying a lavish dinner at the home of Henry Crown, a legendary investor who, in his day, owned everything from General Dynamics Corporation to the Empire State Building and who, at his death in 1990, was said to preside over the eleventh-largest family fortune in the United States. Also present were Derald Ruttenberg, chairman of the Madison Fund; Nathan Cummings, founder of Consolidated Foods (including such popular brands as Sara Lee), and several other luminaries from the world of high finance.

In the midst of our revelry, Crown's butler walked in and whispered a discreet message in his employer's ear. Crown stood up and headed for the door, saying, "I have to excuse myself for a moment." When he returned a few minutes later, he announced proudly, "That was Howard Hughes on the line." He was clearly as impressed to be in Hughes's circle as we were to be in his—a reflection of the ever-present pecking order. I've never forgotten that vivid illustration of the way ego—even more than money—often serves as a powerful determinant and motivation among highly successful businesspeople.

* * *

But change in the weather is inevitable, and even the bluest sky eventually gets its share of clouds. In the midst of our great success in the late 1960s and early 1970s, signs of dissension began to appear in the once solidly unified DLJ team.

The first of these signs was a painful battle over the direction of the company that was instigated by two of our best and brightest young leaders, Joseph Reich and Oscar Tang. A Shanghai-born émigré to the United States, Tang was a brilliant investment strategist who'd done much of our original research work on Xerox. He became a close friend and ally of Joe Reich, one of the first experts in investment banking and mergers and acquisitions to join DLJ as we began to explore getting involved in that side of the financial industry.

Like many of us at DLJ, Reich and Tang were ambitious, creative, and entrepreneurial in spirit. For a number of months prior to the launch of our plan to offer shares to the public, they'd been quietly agitating for a dramatic, large-scale expansion of DLJ's business strategy. Finally, feeling increasingly impatient and frustrated, they decided to take a public stand before the entire company at an off-campus retreat one weekend.

The two men got up and made their case. In effect, their message was: *DLJ is a great company. But we're doing some things that are just plain shortsighted. Relying on institutional research and revenues from our Alliance management fees is too limiting. Deal-making is where the money is. We could make so much more revenue if we got into the private investment business, the investment banking business, and the merchant banking business. What's stopping us?!*

Their views caused quite a stir. It was practically a declaration of revolution, with Reich and Tang basically denouncing Dan, Dick, and me as blind to the obvious path to progress.

Later, after the off-site meeting ended, we all returned to the city. During the whole trip back, I was consumed with thoughts about what had happened along with strong, mixed feelings. The ideas Reich and Tang had put forth didn't surprise me. But the fact that they'd chosen to expose their views challenging the direction we'd chosen in front of the whole company rather than in private had left a bad taste in my mouth.

When I got home, I went straight to the phone and called Dick. As soon as he picked up the phone, we both said, almost simultaneously, "Those two have got to go."

The next morning, I went to visit both men in their offices. "We think you should leave the firm," I said, making it clear I was speaking on behalf of DLJ. It was a significant loss for us—both guys were very bright and talented, and we hated to see them go. But allowing them to stay would have seriously disrupted our carefully planned program of diversification—not to mention the atmosphere of collegiality, teamwork, and mutual respect that we'd worked so hard to create.

They ended up launching their own firm, under the name of Reich & Tang—not a private equity specialist as they'd advocated for DLJ but rather an investment management firm that turned out to be very successful. Years ago, we all put our hard feelings aside. I now think of Joe Reich and Oscar Tang as two of the many great DLJ alumni who have made their mark in so many corners of the financial world, despite the fact that our parting of the ways was so traumatic. Both of them have gone on to be not only successful business leaders but remarkable philanthropists.

Another sign of disharmony in the formerly placid halls of DLJ was the way our cofounder Dan Lufkin was slowly drifting farther and farther away from the rest of us.

As I mentioned in Chapter 1, even as we were laying the foundation for our public equity offering, Dan had been showing increasing disinterest in the firm's activities. One of our original shareholders was Louis Marx, whose father had founded the Marx Toy Company (famous in the 1950s and 1960s for their classic electric train sets). Marx was a close friend of Dan's, and we began hearing stories about how the two of them were undertaking personal investment projects together, unconnected to DLJ. This wasn't any sort of ethical or legal infraction, but Dick and I were troubled to see Dan getting distracted from his duties of behalf of DLJ.

The three of us had a heart-to-heart talk about the issue shortly before our plan to go public was announced. Dick and I and the other senior partners told Dan that we'd need all his focus and energy during the critical months ahead, and we asked him to curtail his outside activities at least until the IPO was successfully completed. To Dan's credit, he agreed.

But it was still increasingly obvious that Dan's heart was elsewhere. Just after the long, complex process of shepherding our stock offering through the regulatory process was complete, he informed us that he would soon be leaving DLJ for an outside job—one completely unrelated to our work. He'd decided to accept an appointment as the first environmental commissioner in the history of Connecticut. In the early 1970s, environmentalism was just gaining traction as a serious social cause, and we understood it was something Dan felt passionately about. So of course Dick and I gave him our blessing, though we knew DLJ would miss his talents.

There was one more uncomfortable moment we'd have to live through before Dan's official departure. Just days before our first stock offering, Dan, Dick, and I met to sign off on the final allocation of shares among members of the company's leadership. One of our big concerns was making sure that the second-level executives—some of whom had been key contributors to the success of DLJ—were fully rewarded for their work. To help make that possible, Dick and I, along with the other senior partners, had agreed that Dan ought to make a portion of his partnership shares available for sale to these executives. This seemed eminently reasonable to us, especially considering that Dan had been somewhat disengaged from the daily operation of the business for months.

But when our entire group presented this plan to Dan, he was very upset. Perhaps Dick and I should have expected as much. It wasn't the financial impact that concerned Dan—all three of us had done very well as cofounders of DLJ, and Dan would still profit handsomely from the stock offering. I think it was the symbolic import of our suggestion—the sense that, somehow, Dick and I were disrespecting Dan and denying him credit for all he'd contributed to the success of our firm. It was a very tough conversation.

In the end, Dan agreed to sell the shares as we'd recommended. But I still feel a little sad, all these years later, to reflect on the way our productive collaboration—and a friendship born of genuine admiration and respect on all sides—had come to a close in a moment of acrimony and hurt feelings.

Dan's departure marked an end to the three-way partnership that had made DLJ possible. We didn't know then that, just three years later in 1973, our leadership team would face another transition when I left DLJ to accept a position in the U.S. Department of State under Henry Kissinger, eager to pursue my lifelong aspirations of a role in public service. That's a career story that will require a chapter of its own.

* * *

Having become, in 1970, the first member firm of the New York Stock Exchange to be publicly traded, DLJ was well positioned to take advantage of the growth in the financial world that we anticipated for the coming decade. And to a large extent, that's exactly what happened. But there were quite a few bumps in the road that made the 1970s more challenging than we might have expected.

One source of trouble was the Arab oil embargo of 1973, which triggered a global recession accompanied by double-digit inflation—a period of "stagflation" the likes of which had never been seen in the modern economy. Like other Wall Street firms, DLJ suffered a severe revenue decline as a result.

A second major hit was the gradual disappearance of the long-standing system of fixed minimum commissions on stock trades. Under that system, whether an investor bought one share of stock or a million shares, the commission was the same per share. It wasn't very logical—after all, the amount of work an investment firm had to do to execute a million-share purchase wasn't any greater than the work involved in a single-share purchase. But the system made executing trades for big institutional accounts very profitable, and the revenues it generated helped to pay for the time-consuming and expensive research work we did at DLJ as well as for other labor-intensive services we provided.

During the early 1970s, however, the illogic of the system led to growing unhappiness among investors, and increasing pressures on Congress, the SEC, and the financial services industry to change it. Finally, the SEC acted. In 1973, it deregulated commissions on transactions of $500,000 or more, and then, in 1975, on all stock transactions. Now brokers and investors were free to negotiate commissions as they saw fit, forcing brokers to compete on price for investor accounts and leading to the birth of discount brokers. It was part of a wave of deregulation efforts from that period that were breaking up traditional business arrangements in many other industries, such as the airlines, and introducing intense competitive pressures in once-cozy markets.

The advent of unregulated brokerage commissions was not an unforeseen problem. In our original share-offering prospectus, dated April 1970, we'd outlined, according to SEC rules, all the positives and negatives of our current business position. On the negative side, we pointed to the fact that downward pressure on income from commissions was likely to prove a growing challenge in the years to come, and we announced in the prospectus that if the profitability of the brokerage business eroded, we reserved the right to leave the New York Stock Exchange and charge our clients whatever we wanted to—or, more accurately, whatever the market would bear.

But now that it had finally happened, the demise of fixed commissions posed quite a challenge for Wall Street, including DLJ. Shares of our stock fell significantly in value (causing some consternation at American Express, which had bought one-quarter of our equity just a short time before). DLJ found itself under increased pressure to both trim expenses and find new sources of revenues and earnings. DLJ's gradual expansion into still other areas of financial business, including investment banking, was in part a response to this pressure.

Still, by any measure, our growth and performance as a company had been extraordinary. At the time I departed DLJ in 1973, our 14-year-old firm was ranked the tenth-largest investment firm in the United States, with a net worth of more than $280 million. I was leaving an industry facing significant changes, but I felt sure that DLJ was in far better shape than most other companies to weather whatever storms might be coming.

As for me, when I left DLJ, my history as an entrepreneurial leader was just beginning, with twists and turns to come that I never could have anticipated.

CHAPTER 6

Out of My Element:
Navigating the Political Tides in
Kissinger's State Department

Donaldson, Lufkin & Jenrette was 14 years old in 1973
when I left the firm to join the State Department. I'd
always known I wanted to move on to some sort of public service eventually. At 42, I'd helped to achieve the goal of public
ownership for DLJ and the opportunity for permanent public
capital it brought to the rest of the undercapitalized firms of the
New York Stock Exchange. I'd also accumulated some personal
financial resources that would afford me a measure of independence. I was beginning to feel that, if I didn't break away from
the company soon, I might never get the opportunity to explore
some of the other worlds I was interested in. It was time for me
to make a change.

What's more, the idea of public service had always attracted
me. I'd been a teenager during World War II, not old enough to
serve but completely caught up in the world-shaking drama of
those years and enthralled by the heroism of our gallant armed

forces. Like millions of other Americans, I admired Dwight D. Eisenhower, the supreme commander who led the Allied forces to victory (and who later received my very first vote in the presidential election of 1952). Later, as I've recounted, I served as an officer in the Marine Corps during the period of the Korean conflict, which ended with an armistice soon after President Eisenhower took office in 1953. My tour with the Marines was a profoundly formative experience—one that taught me more about leadership than any other, including my years at Harvard Business School.

Experiences like these left many people of my generation feeling grateful and admiring of those who devoted themselves to public service (as opposed to the widespread cynicism directed toward government service nowadays). So for me, a move into government felt like a natural step and a valuable way to give something back to my country. But as it turned out, it took quite a bit of persuasion on the part of one of the world's most colorful and controversial statesmen to convince me that this was the right time and the right place for me to make the leap.

It was a tumultuous time in Washington. Nixon had been reelected by a landslide in 1972, but no sooner had the votes been counted than the complicated network of interlocking scandals that came to be known as Watergate began to gain more and more public attention. Soon the rising tide of scandal and acrimony was affecting everyone's behavior and planning in Washington—including that of Nixon's foreign-policy éminence grise, Henry Kissinger.

It was shortly after the start of Nixon's second term when my executive assistant at DLJ came to my office door with a funny expression on her face. "There's someone on the phone for you who's claiming to be Henry Kissinger. And I think it's really him!"

Sure enough, it was Kissinger, with his unmistakably gravelly voice and Teutonic accent, calling to introduce himself and to ask me to visit him in Washington.

The invitation had come about in a slightly strange manner. In the late 1960s, as I've mentioned, my friend Lou Harris, the well-known public opinion pollster whose business DLJ had bought, had been introducing me to a number of his political acquaintances. They included Alex Rose, then head of the Liberal Party of New York State. One Sunday afternoon in 1969, Alex came to visit me.

"We're searching for a candidate to run for mayor of New York," Alex said. "Someone whose name can appear on a fusion ticket. We're looking at Jacob Javits and Robert F. Wagner as possibilities, and we think you'd make a great third option. Are you interested?" At that time, Javits was the Republican senator from New York, while the Democrat Wagner had retired in 1965 after three terms as New York City mayor.

"Honestly, Alex, I'm not interested," I said. For some reason, though, Alex didn't get my message, or perhaps he didn't believe it. It may also be that he and Lou Harris thought that floating a rumor about my supposed interest in a mayoral race might convince me. At least, it would garner some good publicity for DLJ. Whatever the reason, a couple of newspapers soon published items about businessman Bill Donaldson and his intention to launch a fusion candidacy for the mayoralty of New York—all without even calling me to confirm the story.

I found the whole thing a bit far-fetched and basically ignored it until one day when I received a phone call inviting me to a meeting with Nelson Rockefeller, scion of one of America's wealthiest families and the governor of the state of New York. I accepted the invitation and found myself a few days later in Rockefeller's office.

Having read the newspaper stories about my budding political career, Rockefeller had decided to meet with me personally to learn about my intentions. "I assume you want to ask for my endorsement in the upcoming race," he remarked.

"Not at all," I replied. "In fact, I don't have the slightest interest in running. And I think both Jack Javits and Bob Wagner would be much better candidates and mayors than me."

I explained how the newspaper items had come to pass, and the two of us had a brief chuckle over it. But in this way, Rockefeller and I became friends. And when Henry Kissinger, then the head of Nixon's National Security Council (NSC), mentioned to Rockefeller that he wanted to recruit an outsider to help him manage the State Department, Rockefeller suggested my name. So Kissinger called and invited me to meet with him in his D.C. office at the department to discuss the possibilities.

Kissinger greeted me in his office, we exchanged a few pleasantries, and then he promptly launched into an explanation of his situation. "The president wants me to become his secretary of state," he said. "Frankly, I don't want the job. I'm in a good position at the NSC. I don't have to deal with the State Department bureaucracy, but I have the president's ear and I can have almost a free hand on the foreign policy front. I've opened the doors to China, helped manage the Southeast Asia situation, maintained the balance of powers on the world stage, and so on. I've had a real impact, which is exactly what I came here to do."

Kissinger sighed. "But the president wants me at State, and I think I have to do it." The reason, he explained, was Watergate. "A typhoon is going to hit this country," he said. "It's going to get very messy—much more messy than anyone knows right now. And when that happens, we're going to need the State Department to be a Rock of Gibraltar. Otherwise, there's no telling what our adversaries overseas might do to take advantage of our political disarray. So this is my duty as I see it. And that's where you come in. I'm going to need a strong team to manage things here in Washington while I'm on the road talking with the Russians and the Chinese and dealing with the Middle East. And I think you could be a crucial member of that team."

Naturally, I was flattered. But I was also surprised. "Dr. Kissinger," I asked, "Why me? Aren't there people you've been working with at State and at the National Security Council who have the right experience for an assignment like this?"

Kissinger waved his hand. "Of course I have some very able men at the NSC. Some of them are going to follow me to State. Hal Sonnenfeldt and Win Lord will be joining me there." (I'd heard of Helmut Sonnenfeldt—the press sometimes referred to him as "Kissinger's Kissinger," meaning he was one of Henry's closest confidants and advisors. As for Winston Lord, he was a former Yale scholar, a distinguished diplomat, and a noted expert on Asia policy and China.) "Others, too. But the State Department is a big, complicated affair. Very bureaucratic, with career staffers controlling their own fiefdoms who need to be managed. You are a manager, and a talented one. This is something I need if we are going to tame that monster at Foggy Bottom."

Kissinger leaned forward. "What's more," he said, "you are an outsider—a businessman with experience in the real world. You have enormous financial acumen, a major asset in a world where economics is increasingly important. And you are young, with creative flair and a fresh perspective on the world. You can be an antidote to the Beltway worldview that people inevitably develop after too many years in government. We need your entrepreneurial talents—your willingness to shake up old institutions, to try new things. Change is sweeping the world, Bill. Our government needs to change with it."

This pitch evoked mixed emotions in me. Kissinger's reference to the bureaucracy of the State Department had put me off. I didn't relish the idea of spending months or years trying to master a new and arcane set of political rules and rituals while having minimal impact on events on the ground. I've never enjoyed power games for their own sake.

But his use of the E-word—entrepreneurial—helped turn me around. Could he be serious about it? Was his true intention to generate meaningful, lasting change in one of Washington's most hidebound and powerful institutions—and was he willing to handle the acrimony such an effort would inevitably spark? If so, I might be interested.

I told Kissinger so, but asked for a few days to think about the proposition, to which he agreed. Back in New York, I spoke about the possibility of moving to Washington with my wife, Evan. I also discussed the job in confidence with McGeorge Bundy and Robert McNamara, both of whom I'd met while serving as a trustee of the Ford Foundation. Bundy was then president of the Foundation, while McNamara, the former secretary of defense, was president of the World Bank. I also spoke with a few other acquaintances who knew Kissinger well. When I returned to Washington for a second interview, I was straightforward about this with Kissinger.

"I've been doing a bit of checking, Henry," I said (we were now on a first-name basis). "And everyone who knows you says the same thing: Henry is a very talented and interesting man, but be careful—he can be difficult to work with."

Kissinger seemed surprised. "Difficult? What do you mean?" From the look on his face, you'd think he had never heard or imagined any such thing.

"Just a moment," Kissinger said. He poked a button on the big call director on his desk, picked up the receiver, and had a very brief, hushed conversation with someone on the other end of the line. He did the same thing twice more. Then he hung up and said, "I've got three guys I want you to see."

"When should I call them?" I asked. I'd flown down to D.C.

to see Kissinger at the end of a busy work week at DLJ; it was now ten o'clock on Friday night.

"Don't call them, go to see them. They're waiting for you. They'll tell you what it's like to work with me." And he handed me a slip of paper with three names scrawled on it: Hal Sonnenfeldt, Larry Eagleburger, and Brent Scowcroft. The first two had offices at the State Department, while the third, a distinguished retired Air Force general now working as a civilian in the national security apparatus, was at the White House.

Following Kissinger's suggestion, I visited all three men that night. Scowcroft was the last one on my list. By the time I was waved into his office at the White House, it was around midnight. I still recall the room in the West Wing where General Scowcroft sat under the dim glow of a neon fluorescent light, surrounded by piles of paper.

When I explained the purpose of my visit, Scowcroft gave me a wry grin and asked, all innocence, "What do you mean, difficult?" And I thought to myself, *It's just past midnight on Friday night; he's up to his elbows in paperwork; he's probably going to spend the night in this office, and when tomorrow comes he's going to be spending it here too. Working with Kissinger may not be "difficult"—but I'm damned if it looks easy.*

It later turned out that both Sonnenfeldt and Eagleburger (who subsequently became secretary of state) became close allies of mine in the State Department—in particular Larry Eagleburger, who recognized the difficulties of being inserted into the department from my very different background.

All three men gave me their candid but basically positive accounts of what it was like to work with Kissinger—as Henry had known they would, of course. They also pointed out with some enthusiasm that the job Henry envisioned for me, as an undersecretary with significant power and responsibility, would give me the opportunity to have a real impact on government policy, something relatively few newcomers to Washington can have. So I found myself edging closer to the possibility of leaving DLJ to serve under Kissinger.

Kissinger offered me my choice of three jobs. One was "ambassador at large," which struck me as a poor fit for my personal talents and tastes. I think of myself as more of a manager than as anybody's spokesperson or representative, so I turned that one down. Then we discussed the role of undersecretary of state for economic affairs, which seemed logical for a person with my business background. However, there was an incumbent already in that position. Kissinger shrugged that off: "We can get rid of him," he said. But the notion of pushing someone aside to make a spot for myself didn't sit very well with me.

Finally, Kissinger proposed naming me undersecretary of state for security assistance. "It's like being the head of the state department's defense department," he explained. "Your focus will be on military matters. But I also want you to tackle national energy policy. And that's no stretch. In today's world, energy supplies are very much a matter of national security. If you can help us solve that dilemma, you'll be performing a huge service to your country."

At one point in our protracted discussions, I invited Kissinger to a Sunday night dinner in New York; he had a trip to the city planned for the UN General Assembly meetings in October 1973. "I'd like you to meet my wife, Evan," I remarked.

"Of course!" Kissinger agreed, all charm. "What a nice idea. And if I may, I will bring along Miss Maginnes. She will be delighted to meet you." Nancy Maginnes was a former student of Kissinger's at Harvard who'd worked as an aide for New York's Governor Rockefeller and would shortly become the second Mrs. Kissinger.

But late on Saturday night, I received a call from the White

House, canceling our dinner plans. The conflict that would become known as the Yom Kippur War had broken out in the Middle East.

Later that week, Kissinger interrupted his whirlwind of diplomatic and military meetings to phone me. "Have you moved any closer to a decision about my offer?" he asked.

I had, in fact. "You know, Henry," I told him, "I've never worked for somebody else. I think that working for you would be really interesting, but I'm not sure I'd be very good in that role. I'm not saying that I can't take orders from somebody, and I'm not saying I have to be the boss or anything like that, but the fact is that I've just never done it."

Kissinger said he understood. "And yet you are willing to give it a try?" he asked.

"I'm willing to give it my all," I replied.

"This is wonderful!" Kissinger exclaimed. "And the timing is perfect. Why don't you fly down here to Washington tomorrow morning and join me at the department. You can see exactly what we do and discover just how remarkable it is to work at the State Department."

The next day, I was in Washington, trailing Henry Kissinger around as he raced from one office to another, working with his staff as they monitored and managed the fallout from the Yom Kippur War. I was now officially one of "Kissinger's guys" in the State Department.

Evan and I bought a house on Kalorama Road (while keeping our apartment in Manhattan) and moved ourselves and our two small children to D.C. I felt I was embarking on the next big adventure of my life.

At first, it was exciting and very positive. As one of three undersecretaries of state, I would have a wide-reaching portfolio of assignments. I'd be expected to help oversee several key offices within the department, including the Bureau of Science and Technology, the Bureau of Environment Affairs, and the Bureau of Cultural Affairs. I'd also be officially named the first chairman of the State Department committee on U.S. international energy policy.

Henry was gracious and supportive, saying all the right things about the closeness of the partnership we would have and the major projects he wanted me to tackle, beginning with the American response to the Arab oil boycott following the Yom Kippur War. He described the multifaceted role that attorney Cyrus R. Vance had played as deputy secretary of defense under President Lyndon Johnson, and he told me, "I'm picturing you as 'my Cy Vance' at State—someone with great judgment and leadership ability that I can rely on to handle a range of issues on my behalf." I could see that I would have a lot of new things to learn as I tackled the intricacies of public service for the first time.

Evan and I found ourselves being feted as newcomers on the Washington, D.C., social scene, receiving invitations to cocktail parties and dinners at the homes of diplomats, columnists, agency directors, and other luminaries. I was feeling confident, and I was hopeful this assignment could be the first step in a long and successful career in public service. I believed my entrepreneurial experience would enable me to bring a unique new perspective to the world of U.S. foreign policy, perhaps even helping to make the State Department more agile, creative, and resilient in an increasingly volatile and complicated world.

I set to work with all the energy I could muster. But soon, little by little, things began to turn sour.

Some of the problems that developed were probably inevitable. Kissinger hadn't been kidding when he warned me about the intractability of the State Department bureaucracy. In addition to working with several high-ranking political appointees, such as the deputy secretary of state, I had to deal with lifetime employees of the department, experienced foreign service hands, military experts, and others with long track records at State, all of whom were past masters at managing red tape, dealing with Congress, and blocking the administration's agenda when they saw fit. Many of them nominally reported to me in my role as undersecretary, but their idea of serving me was to feed me reports and talking points that supported pre-agreed departmental policies I'd had no influence over. Eventually, I began to feel as if I was working for them rather than vice versa. This was not what I'd had in mind when I accepted Kissinger's job offer.

In other cases, I found myself bogged down in administrivia of the kind I'd always done my best to avoid in the business world. Applying principles of entrepreneurial leadership in Washington turned out to be easier said than done. Finicky details of protocol sometimes seemed to take precedence. One time, on a trip to England with Henry, I was getting off his plane with my bag in my hand. Henry glanced at me and remarked, "Bill, undersecretaries do *not* carry their own bags."

It was on this trip that Henry gave a rousing speech before the Pilgrim Society in London, calling for leaders of the Western nations to unite behind an energy policy in response to the oil boycott. The foreign dignitaries in attendance responded favorably, and Henry invited them to convene in Washington to work on the details.

Then he turned to me. "You arrange it," he remarked. And soon I was immersed in the complexities of organizing a high-level international conference, with all the niceties and diplomatic sensitivities that implies. During one planning meeting, having grown exasperated with the seemingly endless bargaining over details like the shape of the conference table, I threw up my hands. "We've got important work to accomplish," I declared. "Can't we please concentrate on the issues at hand?"

The French deputy minister fixed me with a frosty glare.

"Obviously," he responded, "the undersecretary of state does not understand how things work in the real world."

Over time, making matters worse, Henry was absent more often than not. The Arab oil embargo and the global economic crisis it triggered lasted for months. Henry was on the road almost constantly, making it impossible for him to counsel me or even to intervene on my behalf when I was struggling to deal with recalcitrant staff members. And when he was present, he often seemed distracted and disengaged. One evening, during the final run-up to the energy conference he'd asked me to organize, we held an important session to discuss our goals and strategy for the meeting. Henry wandered in several minutes late and irritably demanded, "What is this meeting about? And where are my notes?"

I exchanged glances with a couple of the cabinet officers who'd been summoned to the meeting. I swallowed hard and quietly replied, "It's the meeting you asked us to schedule about the energy conference, Henry. And your notes are on your desk—where I left them this morning."

I found myself spending little or no time on the big-picture assignments Henry had asked me to tackle. Instead, most of my energy was devoted to visiting Capitol Hill to testify before Congress about various military and diplomatic initiatives that the House members were investigating. In these sessions, I was expected to parrot the official lines printed on my briefing papers, which sometimes differed from the direction that Henry wanted to take—and which I'd had little opportunity to review or discuss with him in advance.

This certainly wasn't what I felt I'd been hired to do. But when I protested the situation to my State Department handlers, they'd shrug and say, "This is what needs to be done today—and Henry's not here to say anything different. He's on a jet, flying around the Middle East."

That was true, of course. Which meant I was in a position that I found increasingly unsatisfying and frustrating. And the State Department bureaucrats were as unhappy with me, since I obviously wasn't interested in playing along with the game. I began to pick up small, subtle hints that they'd be glad to see me depart—including, eventually, occasional comments at my expense in the newspaper, quoting an anonymous "State Department insider" or "well-placed official" about the "problems" Bill Donaldson was having, my "struggles" to master the challenges of foreign policy, and Kissinger's reported "unhappiness" with his once-promising young associate. "Donaldson's days at State may be numbered," was the underlying implication—a way of both greasing the skids under someone the bureaucrats disliked and making sure that the blame for his departure would be placed squarely on his own shoulders.

After some eight months of this, I decided I wouldn't take it any longer. I drafted a note to Henry saying that I wanted to leave the department, labeled it "Confidential," and had it delivered to him in the daily courier bag sent to him wherever he was in the globe the next day.

That evening, I was having dinner at the home of one of the leading Washington columnists when someone tapped me on the shoulder and said, "There's a call for you, Secretary Donaldson." I picked up the line in the kitchen and heard Henry's unmistakable voice on the other end.

"I don't want you to leave," he declared. "And you *shouldn't* leave." He went on to offer his personal experience when facing a similar situation many years earlier. "You know, I had a small job in the Kennedy administration as a consultant to the White House. And like you I found it frustrating. It was so hard to get things done—so hard to get people to pay attention to my ideas. And so you know what I did? I left. I quit. I went back to Harvard. That was a mistake, and I don't want you to make the same mistake."

"I hear you talking," I answered, "and I appreciate what you're saying. But I've made up my mind. I want to go. I'm not going to make a big thing out of it. I'm just going to go quietly, and I'm not going to blast you or the people in the State Department. There'll be no embarrassment or scandal."

I sent Henry a formal letter of resignation and quietly left the State Department early in 1974. It was just a few months before Richard Nixon wrote his own, more consequential, letter of resignation, also addressed to Henry Kissinger in his role as Secretary of State.

Many years later, in 2013, Henry and I looked back on our brief partnership together. He actually apologized to me. "That job was never what I intended it to be," he said. "I wasn't there for you, and I'm sorry about that."

Actually, there was no need for Henry to apologize. I understood full well what had happened—that world events had overtaken Henry's plans, and that my role in government had been one of the smaller casualties. The grand plan for me to become "Henry's Cy Vance" was never meant to be. Instead, my stint at the State Department turned into an object lesson in the challenges of applying entrepreneurial thinking in the complex political environment of a federal government department. Trying to bring about such a drastic cultural shift in a big, tradition-bound institution is profoundly difficult—particularly when you are not the leader of the organization, with a mandate to drive change and with access to all the levers of power, but simply one of many middle-level managers jostling for influence.

I would be better prepared to tackle a similar set of challenges and bring about meaningful policy and cultural reforms a number of years later, when I had the opportunity to take the helm at one of Washington's most important regulatory agencies—the Securities and Exchange Commission—during a time of crisis.

* * *

Meanwhile, having resigned from Kissinger's State Department in 1974, I was wondering what to do next.

The answer—at least in the short term—turned out to involve Nelson Rockefeller, the longtime governor of New York, who I suspect had been one of the reasons I'd been nominated for a job at the State Department in the first place.

In the waning days of the Nixon administration, after Vice President Spiro Agnew had resigned in disgrace due to a bribery scandal, Michigan Congressman Gerald Ford had been named vice president to replace him. And when Ford ascended to the presidency upon the resignation of Nixon in August 1974, he in turn nominated Nelson Rockefeller to serve as his vice president in accordance with the twenty-fifth amendment to the U.S. Constitution, ratified in 1965, which created a procedure for filling a vacancy in that office.

Now that I'd left the State Department, Rockefeller called me up. He was assembling a staff of advisors to help manage his transition from Albany to Washington, and he invited me to serve on that team. I liked the idea. Rockefeller and I got along well, our philosophies and styles were compatible, and I was attracted to the notion of a short-term assignment while I considered other options for the longer term. I accepted the job.

My most vivid memory of my months as a "special advisor" to Vice President Rockefeller dates from the early fall of 1975, a little more than eight months after his accession to that office in December 1974. Rockefeller had asked me to spearhead the development of a proposal for a national Energy Independence

Authority, whose role would be to help finance and direct the development of alternative sources of energy to help wean the United States from dependence on fossil fuels. We were in the process of seeking support for the project from President Ford and his chief advisors.

On this particular day, we were meeting in the White House to review the latest draft of the proposal that I'd written. In attendance were President Ford, Vice President Rockefeller, George Woods, the former president of the World Bank, and a number of administration officials, including Donald Rumsfeld, who was Ford's chief of staff. (I knew Rumsfeld slightly, having met him in Belgium during my time at the State Department; Rumsfeld then served as U.S. ambassador to NATO, and I was visiting Brussels in support of the global energy initiative Kissinger had asked me to oversee.)

President Ford invited everyone in the room to give their opinions about the proposal. Each member of the group offered enthusiastic support, with the exception of Rumsfeld, who considered it a worthless boondoggle and made no bones about his hostility. When everyone had had a chance to speak, Rumsfeld began to pipe up again, eager to amplify the reasons for his distaste. Ford silenced him by simply holding up his hand and remarking, "I heard what you said the first time, Rummy." (Even then, Rumsfeld was feisty, a quality he would later display in full measure during his term as secretary of defense under President George W. Bush.)

The meeting broke up, and Ford, Rockefeller, and I were alone in the room.

"Nelson," Ford said, "I'm going to think this over. I'm flying to California tomorrow, and I'm going to think about it on the plane. I'll let you know when I get there."

The next day was September 5, 1975, and President Ford was scheduled to meet with California Governor Jerry Brown in Sacramento. But shortly before that, Ford had promised to call the vice president with his decision on the energy proposal. Rockefeller called me in. "Sit in my office. The president's going to call at one. We'll have a sandwich and wait for the phone to ring."

We were eating our lunch when the door to the vice president's office flew open. An aide was standing in the door. His face was ashen. "The president's been shot," he announced.

You can imagine our reaction. The first feeling, of course, was shock and horror. Remember that, during the previous decade, America had experienced a rash of assassinations that had shaken the nation to its core—John F. Kennedy, Martin Luther King, Robert F. Kennedy, and others. Yet another killing would have been almost too much to bear. And my second thought, naturally, was the startling realization that the man I was sharing a sandwich with might be moments away from becoming the president of the United States.

A period of confusion followed. Televisions were switched on everywhere, staff members were clustering to swap news bulletins, and phones were ringing off the hook. After an agonizing few minutes, the worst passed. An aide to Rockefeller appeared with the latest news from the president's entourage: "Ford is not hurt. The gun didn't go off. They're rushing him from the scene. And he said to tell the vice president that he will call him as soon as he can." Rockefeller, and the rest of us, breathed a deep sigh of relief. We later learned, as did the world, that the president had been confronted in Sacramento's Capitol Park by a deranged young woman named Lynette "Squeaky" Fromme, armed with a .45-caliber semiautomatic pistol. Thankfully, there was no cartridge in the chamber of the gun she wielded. Fromme was convicted of attempted assassination and served thirty-four years in federal prison for her crime.

Rockefeller and I were a bit startled when, just a few minutes later, the phone on his desk rang and the operator announced, "Mr. Vice President, the president is on the wire."

Rockefeller stood up to take the call. Reflexively, I did the same. So the two of us were standing there, at attention, as Vice President Rockefeller listened to President Ford on the phone. Of course, all I could hear was Rockefeller's words: "Yes, Mr. President. Yes, Mr. President. I understand, Mr. President. Yes, sir. Thank you very much. Good-bye, Mr. President."

Rockefeller hung up the phone. And then he turned to me with a smile and said, "He's going to propose the Energy Independence Authority."

It was an amazing moment—not just because of the historic nature of what the nation had been through, but because of what it revealed about President Ford's remarkable qualities of resilience and focus. Imagine surviving an assassination attempt, and then simply, calmly resuming the people's work as if nothing unusual had occurred!

Gerald Ford may not be viewed as one of our nation's most significant presidents—but his steadiness and dedication represent two of the qualities that illustrate why public service can be, and often is, one of the most noble endeavors one can undertake.

The Energy Independence Authority bill that Gerald Ford proposed in 1975 failed to make it through Congress. As a result, efforts by the United States to lead the world in developing sustainable energy sources and reducing our dependence on fossil fuels were delayed by a number of years. Who knows where we'd be today if Congress had had the foresight to respond more decisively to the energy challenges of the 1970s?

Unfortunately, there's only so much that determined leaders can achieve by themselves. Wise and far-sighted followers and supporters are needed as well—and as history shows, those are not always in great supply.

CHAPTER 7

Back to Yale: Creating a
New School of Management

Having worked in the fields of finance and government, my next major assignment would be in yet another economic sector—the world of academia. But that opportunity did not arise immediately. I returned to New York from Washington, D.C., and began pondering my future. Fortunately, I wasn't under great pressure to make a quick choice, so I was free to take my time to consider a number of options.

One possibility I considered was the idea of owning a newspaper. To be specific, I played seriously with the idea of purchasing the *New York Post* from Dorothy Schiff, who had owned the venerable paper (founded by Alexander Hamilton in 1801) since 1939.

Under the leadership of Dolly Schiff and her editor, James Wechsler, the *Post* had become New York's most liberal newspaper, a far cry from today's very conservative paper. The *Post* ardently defended FDR's New Deal programs and the interests of labor unions and racial and ethnic minorities while covering the arcana of city politics and the latest celebrity gossip with typical tabloid flair. According to a 1976 biography, Schiff may even have had a love affair with President Roosevelt, although she always denied that rumor.

By the time I got interested, Dolly was getting on in years and she was beginning to think about selling the paper. The newspaper business was already contracting and consolidating, and afternoon papers (like the *Post*) were especially hard hit, which meant the value of the paper was likely to decline further, the longer she held on to it. Dolly was also concerned about the impact of the (then-draconian) federal estate tax on her wealth if she died with the *Post* in her portfolio, another factor that pushed her toward divestiture.

As for me, I'd always been fascinated by journalism and intrigued by the possibility of having a hand in the newspaper business. Back in college, I'd been part of a three-man team that ran the *Yale Daily News*, a nearly full-time job for which you had to compete. And as I've previously recounted, during my senior year, we published a book called *Seventy-Five: The Study of a Generation in Transition*, which led to my interviewing Henry Luce about his founding of *Time* magazine in partnership with his classmate Briton Hadden.

So my interest in journalism goes way back. In fact, when I graduated from Yale in 1953, a senior manager for *Time* magazine, Bernhard Auer, invited me to apply for a job because of my experience at the *Yale Daily*. I joined the U.S. Marines instead, but when I got out three years later, Auer called to say that he was still interested in me. I chose instead to go to Harvard Business School and took a different life path, but I sometimes speculate that if I'd accepted Auer's invitation, I might have ended up helping to run what became the Time Warner conglomerate.

Now, in the mid-1970s, as I considered possible next steps in my career, it seemed natural to think about the media business as an option. I respected the newspaper industry because of its public/private dimension—its role in helping to inform, enlighten, and shape public opinion and to influence debate on the great issues of the day. And within the evolving journalistic landscape of the era, I thought I could see an opportunity centering on the *New York Post*.

Back in 1966, in the wake of a devastating strike by the New York Newspaper Guild—one of several crippling newspaper strikes in that era—the historic *New York Herald Tribune* had been shut down. Its president, Walter Thayer, in collaboration with the paper's owners, the Whitney family, decided to invest their remaining assets (including the paper's name) in a collaborative agreement with *The New York Times* and *The Washington Post* to publish an international edition based in Paris. But Thayer still had deep roots in New York, and I had the idea that he and I might be able to work together on resurrecting the paper for the city.

I spoke with Thayer and made a proposal: "Suppose I buy the *New York Post*. Then you and I can make a deal together to create a new venture that will include both a morning paper, using the assets of the *Herald Tribune*, and an afternoon paper, built on the assets of the *Post*. Imagine combining the serious journalistic chops of the *Tribune* with the flashy glitz and sizzle of the *Post*. The result could be dynamite! We could have a paper that would seriously compete with the *Times* for top billing in New York."

Thayer liked the idea—but talking Dolly Schiff into selling me the paper proved to be the sticking point. She was a flighty woman, significantly older than I, and I got the feeling that she enjoyed the interplay of offer, counteroffer, and negotiation without necessarily ever having any serious intention of making a deal. At times, we appeared close to an agreement. But then, Dolly would disappear for days at a time, and I'd see stories in the press about various other "glamorous suitors" who were competing for control of the *Post*. I think Dolly loved the attention, but the game-playing was frustrating for me.

Ultimately Dolly Schiff sold the *Post* in 1976 for a little over $30 million to an extremely self-confident Australian named Rupert Murdoch, who was in the process of expanding his media empire into the United States. Today, the *Post* is just a small part of Murdoch's News Corporation, whose Fox News Network has become a major player in conservative politics in this country. I wonder what the ultra-liberal Dolly Schiff would think about that? Maybe she'd wish she'd sold the paper to me when she had the chance!

As for Walter Thayer, his Paris-based *International Herald Tribune* (renamed, in 2013, the *International New York Times*) has long been the premier English-language daily published in continental Europe.

* * *

At the same time that I was trying unsuccessfully to negotiate my way into the newspaper business, I was being courted from another, very different direction. Kingman Brewster, then the president of Yale, had approached me to explore my interest in joining him as part of the leadership team at my alma mater.

Of course, I was intrigued. I'd already been active as a member of the Yale Corporation, the University's board of trustees, so I was well aware of most of the strengths and weaknesses of the institution as well as some of the goals that Brewster had been pursuing since being named its president in 1963. My love of the University and my fond memories of my years in New Haven, combined with my desire to carve out a constructive role for myself in the sphere where public and private interests intersect, made the possibility of serving in a more active role at Yale very attractive.

Brewster's first thought was that I might help him launch and guide an effort to reform the organization of the entire University, a mission that Brewster had been contemplating for some time. A reform-minded, liberal Republican (in an era when such beings were far more common than they are today), Brewster had already guided the transformation of the admissions process at Yale, admitting women for the first time and greatly expanding the numbers of public school students as well as racial minorities at the University. He'd also courted controversy by supporting protests against the Vietnam War on campus, including publicly defending the antiwar activist clergyman William Sloane Coffin, who'd been the chaplain at Yale since 1958. Brewster also expressed doubts, while speaking to the Yale faculty in April 1970, about whether Black Panther leaders then on trial in New Haven could "achieve a fair trial anywhere in the United States."

Now Brewster wanted to consider making sweeping changes to the overall structure of the University, and with my background in finance, business, and management, he felt I might be the perfect partner for such an effort. He envisioned creating a position that would let me work directly with him, with a new senior title yet to be determined.

The idea of playing an important role in modernizing Yale for the challenges of a new era was exciting. But I was reluctant to take on another job that involved battling an intractable, tradition-bound bureaucracy—especially since I suspected that the faculty and administration of a great Ivy League university was likely to be even more hidebound than the staff of the State Department. I told Brewster as much.

"Well," he said, "if that's not the job for you, here's another possibility. As you know, we've been thinking about starting a new graduate school at Yale—a management school to compete with Harvard in preparing the business leaders of the next generation. How would you like to be part of it? I'd be happy to name you as the school's first dean."

"Now that is really interesting!" I responded, feeling very enthusiastic. "But I'm not sure it will really work. Think about me and my background. I don't have a PhD, I served in the Marine Corps, and I worked on Wall Street. I have a feeling that, in the eyes of your faculty, those will be three big black marks against me! Is there any way you can convince them that I'm qualified?"

Brewster laughed. "It's a risk, all right," he agreed. "But let's worry about that later. The first question is, are you interested in the job? If you are, we can figure out how to sell you to the faculty."

So the two of us talked in more detail about the kind of management school Yale was interested in creating. The notion of launching a program to offer a master's degree in management at Yale wasn't a natural or obvious one, despite the precedent set by great institutions like Harvard and the University of Pennsylvania, with its prestigious Wharton School. Yale prided itself on its deep intellectual roots and its commitment to the liberal arts; professional training, even at the highest level, was regarded as somewhat *undignified*. Even the top-ranked Yale Law School, which dates all the way back to 1824, was sometimes considered slightly separate from the "real" Yale as cherished by the humanistic scholars who dominated its faculty.

Yet at the same time, growing numbers of Yale alumni—themselves successful in business—had been urging the University to launch a graduate business program, and many had indicated they'd be delighted to help fund such a school. In fact, in 1971, the University had received a generous bequest from the estate of Frederick W. Beinecke (one of the leaders of the Sperry & Hutchinson Company and among the world's greatest collectors of rare books) earmarked for this very purpose.

Under the circumstances, Brewster and the University trustees had been thinking about creating a Yale school of management with a unique set of characteristics. After all, having waited three hundred years before launching a school of management, Yale might as well take the opportunity to create something truly unique!

First, the thought was that it would be a division of Yale's Institution for Social and Policy Studies rather than a freestanding unit. Furthermore, it would have a special emphasis on combining public and private service, offering training not only for corporate executives but also for leaders in the nonprofit and government spheres, as well as in-depth analysis of the ever-deepening interconnections among these sectors. In this sense, the new Yale School of Management would resemble Yale Law School, which emphasizes the importance of devoting a portion of one's legal career to public service, as well as Harvard's Kennedy School of Government, which prepares students for careers in public service.

As we talked, I grew more and more intrigued by this idea. The blending of public and private interests appealed to my desire to combine both kinds of service in my own work. And the opportunity not to try to reform a long-established organization but to create something from scratch appealed to my entrepreneurial instincts. Here, I sensed, was the chance to leave my mark on something exciting and valuable that might make a meaningful contribution to the world—and to Yale—for generations to come.

Still, I didn't want to accept Brewster's offer without feeling certain that I was the right person for the job, and that my vision for the new school was likely to set it on the best course for its future. So I made a counter-proposition. In my role as a trustee of Yale, I would visit leaders of some of the top schools of business and public policy in the country and ask their advice about launching a new school. Based on their feedback, I would be able to offer Brewster some solid recommendations about the opportunities and risks Yale faced—as well as to decide whether or not the job and I were a good fit.

Brewster agreed, and so I launched my personal "listening tour." I flew out to California and visited Arjay Miller, dean of the Stanford Graduate School of Business and former president of Ford Motor Company. The two of us had a long and cordial session in which I described Yale's plan to launch a new management school with a strong emphasis on the connections between private enterprise and public policy.

"That's just the kind of focus I wanted to introduce here at Stanford," Arjay told me. But he'd found it very difficult to do. He encountered the same problems of dealing with a set of entrenched leaders that I'd experienced at the State Department. In the end, he'd managed to introduce one new section within the business school that focused on public policy—the kind of modest, incremental change one often has to settle for when trying to reform a successful and long-established institution. However, I found the fact that Arjay had sought to reshape Stanford in the same direction we were considering at Yale encouraging; it suggested that we were on the right track with our thinking.

Arjay helped me in another way. "I've got one piece of advice for you," he said. "If you decide to take this job, tell Kingman Brewster that you've got to be not only the dean and a professor, but a *tenured* professor. It sounds like a small matter, but it makes a big difference. If you're a tenured member of the faculty, not only can you teach classes and lead the shaping of curriculum and programs, but nobody can ever call a faculty meeting without including you." This was the kind of information that only someone like Arjay—a former business executive now ensconced in the very different world of academia—would know enough to share with me, and I was grateful for it.

I had similarly informative conversations with some other business school deans, as well as the dean of Harvard's Kennedy School of Government. Armed with insights and ideas from these discussions, I returned to New Haven and visited with Kingman Brewster.

"I'd be delighted to take on the job," I informed him, "so long as I can be named a tenured member of the Yale faculty as well as the dean of the new school. Don't worry," I hastened to add. "I have no intention of hanging around after my term as dean is completed. I'll collect my gold watch and be out the door. I just want the designation as a tenured faculty member to strengthen my managerial hand."

Kingman smiled knowingly. "I understand, and I don't think that'll be a problem," he replied. "As far as I'm concerned, you've got the job. But why don't we schedule a time for you to come up here for a day or so to meet some of the key members of your faculty team?"

Kingman made it sound like a mere formality, a pleasant gesture to get my relationship with my new colleagues off on the right foot. But there was more to it than that. Unbeknownst to me at time, I wasn't the first person Kingman had wooed for the job of dean at the new school. Two previous candidates, both major industrialists, had accepted his offer—only to be torpedoed when factions of the Yale faculty rebelled against them and refused to confirm their appointments. The world of academia differs in this way from the typical corporate office. Professors and others in the faculty and administration maintain their own small but powerful fiefdoms, and they expect to be consulted and often deferred to even on personnel matters that don't directly affect them. Having run up against this kind of resistance in the past, Kingman was determined this time to navigate his man safely through the gauntlet. My day of friendly visits with leading members of the Yale faculty would be the first step in the process.

Despite my service as a Yale trustee—not to mention my years as an undergraduate at the college—I had only the vaguest understanding of the complicated political dynamics that churn under the placid surface of any great university. Over time, I learned all about them and came to understand much more about the complexities involved in launching the new school of management.

Historically, the closest thing Yale had had to a business school was the Sheffield Scientific School, founded in 1847 as a school of science and engineering within Yale College. Sheff, as it was known, had played an important role in helping Yale make the transition from the traditional liberal arts curriculum (focusing strictly on languages, history, philosophy, and the arts) to one that included classes in math and science. After World War I, the separate curriculum of Sheff was gradually integrated into that of the college, and in 1956 Sheff ceased to exist as a separate entity.

However, some members of the faculty of the old Sheff program (now part of a program called administrative sciences) were still active at Yale at the time I entered the picture, and they formed one of two groups of teachers and scholars that Kingman suggested could be part of the nucleus of the new management school. These were the operations research (OR) faculty, who were quantitatively oriented and believed in a "hard science" approach to the challenges of management. By contrast, the organizational behavior (OB) faculty, whom I also inherited, were people-oriented, focused on the social and psychological aspects of management, and concerned with issues like team building, motivation, and corporate culture.

Both of these groups of academics were very smart and talented; both were engaged in important research, in teaching undergraduate courses, and in working with PhD candidates in the existing Yale graduate programs. And both had something significant to contribute to the running of organizations in the real world. But their approaches and priorities were very dissimilar, and in many cases they saw the world through different lenses. So when Kingman said, "We'll put the OR faculty and the OB faculty together into the new school, and they'll form the nucleus of your faculty," he was setting up a much more difficult political challenge for me than I understood at the time.

During my visit to the University—when my appointment was very much hanging fire, contingent on my acceptance by the faculty—some of these political cross-currents began to be apparent. I noticed that, rather than arranging some kind of formal meeting or reception, Kingman had selected a handful of faculty members for me to meet in informal sessions at their offices. I quickly sensed that these were crucial influencers whose approval would help shape the climate of opinion toward me throughout the University.

I also noticed that there was an immediate affinity between the OB faculty and me. We shared the same people-centered approach to leadership and the same belief in the crucial importance of teamwork. We swapped stories about the business leaders we'd known and worked with—several of the OB professors, I discovered, had long, successful track records of corporate consulting work, having established reputations as thoughtful, sensitive, and creative analysts of the human factors underlying business success. (In this respect, they were often more highly regarded than their more famous counterparts from Harvard Business School, who were generally perceived as extremely intelligent but sometimes rather arrogant.)

By contrast, I didn't hit it off nearly as well with Yale's OR professors. Their approach to business struck me as more theoretical and abstract, which may have been both a cause and a result of their relative lack of hands-on corporate experience. Most of them had written and published plenty of papers about how companies *ought* to work, but few of them had actually grappled with the realities of making them work. When we met, they seemed to eye me a bit suspiciously; my lack of advanced scholarly credentials concerned them, and I think they considered me an interloper from the world of profit-and-loss into what should be the "pure" sphere of academic objectivity. Our conversations tended to be brief.

By the time my day with the faculty was finished, I was beginning to sense the lay of the land. And Kingman could see that I was catching on to the tricky nature of the political challenge we jointly faced. "Don't worry," he said. "I think you've played your cards very well. The OB folks are on your side—they like you. As for the OR guys—well, I think you mostly neutralized them. They aren't crazy about you; you're not their type. But I don't think they're going to put up much of a fuss. When push comes to shove, I think you've got the job."

Kingman's diagnosis proved to be correct. And his political shrewdness in helping me team up with the organizational behavior professors from the start of my "campaign" was particularly insightful. In fact, one member of the OB faculty—a psychologist named Clayton Alderfer, who helped develop Abraham Maslow's famous concept of the hierarchy of needs—turned into a crucial ally of mine. Clay helped convince his fellow professors to give me a chance and so paved the way for me to get the tacit approval Kingman needed for my appointment. And during my early months on the job as dean, when we were engaged in a battle as to how long we were going to take to plan and organize before throwing open our doors to students, Clay took my side. He joined me in urging that we launch the school with a modest cohort of fifty students as quickly as possible, and he even helped me write the original brochure that we circulated to explain the idea behind the school and our unique focus on private/public leadership and management. That brochure—in combination with the power of the Yale name, of course—helped attract nearly a thousand applicants for that first class of fifty students. In a real sense, Clay was one of the creative forces behind the successful birth of the new graduate school.

Given the unique scope and mission of the school, we made the conscious decision to call it a school of management rather than one of business—hence, the Yale School of Management (SOM). Just as I'd hoped, SOM developed into something quite new in the world of higher education. Unlike other management schools, ours recognized the growing importance of public management as practiced in the government and nonprofit sectors as well as their increasing interconnection with the world of private, for-profit business. I'd seen firsthand the gaps in knowledge, understanding, and respect that existed between people in business and people in public-sector leadership. Those on either side of the divide often failed to grasp the importance of the challenges faced by their counterparts in the opposite arena; many failed to appreciate how much they could learn from one another. To tackle the problem, we built a faculty with deep experience as leaders and thinkers in all three sectors—for-profit, nonprofit, and government—and we developed courses that included case studies, historical examples, disciplines, skills, and vocabulary from across the board. We added veteran business educators and practitioners, whom we dubbed "professors of the practice of management," to the core group of OB and OR faculty, as well as faculty "on loan" from other departments of the University. In an amusingly convoluted way, we initially called this group the Interim Board of Permanent Officers.

Our innovations weren't restricted to the curriculum. We

named the degree we offered a Master's Degree in Public and Private Management—an MPPM as opposed to the traditional MBA. (The students irreverently reinterpreted the MPPM as standing for More Power, Prestige, and Money.) We also developed a new way of teaching leadership, one in which students helped to shape the School's infrastructure, where teamwork and group learning were prioritized, and where hierarchical, top-down power was minimized. We introduced a simplified grading system in which students received ratings of "proficient," "pass," or "fail" in order to reduce the emphasis on grades and encourage cooperation rather than competition. In all these ways, we were ahead of our time.

Building this new kind of management program from scratch posed a heady challenge—especially within a historic institution like Yale, where the eyes of the world would be upon us and where failure was clearly not an option. However, we had tremendous support from the University and a highly creative, deeply committed team of faculty and administrators working to make the vision a reality. We mapped out our innovative curriculum, publicized our new educational concept, and began recruiting students. We didn't talk about ourselves as "entrepreneurs," but the spirit in which we worked was entrepreneurial. There was no grand blueprint for what we were doing. We just tackled the job one task, one day at a time. You might say that we built the School of Management in Yale's garage.

When I refer to "building" the new school, that's not just a metaphor. Like any institution, SOM needed a physical home, which we were responsible for creating. We came up with a plan to build a campus by connecting a series of historic old houses on Hillhouse Avenue with more modern adjacent buildings. This would be done by adding a lower level of glass-clad classrooms, in essence creating a courtyard. Several of the houses would need complete renovations in order to serve as classrooms and offices.

Naturally, all of this work would take money. Although the School had an endowment that certainly helped during the start-up, we had to raise funds to grow the School and become self-sufficient. With no SOM alumni to call on and with many large Yale donors off-limits to us, we felt a bit stymied.

Then Kingman Brewster called to discuss a potential donor—Thomas Mellon Evans, a distinguished alum from the Yale Class of 1931 who'd made a fortune as a financier and become a notable owner and breeder of Thoroughbred race-horses. Brewster had been trying for years to convince Evans to support one or another project, but with no success. "I have given up on Evans," Brewster told me. "I can't interest him in anything. He's all yours."

Evans accepted my request to meet him in his office. I arrived loaded with facts and figures about the new manage-ment school, but throughout my enthusiastic presentation, he gazed over my head at a nearby television watching stock prices scroll by on the screen. It seemed clear that he couldn't care less. Finally, I said, "Mr. Evans, it appears that we are wasting one another's time," and I returned to my office, feeling discour-aged. I called Kingman to tell him that I, too, had struck out.

The next morning, my phone rang. It was Evans. "How much did you say that Hillhouse renovation project would cost?" he asked. I quoted a figure. "Put the shovel in the ground," he declared.

You just never know.

* * *

From my first day on the job, I knew that we wanted to take advantage of the fact that we were starting a brand-new school to rethink everything about the education of leaders for the future. I started to gather a senior staff team that would reflect the energy, excitement, and mission of the school. Kingman recommended Doug Yates, a talented young professor of political science and urban affairs and a Rhodes Scholar with BA and PhD degrees from Yale. Doug joined the School as associate dean for academic affairs. He worked closely with the faculty on curriculum, teaching, and research issues, and weighed in on overall planning and strategy discussions. In the end, however, his considerable contributions to SOM proved costly to his career, as he was ultimately denied tenure in the political science department. In retrospect, I wish I had seen that coming and could have prevented it. After the tenure denial, Doug left Yale for Dartmouth.

I recruited Don Ogilvie, a Yale undergraduate with a Stanford MBA, as associate dean for finance and administration. Don fit SOM's profile perfectly, having worked in the private sector at the Celanese Corporation and in the public sector at the Office of Management and Budget in D.C. After setting up the management side of SOM as well as working on all aspects of launching the School, Don left to head the American Bankers Association for the next two decades.

That left the head of admissions, placement, and student services to recruit. I gathered a small committee to find the right person to run this part of the School, and I vividly remember explaining to the committee members what I had in mind. "To attract the right kind of students," I said, "we need someone who is capable of identifying great candidates from a wide variety of backgrounds, including business, government, and the nonprofit sphere, working with them throughout their training, and then helping them find important careers where their new skills will be valued and can have impact.

"This isn't a job for a typical graduate school admissions or placement officer," I concluded. "It's a job for a guy with fresh ideas and a creative approach."

The committee accepted my mandate and set out in search of the candidate I'd described. At some point, the head of the committee came into my office and announced, "We think we've found the guy we've been looking for. Except it turns out the guy is a woman. Would you like to meet her?"

That's how I was introduced to Jane Morrison—the "guy" who ended up playing a key role in helping to make the Yale School of Management a success. And today, so many years later, that "guy" is my wife.

When I first met Jane in my new office at Yale, I quickly saw how bright, energetic, and talented she was—just as my search committee had said—and we lost no time in making her an attractive offer to jump to Yale from Wesleyan University, where she was dean of admissions. Jane soon became an important part of the leadership team of our new management school.

As any entrepreneur will tell you, the early days of launching a new organization are exciting. People work long hours, energized by the challenge of creating something that has never existed before, brainstorming solutions to unexpected problems, and often discovering personal talents they never knew they had. Team members debate, argue, laugh, worry, and exult together; they egg one another on, squabble like siblings, and challenge one another intellectually and emotionally. The result is the kind of intimacy and camaraderie experienced only by a close-knit group on a shared mission: a military unit, the actors in a play, or the members of a sports team. So Doug, Don, Jane, and I—interacting with other staff, faculty, and students— began to build the Yale School of Management, day by day and literally brick by brick.

There could have been some gossip about Jane and me during my five-year term at Yale. But it never reached the level at which people considered us an embarrassment to the institution. It would probably be different today, as we now live in a more transparent time. Things were different then.

* * *

Through a combination of improvisation, hard work, out-of-the-box thinking, and good fortune, we pulled together the resources, people, ideas, and systems needed to launch our brand-new management school. And we did it all in record time. When I first arrived at Yale, a couple of members of the OB faculty told me, "I suppose you'll take a year or two to figure out what this new school is all about. And then you'll be ready to open your doors to the first class a couple of years after that."

"No," I replied. "I think we ought to admit our first class next fall"—that is, in September 1976. And that's exactly what we did. Fifty entrepreneurial people enthusiastically agreed to take a chance as the Class of 1978—the Charter Class—who dug deep with us to launch the School.

Why did students in that first class choose SOM? There is probably no single conclusive answer. At the beginning, it wasn't a school so much as a powerful idea embedded in a prestigious institution with a core of dedicated and talented faculty. Some students came because of the cross-sector vision that the University and I developed and stamped on every piece of outreach we distributed. Some were attracted by the Yale name. Some liked the entrepreneurial aspect of our vision. And, truth be told, some were probably attracted by SOM's having as its first dean an investment banker who had started his own firm and then gone on to take leadership positions in government and education.

What they all had in common was a desire to learn the

mechanics and utility of global organization. They wanted to learn how to do their jobs better, to change their jobs, to make more money, and to be seen—correctly—as professionals in complex fields worldwide.

In those early days, I remember welcoming the Class of 1978 by observing, "You will forever be the Charter Class." History has borne that out. SOM has subsequently had the Charter Class, the Charter Alumni Board, the Charter 5th-reunion class, and other variants through, most recently, the Charter 40th-reunion class.

Even today, when alums are introduced as members of the Class of 1978, they often elicit responses of awe from later graduates.

I have mentioned the part played by the Organizational Behavior (OB) faculty in the founding of the School. Perhaps the most striking aspect of the initial years was the pervasiveness of OB in the curriculum and the culture. Essential to education at SOM from the first day of class was building a collaborative community of students who would support one another in learning. In addition, the emphasis on individual and group behavior gave students knowledge and experiences that would inform their work as future leaders in organizations where working effectively in groups is required to be successful. Prominent features of the unique SOM approach included an absence of grades, no class ranks, an emphasis on community building and group dynamics, and tutorials given by peers.

In probing themselves and the activities of others in the class, issues of race and gender frequently arose. During the first semester, one woman in a group workshop interrupted the discussion with the observation, "There are a lot of deep voices drowning out the higher-pitched ones." Her point was that competitive men trying to maximize their individual input were tending to silence the contributions of women. Thus, the

My grandfather, Henry Marx (upper right), and his twelve brothers and sisters, all immigrants to the United States who fled persecution in Germany in the 1880s. Henry's daughter, Guida, was my mother.

Me with my father, Eames Donaldson, in 1931. The difficulties of the Great Depression would shape my Dad's career and the challenges of our family life.

One of my earliest entrepreneurial ventures, *Read 'Em and Grin* was a short-lived joke magazine I created with a couple of grade-school buddies and sold door-to-door in our Buffalo neighborhood.

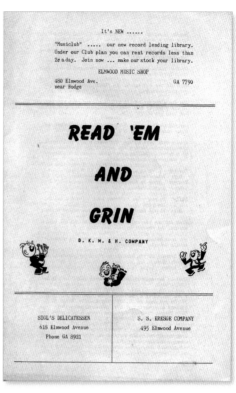

It's NEW ......

"Musiclub" ..... our new record lending library.
Under our Club plan you can rent records less than
2¢ a day. Join now ... make our stock your library.

ELMWOOD MUSIC SHOP

480 Elmwood Ave.   GA 7790
near Hodge

READ 'EM

AND

GRIN

D. K. M. & H. COMPANY

SIGL'S DELICATESSEN
618 Elmwood Avenue
Phone GA 8921

S. S. KRESGE COMPANY
495 Elmwood Avenue

My service in the U.S. Marines provided me with some of my most important lessons in leadership.

The booklet *Common Stock and Common Sense* laid out the investment philosophy that helped our fledgling firm, Donaldson, Lufkin & Jenrette, stand out from the crowd on Wall Street.

Common Stock and Common Sense

DONALDSON, LUFKIN & JENRETTE
INCORPORATED
Members New York Stock Exchange
51 BROAD STREET
NEW YORK 4, NEW YORK

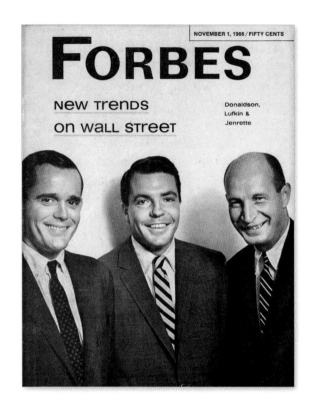

That's me on the left with my partners, Dan Lufkin and Dick Jenrette, posing for the cover of *Forbes* as leaders of one of the fastest-growing investment firms.

The board of governors of the New York Stock Exchange—that's me on the far left edge of the back row.

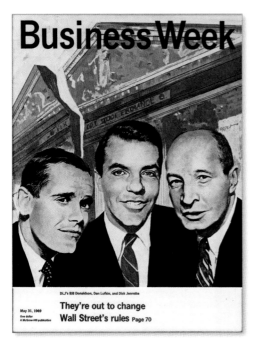

This cover of *Business Week* reflected the controversy DLJ launched with its plan to sell shares of stock to the public: some seemed to think our scheme would bring the stock exchange itself crashing to the ground.

One artist's version of the controversy: DLJ appears as a running back crashing through the old rules of the stock exchange, while other firms cheer us on from the sidelines.

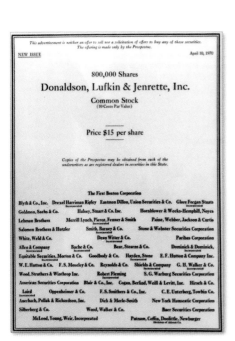

The so-called tombstone ad that formally announced the initial public offering of DLJ shares. It's now a piece of historic memorabilia.

The big day: NYSE president Bob Haack, Dick Jenrette, and I check the ticker tape as DLJ officially goes public.

By the end of 1969, DLJ had matured to the point of being named "investment bankers of the year" by *Finance* magazine.

Consolation prize: DLJ never fulfilled its dream of buying American Express, but in 1972 Amex did buy one quarter of our business. In this shot, Howard Clark, chairman of Amex, signs the historic letter of agreement confirming the deal.

Institutional Investor magazine reports my move from DLJ to the State Department with a drawing that makes me look like a giant ready to take over Washington. It didn't exactly work out that way.

Secretary of State Henry Kissinger welcomes me to his team. Joining the festivities are my wife Evan, our kids Matt and Kim, and my proud mom, Guida.

Enjoying a laugh with Gerald Ford in the Oval Office. I'm in the third seat to the president's left. Others in the shot include Jim Cannon, Bill Ronan, George Woods, and Nelson Rockefeller (seated back to camera).

To Bill Donaldson with deep appreciation and very best wishes from his friend Nelson A Rockefeller

An informal chat with Vice President Nelson Rockefeller, along with my kids Matt and Kim.

A photo from the early 1970s of me as a member of the Yale Corporation. My colleagues included such notables as Cyrus Vance, William Beinecke, John Chafee, Jack Danforth, Marian Wright Edelman, Bill Bundy, Bishop Paul Moore, and Yale President Kingman Brewster.

Me as dean of the new Yale School of Management (SOM).

With Yale President Kingman Brewster,
planning the buildings that would house SOM.

Addressing the academic dignitaries at the official opening ceremony for SOM.

To Bill Donaldson
With best wishes – Friendship G. Bush

I've known members of the Bush family since my undergraduate days at Yale.
Here I am in the White House with then Vice President George H.W. Bush.

MAY

As Chairman and CEO of the New York Stock Exchange (NYSE), I was
privileged to welcome distinguished guests—in this case, the powerful world
leaders President Ronald Reagan and Soviet Premier Mikhail Gorbachev.

Celebrating the 40th anniversary of DLJ (1999) with a bell-ringing ceremony at the New York Stock Exchange.

Addressing the crowds gathered on Wall Street at the 200th anniversary celebration for the NYSE in 1992.

When the insurance giant Aetna fell on hard times, as a director I was called upon to take over as chairman and CEO to help lead a turnaround.

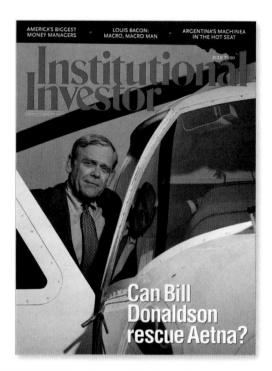

In 2002, in the wake of Enron and WorldCom scandals, President George W. Bush asked me to head the Securities and Exchange Commission (SEC). On the day of my swearing-in, I posed for this shot with the president and my family: wife Jane, our kids Matt, Kim, and Adam, and grandson Lars (on the way).

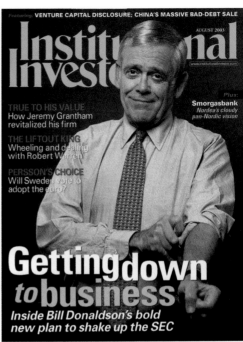

Two magazine covers reflected some of the challenges I'd be undertaking as new chief of the troubled SEC.

Posing with SEC staffers and, in the foreground, my fellow commissioners. A number of split 3-to-2 votes over regulatory issues fueled rumors of "civil war" among the commissioners.

With Patrick Von Bargen, Laura Cox, and Peter Derby, the triumvirate of managing directors I recruited to help spearhead reform at the SEC.

Do the right thing Mr. Donaldson!

When I took a tough stand against financial abuses, some conservative critics worried I was going too far, as this *Wall Street Journal* cartoon (July 27, 2004) illustrates.

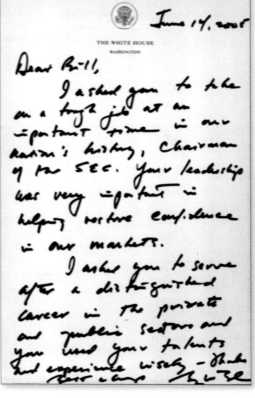

Despite the attacks I received from some on the right, President George W. Bush never wavered in his support.

To Bill – Thanks for your good counsel!

In the aftermath of the 2008-09 financial crisis, President Barack Obama appointed former Federal Reserve Chairman Paul Volcker to head the Economic Recovery Advisory Board. Here I am as a member of the board in the Oval Office with Obama, Volcker, Timothy Geithner, Barney Frank, Austan Goolsbee, and Vice President Joe Biden (closest to camera).

The Donaldson clan as of Christmas, 2017. Back row: Lars, Eric, Adam, Matt. Front row: Kim with Henrik, Bill, Willy, Jane.

It has been a life and career of challenges, achievements, setbacks, and discoveries—but always fun!

entire group was sensitized to "group discussion etiquette"—not a common topic in 1976, and one that the students at SOM, not the faculty, identified and addressed.

Perhaps empowered by the OB framework and culture, students in those early classes took an unusual degree of ownership over the unfolding progress of the School. They often worked alongside faculty and staff to analyze everything from how courses were being taught and received to the grading system and the kinds of extracurricular initiatives made available. It was a heady and sometimes tense process, but one that enabled the School to course-correct more effectively than would otherwise have been possible.

For the Class of 1978, the whole experience was an intense one, made more so than at the typical business school by the School's small size and the impact of OB on its norms and culture. Toward the end of the second year, one member of the Charter Class did a (necessarily imperfect) poll that concluded that, of all the nonmarital relationships students had when they entered SOM, not a single one had survived the two years. Some of the preexisting marriages also failed. And perhaps not surprisingly, many SOM students ended up getting married to one another over time.

The fact that we created a new school of management based on groundbreaking cross-sector approaches and analysis, and that we did so in just twelve months, was remarkable enough. Even more unexpected was the strength of the OB culture. Not everyone on the faculty was enthusiastic about the idea of yielding the academic high ground that characterizes a traditional business school approach. And while most of the students were favorably disposed to the OB approach, many felt uncomfortable with the group-oriented analysis it involved. But for me, this unique style of management training was a revelation. I found it to be the most dramatic and compelling pedagogical and cultural aspect of my tenure as dean. It was entrepreneurial, it made sense, and I embraced it.

We all tried to instill SOM with a culture that students, faculty, and other community members could enjoy and cherish. As I mentioned earlier, one of the tenets of DLJ's philosophy was "having fun," and I tried to embed the same spirit at SOM. One result was the SOM Follies, a comedy show held annually in the early years of the School. The Follies routinely roasted SOM along with its faculty, staff, and students—including me, of course.

The Charter Class produced the first Follies in the spring of 1977. The next-to-last scene, a combination of *Star Trek* and *Romeo and Juliet*, featured a clash between Romeo and the crew of the "Entrepreneurians," representing private enterprise, and Juliet and the "Pro-Bonoians," representing public services. A character known as Prince, The Don, strove to bring the warring factions together, adapting a few lines borrowed from my welcoming address to the class the previous fall. (I know, you had to be there.) Much to the surprise of both the audience and the rest of the cast, The Don was played by none other than me, having allowed myself to be talked into it by Jeffrey Yudkoff, the Follies' producer.

That first Follies ended with a chorus line rendition of "Hurray for Management," with the melody and spirit borrowed from the classic Richard A. Whiting/Johnny Mercer tune "Hooray for Hollywood":

> Hurray for management!
> It's not a question now of us and them,
> But you and me:
> Hurray for management!

Hurray diversity!
This is the only place for you and me,
And though our ideas are hazy,
We're not lazy.
I'll make a home for every crazy! [This was
my solo line.]
Hurray for management!

Hurray for management!
We know our final year will be well spent,
And what seems so unclear
We'll learn next year—
Hurray for management!

That first Follies proved to be a great bonding experience, stress reliever, and welcome respite from the class's hard academic slog through the winter. My cameo appearance set a precedent for later productions—and one of the Follies along the way gave me the enduring nickname "Dollar Bill."

We didn't recruit SOM students because of their song-and-dance abilities, but we quickly discovered that a number of them were multi-talented. In fact, at least two Follies impresarios, after careers in business, became significant theatrical luminaries: Jed Bernstein, former president of the Broadway League and of Lincoln Center for the Performing Arts, and Todd Haimes, artistic director and CEO of New York's acclaimed Roundabout Theatre Company. And Jeffrey Yudkoff, who produced the first Follies, went on to a career in finance which included work with several leading media companies.

* * *

One of the benefits I enjoyed as the founding dean of the School was the opportunity to teach a course of my choosing. I'd never taught before, but I'd always enjoyed the aspect of leadership that involves nurturing the knowledge and skills of others. And I believed I'd developed some insights into the nature of leadership from my experiences at DLJ and the State Department.

I decided to teach a course on entrepreneurial leadership. Today, entrepreneurship is one of the most popular courses of study at practically every business school. That wasn't the case back in the 1970s, when the traditional assumption was that most business students aspired to rise through the ranks of one of the great Fortune 500 companies. But I'd become convinced of the importance of being able to build something new, valuable, and lasting—whether in the for-profit, government, or nonprofit spheres, and whether starting an organization from scratch or infusing an innovative spirit into a pre-existing structure. So I set to work at formulating my ideas as to what entrepreneurial leadership was all about. It was the first time I'd actually tried to analyze and define entrepreneurship—despite the fact that, in one way or another, I'd been practicing it since my teens.

I summarized my thoughts on the subject in a simple one-page document that I used as a class outline. It read as follows:

Entrepreneurial Leader

1. ability to conceptualize—see what others see but from slightly different perspective

2. internally motivated—self-wired demand for excellence that comes from within

3. sense of anticipation & fall-back—not unusual—all or nothing

4. act like owner—your own CEO—whether you are just you—or CEO

5. operates on bifocal level—big picture and attention to detail

6. bestowed with energy—sense of well-being—physical / mental fitness

7. sense of optimism

8. sense of fun

9. defines system vs. being defined by it

10. moral DNA—integrity

Entrepreneurial Leader Creates Entrepreneurial Organization

As my notes show, I focused mainly on the personal and intellectual characteristics of the entrepreneurial leader rather than on any technical skills he or she might have. Of course, an entrepreneurial leader needs to know about subjects like financial management, competitive strategy, market analysis, and the like. But I think those topics are distinctly secondary. More important are the human qualities that the entrepreneurial leader brings to the job—the ability to see the world through fresh eyes; the ability to pay attention to both the big picture and the small details that define a particular situation; a high degree of personal energy, optimism, and a sense of fun; the readiness to shape and define the system in which he or she operates rather than being controlled by a system someone else has created; and, most important, a strong sense of integrity.

It's noteworthy that I did *not* refer to any of the elements that most people today think about when they hear the word "entrepreneur." To me—back in the 1970s, and still today— an entrepreneur is not, or shouldn't be, someone who launches businesses one after another, with the goal of quickly building them up and then selling them off for a fast profit. An entrepreneur should be focused on creating organizations with lasting value, as we did with DLJ.

And I don't believe that entrepreneurial leadership is all about taking risks. Some people talk as if the entrepreneur is above all a gambler, someone who puts his money on ventures almost at random, like a craps player risking his fortune on the next roll of the dice. Sure, there is risk whenever you launch a new enterprise. But the smart entrepreneur uses careful planning, intelligent strategy, and lots of hard work to minimize the risk as much as possible.

The fact that I was, and remain, more interested in the *spirit* of entrepreneurial leadership than in technical business skills is reflected in the fact that two of the role models I mentioned in my class discussion weren't businesspeople at all. Rather, they were great athletes—Michael Jordan, the brilliant basketball star who led the Chicago Bulls to an unprecedented six NBA championships in the 1990s, and Muhammad Ali, the boxing legend who captured the heavyweight crown on three separate occasions. I consider men like these entrepreneurial geniuses because of the creative vision, strategic insight, tactical flexibility, and intense competitiveness they bring to the arena. And while Ali, as a boxer, competed on his own, Jordan was able, through his immense talent and his unmatched will to win, to inspire teammates to perform better than they ever had before—an ability that great entrepreneurial leaders in every field try to develop.

In teaching my class in entrepreneurial leadership at SOM, I drew on my personal experiences at DLJ and at the State Department. But I also brought in guest lecturers who greatly enriched the conversation by describing the entrepreneurial challenges they'd faced and some of the lessons they'd learned in tackling them.

For example, I invited Fred Smith, the founder and CEO of Federal Express, to explain how he revolutionized the shipping business by recognizing an opportunity no one else had noticed (the need for reliable overnight deliveries of urgent business documents and packages) and a simple yet clever way to address it by creating a hub-and-spoke air delivery network to route packages everywhere in the country within a few hours. Smith is a classic example of the entrepreneurial leader who "sees what others see but from a slightly different perspective."

For another class session, I asked Robert McNamara to address the students about the challenges of reforming vast, complicated bureaucracies—first at the Ford Motor Company, then as Secretary of Defense under Presidents John F. Kennedy and Lyndon B. Johnson. He was a controversial guest because of his role in leading the American effort in the Vietnam War, which many of my students strongly opposed. But McNamara's honest, reflective evaluation of what he had done right and wrong in his leadership positions and his willingness to address students' questions candidly and honestly won the respect of the class and taught us all some hard lessons about the painful difficulties that true leadership often entails.

* * *

In an entrepreneurial setting, one must expect the unexpected. At the fledgling SOM, one area where we experienced some surprises was in student placement. Our original plan was to admit a roughly equal number of students from the corporate, government, and nonprofit sectors (we rarely accepted applicants right out of college). We expected that most students would return to their original sector after completing SOM. How wrong we were. A much higher percentage than we thought immediately entered the corporate sector upon graduating.

Seeking an explanation for this pattern, we speculated that perhaps students coming from government and nonprofit organizations wanted to try their hand in corporate settings using the management tools they had acquired at SOM. Another factor was the way companies actively recruited our students, often wining and dining the most attractive job candidates. Government agencies and nonprofits didn't do that. And last—though this may be pure speculation—there's the fact that SOM did not give grades. So for two years, our highly intelligent and motivated students couldn't compete with each other. In fact, they were rewarded for their collaboration. This meant that the first time they could compete was when they applied for jobs—and many viewed being offered a high-paying corporate position as a sign of success.

Over time, SOM was able to offset the corporate recruiting advantage, as students formed affinity groups and invited government and nonprofit luminaries to the campus to speak, sit on panels, and teach in classes. And as the alumni network increased, SOM graduates in government and nonprofits actively began to recruit students.

An early innovation at SOM was the Student Internship Fund, patterned after a similar fund at the Yale Law School. Students accepting high-paying internships in the corporate sector between their first and second years would pledge a contribution to the Internship Fund to be used by their classmates choosing internships in government and nonprofit organizations. The fund was highly successful and underscored the students' commitment to the mission of the School. As the years went by, alumni also contributed to the fund, especially those who'd used it during their own student years.

It was clear to everyone associated with SOM that the success or failure of the School would be played out in the acceptance of our alumni in the marketplace. It was also important, given the School's mission, that students gravitate to all three sectors. We hoped that, over time, there would be a fair amount of switching among the corporate, government, and nonprofit sectors, as the students had been trained to understand the important work being done as well as the specific management challenges and opportunities in each. At least, we hoped that SOM graduates would shift the management paradigm wherever they were, as they understood better than their peers from other institutions the increasing interplay among all the sectors.

* * *

When my contracted term as dean ended in June 1980, I was asked by the University to stay on. By then, the School of Management was well under way. In retrospect, if I'd stayed on for another term, I might have been able to help solidify the accomplishments of the fledgling school. But for me, the entrepreneurial excitement of launching the new school had subsided, and I felt I'd had enough of the academic life.

I turned down the offered extension and returned to New York. I had no specific plans as to what I would do next. But I had a strong feeling that something interesting, challenging, and new would come my way before long. I was right about that.

CHAPTER 8

Shaking Up the Street:
Heading the New York Stock Exchange

It's not common for someone who has challenged the rules of one of our country's most iconic institutions—as my partners and I did at DLJ when we announced our intention to go public back in 1969—to be invited back later to head that same institution. But that's exactly what happened to me with the New York Stock Exchange (NYSE) in 1990.

First, however, I took some time to ponder my next career move, after I returned to New York from Yale. During the next several years, I undertook a number of initiatives and projects. In 1980, I created Donaldson Enterprises, an umbrella structure for managing my private investments, as well as for forming a separate pool of money that I managed for several foreign investors and friends. It performed well, but it was hardly a full-time occupation.

I was looking for something more impactful to take on. In 1981, I seriously considered a run for elected office. My brief stint in the bureaucracy of the State Department had not been very satisfying, but I continued to be a strong believer in the challenge and value of public service, and I wanted to find a role in which I could contribute significantly to the country. At the same time, my experiences at Donaldson, Lufkin & Jenrette and at the Yale School of Management had shown me that I enjoyed creating and leading an organization, especially shaping its agenda and molding its culture. I also liked the entrepreneurial challenge of creating something new. So simply filling a mid-level slot in one of the vast federal cabinet departments or even serving as one of several hundred members in Congress didn't appeal to me. If possible, I wanted to lead an organization with the mission of really making a difference, only this time in the public arena. My entrepreneurial urge surfaced in the area of elective politics.

There were just two elective offices I thought I might seriously consider—the presidency of the United States (then hardly considered a realistic place to start a public service career), and perhaps the governorship of one of the fifty states.

I decided to explore the possibility of running for governor of my home state of New York. The incumbent, Democrat Hugh Carey, had invited me at the beginning of his first term to join his new administration in the traditional senior role of secretary to the governor. Though honored by the suggestion, I'd respectfully declined. Now Governor Carey was scheduled to leave office in 1983 on the completion of his second term in Albany.

Never having run for office before, I knew I needed guidance from an experienced source. So in early 1981, I hired John Steel, a veteran political operative, to initiate and manage my fledgling campaign. John's first question to me was, "What party are you affiliated with?"

"My first vote," I said, "was for Dwight Eisenhower, so I guess I am a Republican. But I'm registered as an independent. I dropped any party affiliation when I moved to New Haven to work at Yale." As dean of Yale's newest graduate school, I'd felt that my role should be devoid of any hint of political bias.

"Well, pick it back up, pronto," John told me. "You can't run for office as a Republican without being a member of the party." So I filled out the required paperwork and embarked on the arduous process of making myself known as an aspiring candidate.

John had the experience and the connections I needed to begin building a political network and organization. He and I began traveling throughout New York State together. The plan was to visit with the Republican county chairs who headed party operations in each of New York's sixty-two counties. I had countless conversations in every corner of the state. Occasionally the meetings were a bit unusual, like the time I met a county chairman who happened to be the town undertaker. John and I visited him in his funeral parlor, where he had just come from working on the remains of a "client"; I recall how he carefully peeled off his rubber gloves, smelling of chemicals, before shaking my hand. Our travels across the state would also include a stop at the local newspaper office for a conversation with the editorial board.

At the same time, with John's guidance I started to build the basic framework of a campaign operation. Lou Harris, my pollster colleague and friend from DLJ, offered the services of his phone bank, and a number of my former students from Yale had signed on as volunteers to begin making canvassing calls on my behalf. We began printing flyers and other promotional materials, and sketching plans for a statewide speaking tour starting on the tip of Long Island. "Donaldson for Governor" was beginning to morph from a vague dream into a concrete entrepreneurial effort.

But as I gained experience with the realities of being a candidate, it began to dawn on me that running for office might not be my cup of tea.

One of the first eye-opening moments for me came at a big Republican dinner in New York City hosted by the state party. John was very proud of the fact that he had managed to get a seat for me on the dais at the banquet, despite the fact that I was a political novice. Luminaries from throughout New York would be present, including many of the party's major financial contributors as well as my potential rivals for the gubernatorial race. My appearance at this dinner would be my first big moment in a political spotlight—an audition of sorts. "This is a great thing for our effort!" John declared. I was suitably grateful.

On the night of the dinner, I took the seat on the dais that John had arranged, where I sat through a series of diverse religious blessings and a seemingly endless litany of introductory speeches by party officials. At long last the speeches ended and the waiters began to serve dinner. But I'd taken just a single bite of my rubber chicken when John hustled up to me. "What are you doing?" he demanded.

"I'm trying to eat my dinner," I replied.

"You can't do that!" he responded, aghast. "You're here to work the room!" He proceeded to drag me from table to table, introducing me to everyone as "Bill Donaldson, the next governor of New York."

By the end of the evening, I had shaken many hands, smiled at hundreds of faces, heard and forgotten countless names, and engaged in not a single conversation of any substance or interest. As I left the banquet hall, I commented to John, "Well, I'm glad that's over with!"

"Get used to it!" he replied. "Between now and the election, I'm hoping to get you to luncheons and dinners like this practically every day. That's politics!"

I began to wonder whether being governor of New York was worth the price. I gamely followed the schedule John set for me, attending gatherings of Republican officeholders and supporters around the state and giving short speeches about myself and my views in venues ranging from Rotary halls to half-empty gymnasiums. I learned how to glad-hand with the best of them and even got pretty good at delivering an inspiring stump speech. I knew I'd hit my stride one afternoon after giving a talk before the Republican Women's Club in Albany. Afterward, I was besieged by the Republican ladies, all eager to shake my hand and declaring enthusiastically, "Mr. Donaldson, what a wonderful candidate you'll be!"

For a moment, I was elated. But that evening, as I lay on the bed in my dreary hotel room and looked over the schedule for the next day's appearances, I found myself thinking, Do I really want to do this for the rest of my life?

But the clincher was when John began to tailor my ideas to make me a better fit with the image of a proper Republican candidate. "You're coming out of nowhere, Bill," he said. "You gotta realize that these Republican primaries are run by the conservative wing of the party, and you gotta have views consistent with that. Your entrepreneurial background is pretty attractive. But I've heard you say some liberal things about issues like abortion. You gotta be in the right place on the abortion thing." The notion of taking political positions I didn't really believe in was uncomfortable.

Soon after that, I had a visit from Lew Lehrman, a businessman who'd resigned his post in 1977 as president of the Rite Aid drug store chain founded by his family to mount a serious campaign for governor of New York. He'd already spent more than three years befriending local political leaders and buying tables at Republican events. Now he came to see me and said, "Are you really going to make a run at this thing? I'm going to put a lot of money into this race. And I have a feeling that your constituency and mine could be pretty much the same." The more we chatted, the more I came to feel that Lew would be a strong candidate, given his family wealth, his three-year head start in campaigning across the state, and perhaps his unquestioning acceptance of conservative Republican orthodoxy.

Several days before the date when I was due to launch a statewide tour as an official candidate, I pulled the plug on my campaign. Lew Lehrman ended up heading the Republican state ticket in 1982. He lost the November election to a young Democrat named Mario Cuomo, who went on to serve three terms as a popular liberal governor of New York.

That was the end of my career in elective politics—though not in public service.

From 1982 to 1984, I served as a member of the Grace Commission, a public-private group headed by J. Peter Grace that was asked by President Ronald Reagan to tackle the problems of government debt and waste. The members of the commission—formally known as the President's Private Sector Survey on Cost Control—spent two years studying such problems as the misallocation of tax moneys, the vast amounts of taxable income that go unreported, and the burgeoning interest payments on the steadily rising federal debt. In 1984, we presented to Congress a report that recommended a series of carefully thought-out reforms that probably would have dramatically improved the efficiency of the federal government—all of which Congress completely ignored.

Later in the 1980s, I became embroiled in one of the stranger and more unpleasant episodes in my life. It all began in September 1987, when my friend Henry Ford II, the grandson of the great innovator and company founder, died rather suddenly from complications of pneumonia in a Detroit hospital.

I'd gotten to know Henry through my service on the Ford Foundation board, of which he also was a member. Like all who knew him, I was shocked and saddened by his passing. But

the matter became far more personal several months later, on
April 9, 1988, when a close friend of Henry's, a Detroit businessman named Martin Citrin, killed himself.

Citrin had been one of three people named by Henry to serve
as trustees of his complex estate, valued at more than $350 mil-
lion and including control of 10 percent of the voting stock of
Ford Motor Company. The other two were Henry's widow—his
third wife, Kathleen DuRoss Ford—and his son, Edsel, one of
three children by his first wife, Anne McDonnell Ford. The two
had never gotten along—in fact, none of Henry's children had
even attended his wedding to Kathleen. With the proceeds from
a huge trust fund at stake, their relationship had become even
more hostile. That meant Martin Citrin, as the third trustee,
had been the "swing vote" forced to adjudicate the battles that
had already begun to rage in the months since Henry's passing.
Now, with Citrin's tragic death, that role passed to the person
named in Henry's will as an alternate trustee.

To my shock, that person was me.

I suppose Henry must have asked my permission before
naming me for this important role, but I hadn't paid much
attention; I assumed that alternate trustee was a purely honor-
ific title that would never take effect. I was wrong—and now
I was thrust into the middle of a family squabble that grew
increasingly bitter, and public, with every passing month.

I quickly became the target of a tug-of-war between the two
chief combatants. When Citrin's death became known, Kathleen,
an attractive 48-year-old former model, promptly invited me to
visit her at her palatial home in Palm Beach, Florida, and in her
charming way she hoped to make me an ally in the coming legal
battle. (Henry's will had provided a minimum income of $1.5
million per year from the trust for Kathleen, but she regarded
this as woefully inadequate—and it certainly wasn't enough to
sustain the jet-setting lifestyle she'd long been enjoying.) I was

polite but businesslike and refused to be drawn into collusion with Kathleen against Edsel, representing the grandchildren's interests. I promised to try to help the disputants find a reasonable compromise that would be fair to all—a position that I'm sure Kathleen considered tantamount to betrayal.

Over the next six months, the Ford heirs did battle in the courts, in conference rooms around the country, and in the pages of the tabloids. The situation had all the makings of a juicy gossip story: a deceased multimillionaire and his glamorous widow; a sudden death by suicide; and a disputed estate that included yachts, jets, fabulous artworks, and magnificent homes in locations around the world. Charges and countercharges flew back and forth, with some of the points at issue seeming amazingly petty. The minutes of the trustees' meeting of May 26, 1988, as reported in *The New York Times*, included this note:

> Mr. [Edsel] Ford stated he was not satisfied with the allocation of expenses. He cited the example of certain "terry cloth furniture covers." He thought they should be paid for exclusively from Mrs. Ford's income. Mrs. Ford disagreed in as much as the covers had been made to cover existing furniture which had deteriorated to the point where it was necessary to recover them.[5]

While these arguments over furniture covers were raging, serious questions about how to invest the millions of dollars held by the trust were going unanswered. And I was caught in the crossfire, including public attacks from Kathleen over the size of the fee I was to be paid for my services as trustee.

In the end, a settlement was reached, obviating the need for an even more embarrassing and painful trial. In October 1988, Judge Vaughn Rudnick of Palm Beach County Circuit Court approved an agreement that gave Kathleen 3 percent per year of the income from her husband's trust—a minimum of $10.5 million—as well as several homes. The rest of the income would go to the other members of the Ford family. Kathleen also succeeded in having my fee reduced—and, more important, in having my term of service as a trustee shortened from life to three years. The latter provision came as an enormous relief to me.

Perhaps the biggest lesson I took away from the Ford estate battle was that no legal document, no matter how artfully designed, can guarantee harmonious dealings between people who simply don't like or trust one another. Forging a group of individuals with varying interests and desires into a mutually supportive team is one of the hardest things in the world to do—and it's as true within families as it is in a school, a military unit, or a business organization.

* * *

Although I had plenty to do during the 1980s, none of the smaller projects I tackled satisfied my hunger for a creative entrepreneurial undertaking.

In 1990, the big new challenge I'd been looking for surfaced. I was invited to become chairman and CEO of the New York Stock Exchange (NYSE). John Phelan, the longtime chairman and CEO of the Exchange, had rather abruptly announced that he was going to retire.

In retrospect, I think John stepped down at a very challenging time—whether by design or by coincidence, I can't say. The Exchange was about to embark on one of the most difficult periods in its history, facing mounting competitive challenges unlike any it had ever encountered. It was also facing significant financial problems—growth had stalled, revenues were down, and expenses were up. Richard Grasso, president and chief operating officer of the Exchange, had appeared to be next in line for the chairmanship.

Grasso was an NYSE lifer with many friends in the industry. A streetwise kid from Jackson Heights in Queens, he'd originally been hired as a floor clerk in 1968 and had spent twenty-two years at the Exchange, rising through the ranks and accumulating great influence and power. He knew everything there was to know about how the Exchange worked and played a valuable role in keeping its operations running smoothly. Perhaps understandably, Grasso assumed he would be named chairman. But there were many people at the Exchange who didn't want him in that role. Some didn't like his brash personality; others believed he lacked the *gravitas* and public presence needed to represent the Exchange on the world stage; still others simply thought that, at age 44, he wasn't quite ready for the job.

So the NYSE delegated the challenge of naming a new chairman to a search committee, which began interviewing top executives from throughout the financial world. One of the leaders they spoke to was my old friend and colleague Dick Jenrette, who'd cofounded DLJ with me. Dick was flattered by the interest shown by the NYSE, but he was deeply involved in helping to run the troubled Equitable Companies, which had purchased DLJ in 1985. "You ought to talk to Bill Donaldson," he said.

The search committee was looking for someone who could bring a measure of stability and focus to the Exchange and to the industry in a time of growing upheaval. They also wanted someone who could effectively represent the Exchange in dealings with corporate CEOs, U.S. government regulators, and financial industry leaders from around the world. In August 1990, the NYSE board offered me the job.

It was an ideal assignment for me: at the crossroads of private enterprise and public service, leading a major institution that was already contributing enormously to the economic growth of the nation and the world but that was in need of a jolt of entrepreneurial creativity and competitive reform in order to survive and thrive in the twenty-first century.

There was also a touch of irony in being asked to help run the organization that, not so long ago, we'd scandalized by the unprecedented act of taking Donaldson, Lufkin & Jenrette public—a move that had ended up revolutionizing the relationship between the stock exchange and the world's biggest financial institutions.

I agreed to become chairman and CEO of the NYSE as of January 1, 1991. But for a time, tumultuous personal issues that were unfolding simultaneously threatened to upend my plans.

* * *

Earlier in this book, I recounted how Jane Phillips Morrison and I met during our time as colleagues at Yale. We continued to stay in touch after my departure from Yale in 1980. Jane would remain at SOM for another year as head of admissions, placement, and student services.

Committed to our longtime spouses, we didn't know quite how to think about or handle our own relationship. Jane's husband Bruce Morrison, then serving as head of the New Haven legal assistance office after having graduated from the Yale Law School several years prior, had launched a political career. Despite being an unknown with no party backing and very little funding, Bruce decided against all odds to run for the Democratic nomination for the third district U.S. congressional seat in Connecticut, representing the New Haven area and the coastal towns along Long Island Sound. Having left Yale, Jane stepped in to run his campaign, out of necessity.

Amazingly, Bruce won the nomination and went on to win the general election. He and Jane spent the 1980s commuting between New Haven and Washington, D.C., as he continued to win reelection and gain considerable prominence in the House of Representatives. In 1990, Bruce won the Democratic nomination for governor of Connecticut, although he was defeated by the popular Lowell Weicker, running as an independent. It turned out that ended Bruce's career in elective office.

During these years, I would see Jane periodically. When not in D.C. or campaigning with Bruce for reelection, she worked at the Ford Foundation, helping them recruit an array of program and administrative officers for their New York headquarters and their field offices abroad. In 1991, she and her partner Debra Oppenheim would found Phillips Oppenheim, a search firm that now has been prominent in recruiting professionals for the non-profit sector for over twenty-seven years.

It was toward the end of the 1980s, more than ten years after we had met, that Jane and I finally began to come to grips with our relationship. I was now in my late fifties and had been married for almost thirty years; Jane was in her early forties and had been married almost twenty years. We lived interesting, complicated lives, mostly separate, but sometimes together. Our relationship worked without much introspection on anyone's part for a long time. But our marriages were starting to fracture for a variety of reasons. Bruce and Jane had separated just as he began his gubernatorial campaign, and she moved to New York and concentrated full-time on her executive search work.

Then, in the summer of 1989, everything changed. Jane, who had never had children, found herself pregnant at 45. Needless to say, it was a stressful time. Her divorce was not yet finalized, her husband was running for governor of Connecticut, and I, our child's father, was chairman of the NYSE.

During all the years of my relationship with Jane, there had been quiet speculation about us, but nothing public. At this point, however, political junkies in Hartford, Connecticut, were watching the gubernatorial race closely, and inevitably rumors began to swirl about the estranged wife of one of the candidates and a prominent New York business leader. Yet somehow, the rumors never made it into print. I attribute that to the fact that most people in and around our two worlds—Connecticut/D.C. politics and Wall Street—genuinely liked and respected both Jane and me. There were few people who were eager to use the taint of scandal to drag us down, and I think most reporters who heard the whispers were content to ignore them. (I suspect that things would be different in today's Internet-driven, feeding-frenzy media world.)

Jane's divorce was finalized without fanfare or press coverage in Connecticut in early 1990, just before our son Adam was born.

As for my wife Evan and me, the final chapter of our story was an extremely painful one. After finally finding the courage to tell her everything, I tried to be supportive as best I could. I moved out but lived on my own, not with Jane. For the next several years, I tried to make things right for everyone, an effort that, in the end, probably did more harm than good. My children, Kim and Matt—at this point in their early twenties—couldn't understand or accept what had happened. Evan was understandably devastated, but she wanted us to put our relationship back together and move forward. Jane, although she wasn't happy, didn't pressure me, letting me know that she would raise Adam alone, if need be.

In the end—inevitably—Evan and I started divorce proceedings. Evan accepted the reality that our marriage was over, and she had begun to date. And then in May 1994, horrifically and without warning, Evan experienced a cerebral hemorrhage while at a Lincoln Center concert and died, virtually overnight.

Evan's funeral service was one of the most emotionally difficult days of my life. The church was packed with hundreds of friends and family, all of whom knew and loved Evan. Everyone was numb with grief over her sudden, shocking death. I felt it was important to offer my tribute to Evan's wonderful qualities and to the long life we had shared, and I did my best to summarize those feelings in my brief eulogy.

Healing with Kim and Matt would take a while. I suppose I, too, needed to sort through my own conscious and subconscious feelings and reactions to it all before I could move on. Jane understood the impact of grief on all of us, having lost her own mother early in life. She let Kim and Matt know she was there for them when they were ready. Over the next year or so, we gradually all came together—not least because of the unwitting help of Adam, an exuberant little 4-year-old whom everybody adored.

Jane and I were married in December 1995, eighteen years after we met, in the old stone Mead Chapel near our home in Waccabuc, New York, the site of numerous future family weddings and christenings. Our families and close friends were there to celebrate with us: Matt was best man, Kim led the readings, and Adam, still a toddler then, was ring bearer and, after the ceremony, the steeple bell ringer with his cousins. Adam's kindergarten teacher, in congratulating us, said that, over the years as she'd looked at pictures of her own parents' wedding, she'd wished she could have been there, as Adam was at ours. Only in New York!

The following February, we held a party for several hundred people that covered all three floors at the Century Association in New York City, resplendent with dance bands, the Yale Whiffenpoofs, flowers everywhere, and all manner of food and drink. Century staff members still refer to it to this day.

Kim, Matt, and Adam have now created with Jane and me a strong, tightly bonded family core. In-laws and grandchildren have joined us and added to our pleasure, but the five of us will always have a unique emotional connection.

Kim inherited two of my lifelong passions: hockey and entrepreneurialism. She jokes that "entrepreneur" was one of the first words she learned growing up in our house. Kim went to St. Paul's for high school, where she ran varsity track, was the captain of the varsity squash team, and was coeditor of the school newspaper. At Yale, she cofounded a literary magazine and played on the women's varsity squash team that won a national championship.

After graduating, she tried her hand at advertising and became the first employee at Grey Advertising to move from account management to the creative side. With an MFA in graphic design and collage, Kim launched her first start-up, Donaldson Design Group, a branding and marketing firm she ran for ten years. In 2005, wanting a new challenge involving the Internet, she and a friend cofounded Bottlenotes, a niche e-commerce and tech company focused on wine. They produced content and events, published a daily email on wine for 450,000 subscribers, and hosted large-scale wine events around the country. Then, in 2015, Kim moved on to cofound Excelle Sports, a multimedia platform featuring editorial coverage of all women's sports. Kim is the mother of our grandsons Lars and Henrik.

While growing up, Matt could always be found where mischief was to be had. And since childhood, he has always loved the outdoors—fishing, hiking, biking, and playing sports. He attended Taft for high school, where he played varsity soccer, hockey, and lacrosse. He was nicknamed The Rhino, which later became the school's mascot because of him.

After graduating from Alfred University, where he was the varsity lacrosse goalie, Matt set out to see as much of the United States as he could. He joined Trek America and spent a decade traveling throughout the country in a van carrying foreign visitors (including a healthy stream of au pairs), who wanted to see America at the grassroots level. These trips generally lasted three to nine weeks. Along with twelve other Trek guides, Matt planned the trips, drove the van, organized the logistics, and made sure everyone had a good time.

After leaving Trek in 2004, Matt took a job working for Northwestern Mutual in New York, quickly proving that he had a natural talent for communicating with people, listening to what they needed, and then selling them insurance and financial products that made sense for them. Having built a vast network of clients, acquaintances, and friends, Matt went on to start his own successful business connecting potential investors with entrepreneurs and companies needing capital. He also raises capital for sizable investment funds and has expanded his network internationally. Still a serious outdoorsman with three Ironman Triathlons under his belt, Matt now lives in Los Angeles and is the father of our grandson Willy.

The youngest of my children, Adam, arrived when I was 59 and has helped to keep me young. A multi-sport athlete, Adam played competitive USTA tennis as a boy and continued that through high school as a ranked U.S. junior and captain of the Taft varsity tennis team his senior year. In 2008, he was recruited by the University of Louisville to their high-ranking NCAA Division I tennis team.

After graduation, Adam combined his love of sports and his interest in media by joining the video production team of the successful sports start-up, Bleacher Report. Adam focused on developing video stories about talented high school, college, and pro athletes, using his considerable talent for asking the right questions and portraying the athletes and surroundings in a creative, exciting way. He is very good at listening to people and communicating with them in a way that instills trust.

After becoming a senior field producer at Bleacher Report, Adam was recruited by the University of Notre Dame in 2017 to upgrade and run the social media production for all the university's sports teams. Consistent with his interest in sports management, Adam will attend Notre Dame's Executive MBA program, while continuing his work highlighting Notre Dame athletes and teams. I have finally gotten one of my children to go to a management school!

Jane and I have now been happily married for more than two decades. Our friendship and love are as strong as ever, and I consider myself as blessed as a man can be. But I can never forget the pain that fundamental life choices can bring when they involve people close to you. And I don't really know that there is one right way to handle those choices. If there was in my case, I didn't find it.

* * *

While my family drama was unfolding, I was in the process of being selected chairman and CEO of the NYSE.

My visibility in the new role actually began even before I took over. Shortly after my appointment was announced, I was invited by James Morton, dean of the Episcopal Cathedral of St. John the Divine in New York—the world's largest Gothic church and a notable center of community life in the city—to give a lay sermon. On October 14, 1990—less than two months before I would assume the leadership of the Exchange—I gave a talk from the pulpit in which I called on American business leaders to do more to help create a greater spirit of sharing and generosity, which stirred up quite a bit of interest and controversy.

My comments from that sermon about the rising tide of economic inequality would be at least as relevant—and unfortunately just as controversial—today:

The '80s, for many, was a decade of abundance, a decade when bulls trotted confidently at us through our television screens, when it was easy to see how good things were for some people and too easy *not* to see how bad it was for others:

- Chauffeured limousines lined up outside fancy new glass towers, while the homeless congregated in Grand Central.
- Lavish Park Avenue parties made headlines, while the lines lengthened at the soup kitchens.

We could have seen that the gap was widening. That many people weren't getting the opportunities we believe everyone deserves. That we were leaving out of the economic mainstream a major portion of society's most precious resource—people.

The Washington Post quoted parts of the sermon and remarked, "William H. Donaldson, the new chairman of the New York Stock Exchange, is Wall Street's highest-ranking spokesman, but sometimes he sounds more like its leading critic . . . Donaldson's self-appointed task on Wall Street is reminiscent of Jimmy Stewart as the idealistic politician who tried to clean up Congress in 'Mr. Smith Goes to Washington.' He appeals to the industry to rebuild a reputation for honesty and fair dealing that he believes it had enjoyed—and deserved—in an earlier era."[6]

One of the first challenges I faced as chairman was forging a positive partnership with my frustrated rival for the top job, Dick Grasso. Both the NYSE board and I recognized Dick's skills and appreciated them enormously—which is why I started my tenure by personally appealing to Dick to remain at the Exchange as president and serve as a critical member of our leadership team. "I really need you," I told him. "I don't know as much as you about this side of our industry. You'll be a great partner, and together we can make the Exchange even better than before."

Dick accepted my proposal. And as far as I'm concerned, Dick Grasso and I worked effectively together as a good team in running the NYSE.

But chairing the NYSE turned out to offer a profound challenge, even with all the skills I'd developed as an entrepreneurial leader.

A long list of complex issues was waiting in my in-box when I started the job. The NYSE was the most venerable and influential exchange in the world, with the most rigorous listing requirements for traded stocks. But it also faced huge challenges. It was still working to recover from the catastrophic market collapse of October 1987, when the Dow Jones Industrial Average fell by 508 points in one day and the Exchange had difficulty keeping pace with the increasing volume of transactions as panicked investors sought to sell their shares. Since then, many in the general public had come to view stock markets as dangerously volatile, a perception we were eager to dispel. Some even feared the markets were rigged in favor of big institutional traders, a view that would be fatal to long-term investment confidence if we didn't succeed in squelching it. And as the years passed, trading volume had continued to increase, creating a desperate need for improved infrastructure to manage the greater flow of transactions.

Other trends were also challenging the NYSE. The world of business was rapidly globalizing, in part due to the 1991 collapse of the Soviet Union and the consequent expansion of capitalist markets across Europe. American purchases of foreign stocks, which had amounted to just $18 billion in 1980, had climbed to more than $200 billion in the subsequent decade. This meant that, to remain competitive, the NYSE had to become more open to listings of foreign companies. Yet these were severely restricted by an SEC rule that foreign company financial statements comply with generally accepted accounting principles (GAAP) as formulated by U.S. regulators. Partly as a result, investors were drifting away from the NYSE and doing an increasing share of their trading business on other exchanges, including the burgeoning over-the-counter market managed by the Nasdaq system.

I was a great believer in the value and importance of the NYSE as the world's preeminent stock market. There are huge advantages to having a single site where fair prices for shares can be readily discovered, rather than having atomized, fragmented markets that provide advantages to those with inside information. During my years as chairman, I promoted this concept in countless speeches, often summarizing the theme with the sentence, "The best market is one that brings all the buyers and sellers together in one place."

Circumstances gave me plenty of opportunities to promote the importance of the NYSE. My first year as chairman happened to coincide with the 200th anniversary of the founding of the New York Stock Exchange, which famously had its origins in a 1792 gathering of traders in the shade of a buttonwood tree on New York's Wall Street. We took advantage of the bicentennial to trumpet the message of free markets around the United States and the world. I visited some twenty-five cities on behalf of the NYSE, meeting with local government officials, speaking to school and university students, addressing business organizations, and giving interviews explaining the role of financial markets in promoting economic growth. Our bicentennial celebration culminated in a gala New York street fair on May 17, 1992, attended by 14,000 stock exchange members, employees, and friends. Treasury Secretary Nicholas Brady, an old friend of mine, addressed the crowd from the steps of Federal Hall, where George Washington had been inaugurated as first president of the United States in 1789, and helped us cut and serve a giant 200th birthday cake.

More important, I got to work with my talented team on tackling the challenges the NYSE faced. We set about developing plans for accelerating the modernization of the Exchange and helping to prepare it for the stiff new competition it faced from overseas exchanges and electronic trading systems here at home. We instituted longer trading hours—first in the form of an experimental program of "off-hours trading," then as a permanent change. This made it easier for overseas traders to use the NYSE to buy and sell stocks. We eased our disclosure rules, which also served to attract foreign participation while maintaining the necessary requirements for transparency to protect investors. We reduced transaction fees for small investors, making the trading floor more of a level playing field for all participants. We created a new Competitive Position Advisory Board made up of representatives from exchange member firms, traders, and senior management of the Exchange, to spearhead initiatives designed to reduce turnaround times on market orders, improve trading accuracy and efficiency, and experiment with new technological tools. And we spent some $125 million on overhauling the technology of the Exchange.

These enhancements rapidly created a noticeable impact on our operations and on public perceptions of the stock market. By October 1992—five years after the crash of 1987, and close to two years into my tenure at the NYSE—*The New York Times* was able to report on the many positive changes we'd wrought in the market systems. They included vastly improved, more efficient trading systems capable of handling 800 million share transactions per day, a fourfold increase from 1987; enhanced computer systems and training programs at brokerage firms;

greater financial strength among the specialist firms on whom the market depended; and improved stability in the markets thanks to the deployment of "circuit breakers" and other tools designed to minimize panics.

"The wrenching changes brought on by the crash," the *Times* concluded, "have created healthier, more resilient and more reliable trading markets."[7] It was a classic example of how the pressure created by powerful external trends and the impact of a crisis can force a traditional organization to implement dramatic change—provided the leadership is in place to conceive and drive that change.

Another crucial challenge involved finding a way for the NYSE to seize the explosive growth opportunity represented by market globalization. With more and more large companies emerging in countries around the world, U.S. investors were eager to put a portion of their money into foreign stocks. A few small businesses from overseas had long been available for trading on the NYSE. But major corporate listings of foreign businesses on the Big Board had long been opposed by regulators, mainly due to concerns over the varying standards of accounting and financial disclosure practiced by companies in other countries. Some took the position that universal accounting standards accepted throughout the world would be necessary before truly global markets could exist. That might be a desirable end goal, but I believed that waiting for universal standards would simply mean that the NYSE would never be able to list the shares of the great foreign companies—a deeply unfortunate missed opportunity for U.S. markets and investors.

During my tenure as CEO, I pushed hard on this front. My main opponent was Richard Breeden, then chairman of the Securities and Exchange Commission (SEC), the chief federal regulator of the stock market. A breakthrough finally took place in 1993 thanks to a settlement we helped to negotiate between Daimler-Benz, the German automotive giant, and the SEC. Daimler-Benz agreed to release most of the financial data required by U.S. accounting rules, thereby minimizing the risk to American investors interested in owning a part of the German firm. In October 1993, we proudly welcomed Daimler-Benz to the NYSE. Within the next few years, many other great foreign companies joined it on the Big Board.

During my years at the helm of the NYSE, I was able to infuse the old, tradition-bound Exchange with a new sense of entrepreneurial risk-taking and innovation. But I didn't solve all the problems the Exchange faced. Most significantly, I wish I had done more to break down the anticompetitive structures the Exchange had accumulated over time, making it needlessly costly and difficult for individuals and institutions to do business on the NYSE. These barriers ultimately led to the creation of complex workarounds by outside organizations— for example, the so-called "dark pools" used today by trading companies to avoid having to bring all their business to public exchanges like the NYSE. The existence of these dark pools, their lack of regulation, and the mistrust and controversy they've engendered in recent years represents a failure of anticipation on my part and on the part of other leaders of the financial industry.

Overall, however, I believe I left the NYSE in an improved competitive position, having significantly increased the proportion of trades in Big Board–listed stocks done at the Exchange versus those done via the Nasdaq over-the-counter market in the years since 1992. When I left the NYSE in 1994, the price of a seat on the NYSE, often viewed as a gauge of the importance of the Exchange, was higher than at any time since the pre-crash boom of 1987. We'd done a lot to modernize the infrastructure, rules, and systems of the stock market, enabling it to effectively handle the big bull market of the 1990s.

And when Dick Grasso, as expected, was named to succeed me as CEO, he told reporters, "The vision of Grasso is a continuation of the vision of Donaldson and Grasso." It was a fine tribute to the success we'd created together and for which I was happy to share the credit.

I never viewed Dick as a competitor. But what unintentional rivalry there was between us would resurface unpredictably a few years later, when I was forced, in my new role as the chief government regulator of the Exchange, to defuse a massive scandal triggered in part by that same Dick Grasso.

CHAPTER 9

Out of the Blue:
The Aetna Turnaround

In February 2000, I was on a family vacation in New Zealand. We were enjoying the America's Cup races as guests of Doug Myers and his wife Barbara, owners of the New Zealand boat. We'd retired to the Myers's farm on the North Island after the races in Auckland when an unexpected call came for me. On the other end of the line was the head of a search committee that had been delegated to identify a new CEO to take the reins at Aetna, the giant insurance company. "The company's in serious trouble, Bill," he said. "Even worse than we'd realized. Would you consider stepping in as CEO to help turn it around?"

I was well aware that Aetna had been struggling. I'd been a member of the company's board of directors since 1977. It was a venerable financial business that had started out as a fire insurance provider back in 1853. Over the generations, Aetna had grown into a huge company with many lines of business, including health insurance, property and casualty insurance, pension and investment management, and significant international operations. For decades, Aetna had prospered, becoming a mainstay of the financial services industry and one of the leading employers and civic pillars in its home city of Hartford, Connecticut.

But during the 1990s, Aetna had gradually lost its way. In 1997, under increasing competitive and financial pressure, it had chosen an outsider named Dick Huber as its CFO and then its CEO, hoping he could give the staid, conservative company a jolt of new thinking. Unfortunately, Huber had chosen a misguided path. A natural-born wheeler-dealer who had cut his teeth in the banking business, Huber had engaged in a series of ill-considered company acquisitions, believing that sheer size would be the key to Aetna's future financial success, particularly in the rapidly changing health insurance business. Some of the companies that Aetna had merged with—particularly the industry darling, the innovative and aggressive U.S. Healthcare—had corporate cultures quite different from Aetna's. Yet neither Huber nor anyone else had dedicated the time and energy needed to truly integrate these mismatched organizations. As a result, the company had become bloated and was basically directionless.

As a member of the board, I bore a share of the blame for allowing this to happen. For a time, Huber's strategy appeared to be successful. In the midst of his acquisition spree, Aetna's stock had climbed to an all-time high of more than $110 per share. But by February 2000, it had fallen to below $39—an eight-year low. A company that had once been solidly, consistently profitable was now losing money by the tens of millions. That was when the board realized that the problems at Aetna were deep and systemic. While I was traveling overseas, they asked Huber to resign, and the search committee they chose to name his replacement called on me for help.

I was startled to receive this invitation. At age 68, I was relishing the prospect of spending more time with Jane, my adult children, and my wonderful young son. My previous careers at Donaldson, Lufkin & Jenrette and the New York Stock Exchange, along with a carefully crafted investment portfolio, had left me comfortably situated from a financial perspective. So I was thinking about ratcheting down my business activities, not taking on a huge new challenge.

But I did have a feeling of responsibility toward Aetna. Most corporate boards take a largely hands-off role when it comes to day-to-day management; they tend to defer to the judgment of the CEO and his team, assuming that he is more in touch with the realities of the marketplace than they are. That laissez-faire attitude had not served Aetna well, and I felt a sense of obligation to my fellow shareholders and directors as well as the employees and policy owners who relied on the company. Under the circumstances, I was willing to consider the possibility of taking the helm of the company, at least until we could get it back on the right course.

I cut short my travels, returned from New Zealand, and attended an emergency board meeting in Hartford on Friday afternoon, February 25. "I've given your invitation a lot of thought," I told my fellow board members. "I'm willing to serve as CEO. I have just one condition. I don't want to be called an 'acting CEO.' I think that just raises questions in everyone's mind as to what my authority, responsibilities, and intentions are. I'd like to be CEO, chairman, and president of Aetna, so there won't be any doubt as to the seriousness of my commitment." The board agreed to my proposal.

In two hours, I had suddenly morphed from a semi-retired family man into chief executive of a 150,000-person company responsible for, among other services, delivering health care coverage to 19.5 million members through a network of more than 330,000 providers.

This was a new kind of challenge for me. I'd never run a

giant Fortune 50 company before. My previous management jobs—particularly at DLJ and Yale—had been about launching something new and nurturing its growth. Now I had to take a long-established organization that had grown big and unwieldy and transform it into a smaller, more focused, more productive entity.

One of the reasons I took on the mission was my concern about the future of America's dysfunctional health care system. It was widely understood that delivering quality health care to all Americans at a reasonable cost was an unresolved challenge facing our economic system. I was worried that a collapse by Aetna would accelerate the momentum toward converting our health care into a totally government-run system. As I said in an interview shortly after taking the helm at Aetna, "This may be the last, best chance to prove that somehow our health system can be run by the private sector. . . . Somehow we have to figure out a way to help the 40 million people in this country who are uninsured. I'm pretty convinced the private sector is the way to do it."[8]

I didn't know how long it would take to fix the problems at Aetna, but I knew that the first thing that needed to happen was to get rid of all the crazy diversification Aetna had done. In the mid-1990s, Aetna had acquired Prudential Insurance Company's health insurance business—a money-loser for Prudential that remained a money-loser after its sale. Aetna had also bought three big health maintenance organizations (HMOs), including giant U.S. Healthcare, for prices that soon proved excessive. U.S. Healthcare alone cost Aetna $8.9 billion, a sum estimated by industry analysts as three times its value.

These poorly conceived, badly managed acquisitions led to painful culture clashes and infighting at Aetna. In particular, U.S. Healthcare's brash leadership team ran roughshod over the more traditional executives from Aetna. They represented the worst of what "entrepreneurial" leadership is often assumed to be—short-term thinking, careless risk-taking, eagerness to boost profits at all costs. Among other missteps, they instituted harshly restrictive new coverage policies that both health care providers and patients hated. The concept of the HMO, once hailed as a brilliant innovation in health care, quickly earned a reputation as a greed-driven business model designed solely for the benefit of insurers. Soon competing health insurance companies that had avoided the worst excesses of the HMO trend were running rings around Aetna in the marketplace.

Aetna's CEO Richard Huber made matters worse through his management style. A perhaps telling story involved Huber's redecorating the executive suite at Aetna, which included a dining room intended for business lunches and dinners. The job was tastefully done and probably needed at the time. When the suite was unveiled, it turned out that a mural had been commissioned for the dining room walls depicting various scenes from early American history, including patriot soldiers proudly on horseback during the Revolutionary War. A close look revealed that one soldier bore the exact likeness of Dick Huber.

Huber was also guilty of more serious leadership missteps. He publicly criticized doctors and other health care professionals who complained about Aetna's restrictive policies, implying that they were lazy and greedy. After Aetna lost a $120 million lawsuit brought by the wife of a deceased policyholder, Huber mocked the judgment in callous, caustic terms, blaming it on "a skillful, ambulance-chasing lawyer, a politically motivated judge and a weeping widow." He later apologized for the remark, but the damage was done. Aetna had gained a reputation as a company that disdained its customers as well as its industry partners.

Huber's attitude encouraged even more lawsuits, including

one supported by the American Medical Association that charged Aetna with routinely delaying claims payments. State attorneys general joined in the legal fray. The problems that plagued Aetna's health insurance business weren't unique—the entire industry was grappling with the challenges created by a world in which health care costs were skyrocketing, putting enormous pressure on insurance company budgets. But Aetna became the poster child for these industry-wide troubles. The company's leaders had believed that the HMO revolution would solve the industry's financial problems. When those hopes fizzled, the company's senior executives found themselves under attack. And as an industry leader, Aetna was particularly visible and vulnerable. As one *New York Times* reporter put it, "At the end of the rainbow there was supposed to be a gold mine of profits wrung from managing away the inefficiencies and excesses of modern medicine. Instead, Aetna found itself the biggest target in an industry under siege."[9]

As of February 25, 2000, dealing with this crisis was my responsibility.

Aetna's annual report for 1999 was on its way to the printer when the decision was made to change the company's leadership. The report was hastily reedited, and a letter from me was inserted inside the cover. It read, in part:

> Aetna's long record of achievement is rare and to be honored. That said, however, it is no secret that in the recent past the company has stumbled in certain key areas. Our financial performance has not been all that we had hoped it would be. There have been fissures in some of the company's crucial relationships, particularly with the physicians who participate in our provider networks. Shareholders are rightfully frustrated and disappointed about the returns they have received

on their investment. The Board of Directors and I share those concerns.

As Aetna's Chairman for less than 24 hours as I write this letter, my overarching goal is to move swiftly to address these problems. With the support and dedication of Aetna's capable people, I am determined to put these issues behind us, and to restore confidence in this great company and in the important work it does to serve the needs of the public for quality health care and financial services.[10]

The first step would be to prune the unwieldy, money-losing structure that Aetna had accumulated over the previous decade. During the final weeks of Dick Huber's tenure, Aetna had begun hatching plans to reorganize the company into two pieces—Global Health and Global Financial Services. We decided to continue this process and, if possible, accelerate it. My goal was to employ entrepreneurial leadership in the truest sense of the term—building an organization for the long haul, one that would be sustainable because it creates value for everyone involved—including employees, customers, suppliers, and the community—not just for a few company executives.

A cover story in *Institutional Investor* magazine summed up the challenges we were facing:

> Doctors, hospitals and medical societies nationwide are in open revolt over the stingy reimbursements and burdensome paperwork requirements of Aetna and other insurers. Tort lawyers, fresh from their victories over Big Tobacco, have filed dozens of state and federal lawsuits, including eight class-action claims; the charges include what plaintiffs say are illegally restrictive treatment policies, slow payments and

fraudulent business practices. Congress is working to
pass a patients' bill of rights, prodded in good measure by problems at Aetna. And local Connecticut
politicians are warning Donaldson not to abandon a
depressed Hartford.[11]

One industry analyst summed it up this way: "The company
is one big colossal mess right now. . . . Donaldson certainly has
his work cut out for him."[12]

It was obvious to me that I needed help in tackling this huge
set of challenges. A fellow director of Aetna suggested that I
contact Robert "Steve" Miller, a well-known expert at turning
around struggling companies, starting with his tenure at troubled automaker Chrysler back in the 1970s and continuing with
two stints at Waste Management Inc. Steve agreed to join me
at Aetna. I made him my second in command, giving him significant control over the internal reorganization, streamlining,
and damage-repair processes, while I focused on the big strategic decisions—in particular, on figuring out which pieces of the
bloated corporation we ought to jettison and which pieces we
ought to retain and build around.

One of the first key decisions we needed to make was how
to deal with takeover bids from outsiders. On February 24,
2000, one day before my arrival in the CEO's office, rival Well-
Point Health Networks and Dutch insurer ING Group made
a joint bid for Aetna at approximately $10 billion. This was
almost double what the company was worth based on its then-
current trading value of $38 per share, but close to its book
value of $75 per share. The board and I talked it over during
the course of a weekend meeting. We decided to turn the offer
down, banking on our ability to make the company more profitable for our shareholders in the long term. When we publicly
announced the decision to reject the WellPoint/ING proposal,

we also confirmed our tentative plans to split Aetna into two independent companies, one focused on health care, one on financial services. We made it clear that we hoped to sell off some less-relevant businesses and use to the proceeds to reduce debt and buy back some of our own stock—a strategy that would boost the share value and thereby improve the morale of the company's understandably jittery shareholders.

Most of our shareholders responded positively to these decisions, though all recognized we weren't yet out of the woods. A collection of institutional investors with holdings of Aetna stock held a meeting in April led by Herbert Denton, president of Providence Capital Inc. Afterward, Denton said that the investors agreed with my contention that the WellPoint/ING offer seriously undervalued Aetna. But he also said that the group was impatient to see how Aetna would improve its stock price and earnings performance. Management, Denton declared, "needs to take steps now to deliver value in the marketplace."[13]

We also moved forward with our plans to reorganize and focus the business exclusively on health insurance. In July 2000, we sold our profitable financial services and international businesses to the ING Group of Amsterdam for $7.7 billion. Aetna shareholders would receive a $35-a-share payout, and most of the divisions' Hartford-based employees would retain their jobs. On December 14, 2000, we spun off the "new Aetna"—a smaller, leaner company singularly focused on the highly challenging, rapidly evolving, but potentially very profitable health insurance business, with a strong balance sheet and some 40,000 employees.

To stanch the bleeding, we had to find ways to cut costs. We created an immediate plan to trim some $150 million in payroll, advertising, and travel costs, which we implemented within a few months. Cuts like these were unavoidable but also traumatic for Aetna, a pillar of the Hartford insurance industry and a community leader long known for its humane corporate style and its reluctance to reduce headcount. "Mother Aetna" was a byword in Connecticut, and it was widely assumed that if you worked at Aetna, you had a job for life—in fact, many people in the area came from multi-generational Aetna families. News of our cost-cutting made many in the state nervous.

Concerns about Aetna's future came to the forefront on April 28, 2000, when I had to lead my first annual shareholders' meeting in Hartford. Many of those who turned out for the meeting were employees and retirees worried about the value of their stock holdings, the security of their pensions, and the future role of Aetna in the life of Hartford. The stories about takeover bids had rattled Connecticut residents who pictured Aetna being purchased and then dismembered, decimating local employment and devastating the community.

At first, the atmosphere was tense. Aetna shareholder Evelyn Y. Davis was a well-known gadfly who'd been launching rhetorical missiles at shareholder meetings of various companies for the past thirty years, and who'd fought for a resolution to make it easier to elect dissident candidates to the Aetna board. Now Davis showed up at the meeting dressed in surgical scrubs to dramatize her belief that "the company needs an operation." Other angry shareholders took the microphone to give brief speeches denouncing the corporate greed they perceived among Aetna's leaders and what they feared was a permanent loss of the traditional values that had once made the company great. The room erupted in applause at several of these volleys.

My job was to reassure the crowd that we'd heard their concerns and that we were serious about getting Aetna back on the right track. In a symbolic gesture that won its own round of applause, I stepped down from the auditorium stage to join the shareholders on the floor and to speak with them face to face. I reaffirmed that Aetna was not for sale and was not actively soliciting interest from buyers, though we would of course be prepared to consider any "legitimate and compelling" offer to purchase all or part of the company. I pledged that our commitment to maintaining Aetna's corporate presence in Hartford and other Connecticut communities remained intact. And I promised retirees concerned about their pensions, "Aetna will stand behind its obligations."

By the end of the meeting, the feisty Evelyn Davis had been won over to the extent that she rewarded me with a hug and a kiss on the cheek. "You did a nice job of answering my questions," she declared. "I really like you very much."[14] Visibly relieved, Aetna spokeswoman Joyce Oberdorf summed up the session this way: "It was a potentially explosive meeting that turned into a love fest."[15]

Another job I had to tackle was changing Aetna's bad reputation among physicians and other health care providers. I toured the country, speaking to medical associations and hospital staffs, saying that Aetna had gone too far in its efforts to cut costs and that a more balanced approach would be developed. We started reaching settlements in some of the lawsuits being brought against us. And we set about mending fences by pulling back on some of the strict insurance coverage policies we'd created.

For example, in our home market of Connecticut, we stopped insisting on controversial "capitation" contracts with physicians, which restricted doctor payments to a single, often too-low monthly fee; we relaxed the mandatory "all-products" rule that required physicians to participate in all Aetna plans; we created a new "Specialist as Principal Physician" program that allowed seriously ill patients to have their care coordinated by a specialist without requiring referrals from a primary care physician; and we made it easier for physicians and patients to appeal our coverage decisions.[16]

I appeared in person at the annual meeting of the state's medical society in May 2000 to announce these changes. "It's a historic first step," said Dr. Michael Deren, the vice chairman of the society's council. The society's president, Dr. Donald H. Timmerman, commented, "[Bill Donaldson] has my profound respect for the courage to walk into the enemy camp and start a dialogue—a dialogue that should have been started years ago."[17]

We followed up by making similar changes in other states as permitted by local regulatory guidelines. And internally, we made it clear to our thousands of employees that Aetna was no longer going to boost its profits by treating policyholders and health care providers unfairly. We curbed the aggressive financial practices promoted by some of the leaders from companies we'd acquired, including U.S. Healthcare. Within months, several of the top executives from our U.S. Healthcare subsidiary resigned, and the company founder, Leonard Abramson, departed the Aetna board. These personnel shifts helped to resolve the culture wars that had shattered Aetna's internal unity.

The changes we implemented in Aetna's business practices cost us some money; in fact, in the short term, earnings in our health care business fell as a result of higher medical costs. In July 2000, when we warned analysts that we expected lower profits for the year's second quarter, Aetna's stock interrupted its recovery to take a short-lived tumble as some nervous investors bailed out. Financial news pundits tut-tutted over the drop, and one stockholder broadcast an email message to fellow share owners saying, "The only hope for Aetna is if Donaldson croaks!"[18]

Local media were all over the news. During one afternoon drive-time radio broadcast, a Hartford station played a satiric piece featuring an actor who identified himself as "William

Donaldson, CEO of Aetna." The actor complained, "We had a few shaky days on the market, if you know what I mean . . . we should have medical technicians standing by with clotting factor, the way this hellhole is hemorrhaging dough!" The actor went on to urge listeners who owned Aetna policies to help boost the company's anemic bottom line by staying away from doctors for a while: "I'm saying, if a monkey bites you, maybe you wash it out with a hose, put some duct tape on it, and go about your business."[19]

Thankfully, our financial woes weren't nearly as serious as the radio lampoon implied. Our share price soon resumed its climb, and the nervousness among Aetna shareholders subsided. We moved ahead with a number of other business reforms designed to streamline our internal systems, improve our financial performance, and enhance our ability to serve customers. These included decentralizing managerial authority to make it easier for regional leaders to adjust to changes in local health care markets; changing our sales compensation program so salespeople would be rewarded for retaining customers, not just signing up new ones; and launching a series of new insurance products to give consumers a greater choice of policies. As the months went on, consumers, health care providers, and industry analysts increasingly recognized the value of our new strategies and rewarded Aetna accordingly.

In April 2000, Steve Miller and I launched a search for a new CEO to run this smaller company, engaging the help of a leading executive recruitment firm to identify top candidates from throughout the industry. Aetna took some fresh heat when we announced the move; *BusinessWeek,* for example, called our decision to recruit from outside Aetna "a stunning admission of the company's failure to develop deep management strength."[20] But it also reflected the realities of the talent pool in a health care industry that was generally in turmoil. Several other big firms in the same business had been searching fruitlessly for CEOs for the previous few months.

In September 2000, our search for top talent bore fruit. We brought in Dr. John Rowe to serve as our new president and CEO, while I was asked to stay on as chairman. Jack was an unconventional choice—a physician who had never run a publicly traded company, knew little about the insurance business, and in fact had never had an hour of management education or training. But he was the perfect person for the job. A highly respected medical researcher who had run the renowned Mount Sinai Medical Center in New York, Jack was a highly credible spokesman for Aetna's efforts to rebuild its reputation among physicians and other care providers. When Jack told doctors and nurses that Aetna's first commitment would be ensuring the best possible care for patients, they knew it was true.

The bumps in the road weren't all behind us. As Jack said upon joining the company, "Aetna is like a patient with a lot of problems." In December 2000, we announced 5,000 job cuts as well as plans to exit unprofitable businesses and customers during 2001. And despite our best efforts, some of our troubles with health care providers continued. In February 2001, the Connecticut State Medical Society filed a suit against us alleging a pattern of unfair and deceptive practices. "We couldn't believe it," Jack commented. "We're doing everything they've asked."[21] He continued the fence-mending process, working internally to identify and fix problematic company policies, and meeting continually with health care providers from around the country to learn about their concerns and promising to address them.

Of course, Jack couldn't complete the job of reforming Aetna without help. We expanded the new leadership team at Aetna with the additions of Dr. William Popik as the new chief medical officer in February 2001, and Ron Williams as executive vice president and chief of health operations on April 1, 2001.

Ron proved to be an inspired choice. He came to Aetna from WellPoint Health Networks, a California-based insurance company where he'd run the national large-group business and was responsible for 4.8 million members and $4.5 billion in operating revenue. With Ron's arrival, Jack added the title of chairman, and I stepped down as chairman while retaining a seat on the Aetna board.

During the next few years, Aetna experienced a remarkable renaissance, first under Jack Rowe (who continued as CEO until 2006), then under Ron Williams (who succeeded Jack and served as CEO until 2011).

Running Aetna was quite an experience for me. During my time at the helm, we thoroughly restructured the business, laid the foundation for refurbishing the company's public image and internal morale, improved its internal processes so as to better serve external customers while improving financial performance, and recruited a capable team of outsiders to complete the transformation of Aetna into one of the world's most respected companies. It all happened a lot quicker than I thought it would—a testimony to the resilience that characterizes a great company like Aetna and enables it to rebound from times of trouble, once entrepreneurial leadership sets the right direction.

CHAPTER 10

The Politics of Regulation:
Challenges at the SEC

The year 2002 marked a new low in public confidence in business. It was the year of the Enron, WorldCom, Tyco, and Global Crossing scandals—cases in which giant, once highly respected companies were revealed to have committed significant frauds against investors and others. As a result, the savings, pensions, and livelihoods of millions of people who'd relied on the integrity of corporate management were damaged or lost. Ordinary Americans, many of whom tend to harbor a degree of suspicion about big business to begin with, saw these scandals as evidence that big corporations—particularly those involved in complicated financial dealings—wouldn't hesitate to violate basic ethical principles in exchange for a few extra millions (or billions) in profit.

The shock to public opinion caused by the business scandals set off a series of repercussions. It led to passage of the Sarbanes-Oxley Act, a controversial new set of regulations that mandated a series of changes in business accounting and reporting practices. Passed in haste by a Congress influenced by a public uproar, Sarbanes-Oxley was signed into law by President George W. Bush on July 30, 2002.

It wasn't the kind of bill that a conservative Republican president might normally be eager to support, but Bush really had little choice in this case. The Enron scandal was particularly difficult for the Bush administration. Enron's chairman and CEO Kenneth Lay was a fellow Texan and a political and financial supporter (though of course the administration moved quickly to distance itself from Enron and Lay in the aftermath of the scandal). Supporting Sarbanes-Oxley and vowing to crack down on corporate malfeasance was essential for any administration with a modicum of political sense—especially with midterm congressional elections looming in fall 2002, and a presidential reelection bid on the horizon two years later.

The Securities and Exchange Commission (SEC) was and is the chief federal regulator of financial markets. In the wake of the scandals, people looked to the SEC for signs that American business still deserved their confidence. Unfortunately, Harvey Pitt, the man then in charge of the SEC, had only made matters worse. A longtime SEC staffer and an accomplished lawyer, Pitt had been named chairman of the SEC by President George W. Bush in 2001. However, in the chairman's seat, Pitt had proved to be a less-than-effective administrator as well as politically tone-deaf. In the midst of the financial scandals—while commentators in the media and experts on regulation were bemoaning the agency's failure to foresee and forestall the problems and wondering how it could have happened—Pitt made the surprising public gaffe of saying that he hoped to create a "kinder and gentler" SEC. The statement left millions of Americans with the impression that Harvey Pitt was planning to render the people's financial watchdog even more toothless than it already appeared to be—precisely the opposite of what they were demanding. Pitt then compounded the problem by publicly advocating that his own job of SEC chairman be elevated to a cabinet-level position, a proposal that seemed self-centered and grandiose under the circumstances.

The final straw came when Pitt nominated William Webster to serve as head of the Public Company Accounting Oversight Board (PCAOB), a new body under the auspices of the SEC that had been mandated by Sarbanes-Oxley. Webster was a highly regarded former director of the FBI. Unfortunately, Pitt put forth Webster's name and persuaded his fellow SEC commissioners to support him without informing them about an embarrassing detail in Webster's background. Webster had served as head of the audit committee of U.S. Technologies, a public company then under federal investigation for possible financial improprieties. This made him a poor choice under the best of circumstances, a disastrous one in the wake of Enron and WorldCom.

This self-inflicted wound would be the last one Pitt would be permitted. The SEC chairman had become a liability to the Bush administration—something they didn't need in the run-up to a presidential reelection bid. After just eighteen turbulent months in office, Pitt resigned his post on November 5, 2002. In the aftermath of Pitt's resignation, I was contacted by members of the Bush team about whether I would consider stepping into the breach.

I wasn't looking for a job. At age 71, I'd recently stepped down as CEO of Aetna after having led the troubled insurance giant through a tough period of reinvention and turnaround. I was looking forward to finally spending more time with my family. When the personnel people from the Bush White House called me in December of 2002 and asked me to come down to Washington and talk to them about running the SEC, I was reluctant.

But it's difficult to say no to a president, and I understood how serious the need was and how important it was to get our nation's financial house in order. And anyway, I reasoned, there's never any harm in talking.

So I flew down to Washington and met with the senior personnel at the White House. Whether they were interviewing other potential candidates for the SEC job, I didn't know.

I knew the president slightly. The Bush family and I go way back; as I've recounted, my first job on Wall Street was working for George H. Walker, senior partner of G. H. Walker & Company, uncle of President George H. W. Bush and great-uncle of the second President Bush. Like both presidents, I'd gone to Yale, and my classmate there (and a close friend) was Jon Bush, the current president's uncle. I'd encountered George W. Bush only briefly, years earlier, during the days when he was regarded as the "wild" younger son of the family and scarcely considered presidential timber.

Shortly after the Christmas holiday, upon my return from a family trip to Morocco, I was invited back to the White House. This time, the president and I were alone together in the Oval Office. We chatted in a friendly way for a few minutes, and then Bush confronted me with a relatively blunt question: "Why would you want this job, Bill?"

It was actually a very good question, one I'd been pondering and discussing with Jane over the Christmas holidays. But now that I was put on the spot by the president himself, I found it surprisingly difficult to give a clear, simple answer. In a rambling sort of way, I talked about my background as a veteran of the financial services industry, a cofounder of one of the leading firms on Wall Street, and a former chairman and CEO of the New York Stock Exchange. I spoke about my deep commitment to the future of our country, my belief in the importance of business, and my concern that a breakdown in trust between the American people and the financial community might cause long-term damage to our social compact.

I knew what I was trying to say, but I wasn't sure that I was expressing it very well. After I'd been floundering for a minute or two, President Bush came to my rescue.

"I know, Bill," he said with a smile. "Semper Fi, right?" He was referring back to my years in the Marine Corps and the commitment to public service that every Marine holds sacred. President Bush's reputation may be subject to debate by some, but when it came to making intuitive connections with people, he was one of the best.

"You got it, Mr. President," I responded.

I told the president I'd be honored to accept the appointment, with the understanding that I would remain in office for a limited period of time, just long enough to try to get the SEC back on its feet. I wasn't eager for a long-term assignment, but I was ready to serve if the president thought I could be of service to the nation.

The initial reactions to my appointment were mixed. Political commentators, business pundits, and politicians complimented the president on moving quickly to fill the SEC leadership gap, expressed relief that the Harvey Pitt era was over, and noted the highlights of my resume—cofounder of DLJ, undersecretary of state, founding dean of the Yale School of Management, chairman of the New York Stock Exchange, CEO of Aetna. The general reaction, on paper at least, was that I appeared to be an ideal candidate.

Of course, there were other, more cynical reactions. I was not a lawyer, which some viewed as a potential problem in a position with significant law-enforcement responsibilities. Many assumed, because of my relatively advanced age and my former ties to Wall Street, that I would be a complacent, passive overseer of Wall Street—a caretaker at best, an enabler of profit-boosting malfeasance at worst. Others pointed out my past ties to the Bush family and concluded that I was basically a crony who would do whatever the president found politically expedient. One investment advisor quoted by *Business Week* remarked, "What's [Donaldson's] agenda? Ask Karl Rove."

Under the circumstances, I knew it was important to set the right tone for my chairmanship from the beginning. So during January, I prepared carefully for the Senate confirmation hearings, trying to anticipate the toughest questions and listening to advice from the administration's spin experts while seeking to clarify my own positions and attitudes as forthrightly as possible. I described the controversial Sarbanes-Oxley law as a positive contribution to good corporate governance and a necessary corrective to the "excesses" of the 1990s (a mild euphemism for the unscrupulous behavior we'd seen in some quarters in recent years). I emphasized the need for a renewed commitment to integrity, transparency, and tough law enforcement while noting that the U.S. financial markets were generally strong, well managed, and globally respected.

Unsurprisingly, I got some pointed questions about my professional history (including some of the challenges I'd had to deal with as chairman of the New York Stock Exchange) and a fair amount of probing into my attitudes toward the big issues I'd be tackling at the SEC.

Several questions focused on my approach to one of the fastest-growing and least-understood segments of the financial industry, the virtually unregulated entities known as hedge funds. I told the senators that, based on my experience, I thought some form of regulation for hedge funds was probably necessary, but that my first step would be to study the research and analysis that had already been done by the experts who worked at the SEC. Naturally, I explained, I would want to be guided by the insights of people who'd been devoting years to studying the issue.

My position on the hedge fund question was deliberately couched in nonideological, pragmatic terms, and it presaged exactly how I would handle the issue (as well as many others) once in office. It seemed to satisfy the senators. I was confirmed by the Senate and took office as SEC chairman on February 18.

Jane and I, along with our three children, were scheduled to fly down to Washington for my swearing-in ceremony at the White House. But a blinding snowstorm shut down the airports, so we traveled by train instead. Making matters worse, poor Adam was clearly feeling unwell on the train. He should have spent the next day in bed, but a visit to the White House would be a rare opportunity for him, so Jane and I cajoled him into making the trek.

The main thing I remember about that morning's event was President Bush's kindness and good humor. He promptly sized up the situation and installed Adam comfortably on a sofa in the Oval Office. We posed for pictures with the president, fielded a few softball questions from the press corps, and then I was officially installed as the twenty-eighth chairman of the SEC.

It was not an easy moment to be taking on the challenge of being responsible for investor protection and market regulation and serving as chief ethical watchdog for the financial industry. In a column titled "Lies My Broker Told Me," investment guru James J. Cramer described the climate this way:

> [A]s someone who speaks to or e-mails literally thousands of investors a week, I can tell you that people have lost all faith in the stock market as an honest place to make money.
>
> The industry itself is in total denial. Actually, it's worse than total denial. The average "leader" in the stock business says that if it weren't for Eliot Spitzer, the New York State attorney general, and his ridiculous crusade, we'd be back to normal by now. That's preposterous, because "back to normal" would simply

mean that we had restored investor stupidity instead of restoring investor trust.[22]

This was the atmosphere into which I was stepping. Cramer summed it all up very simply: "Donaldson comes in at an awful time."

Fortunately, I brought with me some advantages. Perhaps the foremost was the simple fact that I was not Harvey Pitt. Relieved that Pitt's "reign of error" had ended, most people in the worlds of finance and government welcomed me to the SEC and were genuinely supportive, hoping I could begin to rebuild some of the credibility that the SEC, Wall Street, and the business community had lost.

My role in helping to found Donaldson, Lufkin & Jenrette, my reputation as a progressive innovator in financial services, and my previous stint as chairman of the NYSE all combined to reassure people that I understood the industry as only an insider can and was unlikely to demonize it. I'd shown that I was willing to ruffle feathers when necessary—for example, in taking DLJ public in opposition to decades of custom and long-standing Exchange rules. But at the same time, I tried to maintain a low-key and respectful personal manner. For example, I always took the opportunity to speak *last* at commission meetings, thereby giving the other commissioners an opportunity to say what they thought without forcing them to be confrontational.

Perhaps most important, it was generally understood that I had no ideological or personal ax to grind. I wasn't angling for public acclaim or seeking to use the SEC as a stepping-stone to higher office. "He's post-ambition," observed Barney Frank, the ranking Democratic member of the House Financial Services Committee.[23]

And while I was certainly pro-business and a staunch advocate of the free-enterprise system, I was in no way a doctrinaire conservative. I believed government had an important role to play in ensuring the fairness and transparency of the markets, and I would take a pragmatic approach in deciding exactly where the regulatory lines ought to be drawn. The big questions for me, always, were simply, "What is the law?" "What is fair?" and "What will work?"

I would soon discover that this pragmatic approach is *not* universally appreciated in Washington.

* * *

As soon as I arrived at the SEC, I set to work tackling some of the major issues the agency faced.

Two of the most urgent were addressing the SEC's malfunctioning internal structure and systems, and restoring staff morale. The agency's low budget, eroded by years of cutbacks, and the relative neglect it had received under recent administrations, for whom business regulation was not a high priority, had made it difficult to attract the quality of people needed. After all, a bright young lawyer or analytic expert with a head for business could go to work on Wall Street and make a large amount of money—while the same person, working at the SEC and charged with understanding and regulating Wall Street in order to protect investors, could earn only a fraction of that amount. This was not a fair fight.

During my first two years at the SEC, I pushed Congress hard to authorize the funds necessary to remedy this situation. It's a credit to the Bush administration and to leaders of both parties in Congress that they understood the urgency of the need for more modern, proactive systems of oversight and were ready to provide the resources needed to make them possible. As a result, we were able to increase the agency's professional staff by more than 25 percent, hiring 1,100 badly needed accountants, lawyers, and economists. The agency budget, which had been $483 million in fiscal 2002, was expanded to $842 million in fiscal 2004.

In addition, we introduced new, more efficient internal systems within the agency. The old structure had provided the chairman with a single right-hand person charged with overseeing all of the daily activities of the agency. But as the financial industry had grown and become increasingly complex, this simple structure had become more and more inadequate.

I restructured the office of the chairman into three separate areas and recruited three highly talented professionals to whom I gave the new title of managing director—a triumvirate of leaders whom I could count on to keep the SEC running efficiently.

I appointed Patrick Von Bargen, a Stanford Law School alum and one of the earliest graduates from the Yale School of Management, to coordinate policy. Patrick had worked briefly for my abortive campaign for governor of New York. He'd then gone on to serve as founder and executive director of the National Commission on Entrepreneurship. Patrick was also well versed in the ways of Washington, having spent five years as chief of staff to U.S. Senator Jeff Bingaman, a New Mexico Democrat.

I chose Laura Cox for the crucial role of managing external relations with Congress and the press—two groups of influencers whose support I knew would be essential in the challenging months ahead. Laura, like Patrick, was a D.C. veteran. She'd worked on Capitol Hill for eight years, working for Democratic Congressman Charles W. Stenholm and then for Republican Senator Richard Shelby, then joined the office of legislative affairs at the U.S. Treasury.

Finally, I named Peter Derby to oversee SEC operations and to serve as a key "change agent" in strengthening the culture and structure of the agency. Peter had recently returned from Russia, where he'd founded and run DialogBank, one of the first private banks in the country. During his decade in Russia, he'd seen firsthand the damage done when free-market values are corrupted by political influences. Peter tells the story of meeting a Russian legislator who literally posted an influence-peddling price list on the wall of his office: Pay this much to have your opinion heard, pay this much more to have your pet law proposed in parliament, and so on. When Peter expressed his dismay, the legislator defended the arrangement: "This is so much more efficient than in America! There, you have to pay lawyers and lobbyists to make deals with members of Congress—but here, we cut out the middleman!" Peter's personal integrity and his Russian experience served as constant reminders to him as to why the SEC's efforts to ensure the fairness and effectiveness of government regulation of the financial markets were so important.

The creation of this triumvirate, operating under the authority of the chairman, was a first step in my larger managerial strategy, which was to reform the siloed management system that had divided the SEC into a series of disconnected fiefdoms. The agency was filled with staffers who were expert in various financial fields and who spent their days monitoring trends and activities in those fields, the better to propose intelligent regulatory practices that would protect investors and safeguard the integrity of the markets.

I found that, too often, the internal departments working on rules about a particular branch of the financial industry were unaware of how their proposed actions might affect other operations. This was a big problem, particularly in a financial industry that was increasingly complex, interconnected, globalized, and digitized. So I mandated that these departments must include staffers drawn from other relevant units, thereby insuring that the impact of proposed rules on disparate industry segments could be taken into account.

Other internal reforms followed in due course. We arranged to have the Government Accountability Office conduct the first-ever audit in the history of the SEC, vetting our performance in such areas as efficiency, accuracy, timeliness, and transparency. We created a collection of management "dashboards"—nineteen in all, one for each of the agency's operating divisions—that contained crucial metrics, constantly updated. These dashboards enabled the SEC's managers to monitor activities in key areas and thereby rate and improve the agency's effectiveness. And we used our increased staffing to clear up a huge backlog of enforcement cases, which had made SEC personnel feel as if they were continually swimming upstream and left financial professionals and the general public unclear about government policies.

Above all, we worked to embed a proactive attitude toward financial regulation. Many perceived the SEC as having been caught flat-footed by the revelations of misconduct at Enron and WorldCom, and in similar cases. We vowed that we wouldn't let that happen again. Rather than sitting back and waiting for cases of malfeasance to be brought to our attention, we would actively monitor the fields of corporate accounting, finance, and investment, seeking out potential risks and taking steps, when appropriate, to minimize them and protect the public. I told our staffers, "The SEC must learn to look around corners and over hills," a catchphrase that people throughout the agency eventually began using.

I asked Peter Derby to launch a new program called the Office of Risk Assessment (ORA). Its goal was to use every legal and ethical means of intelligence-gathering to figure out what was really happening on Wall Street and in the world of corporate finance so that potential dangers to the public could be identified and averted. Peter recruited Charles A. Fishkin, a distinguished expert of risk analysis, to head the office.

The tools used by the ORA in its efforts to have an ear to ground in the world of finance were deceptively simple. One involved asking every manager at the SEC to list the ten biggest risks he or she was worried about. The risks ranged from the systemic (poorly regulated financial instruments that were prone to fraud and abuse) to the mundane (unprotected keys and passwords that might compromise the safety of SEC offices and information). These lists were then combined into a series of "risk maps" that division heads could use in setting their own priorities and developing risk-reduction programs.

We also created a public tip line that made it easy for anyone—a concerned investor, for example—to phone the SEC's offices to report dubious financial dealings. The tip line served as a kind of early warning system that enabled the agency to get ahead of possible cases of fraud and try to minimize the damage rather than waiting until disaster had struck. It was closed after I left the SEC, but later restarted under the provisions of the 2010 Dodd-Frank legislation.

Another tool of the ORA consisted of a series of ten-minute meetings between Peter and the chief risk officers of five of the biggest financial institutions in the United States. The very idea of scheduling a ten-minute meeting—very unusual in the business world—captured everyone's attention immediately. In the meetings, Peter asked the risk officers a single question: "What is your biggest nightmare?" His goal was to identify the most worrisome area of financial activity—the one most likely to trigger a catastrophic economic meltdown.

It's fascinating to note that, in those meetings with Peter, four of the five risk officers mentioned the same nightmare: the danger of financial losses caused by imprudent investments in credit derivatives. Just four years later, the market crisis of 2008 would be triggered by that very problem. Unfortunately, in the intervening years, the SEC had been dissuaded from mounting a full-scale effort to tighten controls over credit derivatives, thanks partly to the influence of the Federal Reserve, which classified credit derivatives as falling squarely under their mandate and therefore refused to cooperate with us.

We didn't have the luxury of focusing all our attention on possible future dangers, of course. Leading an agency like the SEC is also about putting out fires—responding to short-term problems and public-relations challenges as they arise.

Nominating William Webster to serve as chairman of PCAOB, the auditing standards board mandated by Sarbanes-Oxley, had been one of the errors in judgment that had doomed my predecessor. Inadequate vetting of his background had led to needless controversy and, ultimately, Webster's resignation just one week after Harvey Pitt's. Wishing to avoid a similar problem, I assembled a confidential team of SEC staffers to quietly, professionally screen the candidates to replace Webster.

During this process, it suddenly occurred to me that the right person lived in my backyard. William J. McDonough, a former executive at Merrill Lynch and recently retired as president of the Federal Reserve Bank of New York, was my neighbor in Westchester, New York, where he and his wife, Suzanne, had purchased a home in our small community of Waccabuc. For years, we had socialized at one another's homes.

I invited Bill over for coffee one beautiful April Saturday in 2003 and went about trying to convince him to take on the job of running the PCAOB. Having just stepped down from the New York Fed, Bill was considering an array of offers, many of which I knew were quite lucrative, challenging, and interesting. Bill was very engaged and attentive during our coffee, and as he left he told me he would think it over, talk with Suzanne, and get back to me the next morning. I told Jane sadly, "Bill will never do it. It's really a shame, because he would be the perfect person."

But when Sunday morning came, Bill called and said, "Count me in!" And so began a two-and-a-half-year adventure in Washington that Bill and Suzanne shared with Jane and me. We even had apartments in the same building. Bill succeeded in getting the PCAOB on firm footing, which was not easy at a time when the knives were certainly out. He thus added to his already impressive resume an illustrious stint in public service— at an extremely modest salary for a person of his qualifications. It was a move early in my tenure that sat well with reform-minded observers.

When Bill retired in 2005, Senator Paul S. Sarbanes, the Maryland Democrat who was a sponsor of the Sarbanes-Oxley Act, said he "did an outstanding job in building a first-rate institution with a superb staff," while Representative Michael G. Oxley, the Ohio Republican who was the law's House sponsor, called Bill "the perfect man for the job."

Another thorny public relations issue was dealing with the very public challenge to the SEC being mounted by New York's Attorney General Eliot Spitzer.

Spitzer was a politically ambitious crusader who had become famous by successfully investigating and prosecuting labor racketeering. Now he began using aggressive enforcement of financial regulations to capture headlines, forge an image as a populist hero and the scourge of wrongdoers on Wall Street, and (many said) to pave the way for a run at the governor's seat. His primary tool was the Martin Act, a New York law that empowered the attorney general to bring suit against anyone in the state who was engaged in securities fraud. Armed with this law, and spurred by apparent conflicts of interest at some firms, Spitzer began uncovering biased research reports from Wall Street firms as well as trading abuses in the huge mutual fund industry.

Unfortunately, Spitzer also used his prominence to castigate the SEC as passive and ineffective, thereby further undermining public confidence in business and in the government overseers who were charged with policing it.

In one sense, Spitzer and I were on the same side: I shared his concern about conflicts of interest and improper practices on Wall Street, and like him I wanted the bad eggs to be exposed and punished so that the vast majority of honest financial professionals could regain the respect and trust of the public. But I certainly didn't appreciate his needless grandstanding, his sometimes exaggerated pronouncements about the greed and dishonesty of Wall Street, and his repeated attacks on the efficacy of the SEC itself. I could see firsthand how badly these attacks were contributing to the demoralization of our staff.

I responded with a two-pronged strategy. Publicly, I praised Spitzer. Early in my tenure, I had Laura Cox issue a statement on my behalf that said, in effect, "What Spitzer's doing is terrific. We want him out there, rooting out crime and dishonesty."

But behind the scenes, I took a different approach. One of the first things I did after becoming chairman was to invite Spitzer down to Washington to meet with me—in private.

"Look, Eliot," I said, "I understand what you're doing. You're trying to fight fraud and corruption in the markets, and you're frustrated with how difficult it is. So you're out there in the press every day damning the SEC because you think we haven't been aggressive enough.

"But we're on my watch now, and the SEC is going to do its damnedest to stay ahead of the Street. So you've got to cut out these public attacks. We need each other. It's easy for you to fling around accusations about dishonest brokers and an ineffective SEC, but in too many cases you can't back them up. You don't have the staff. You don't have the background. You don't have the know-how. The SEC does.

"We'll cooperate with you in every way we can. We'll follow

up on cases you expose and we'll support you in your investigations and prosecutions. We'll do whatever it takes. But we can't do that if we have to spend our time responding to your potshots. They're counterproductive, they're affecting our staff morale, and they need to stop."

To his credit, Spitzer heard my message and cooperated. The level of criticism directed at the SEC by Spitzer and his team diminished, and our two organizations supported one another for the remainder of my years in office. From time to time, the press still ran lurid headlines about the supposed "war" between Spitzer and Donaldson, but that's just because some reporters have a habit of turning every policy difference into a matter of personal animosity. It certainly didn't reflect any real antagonism between us.

One of the hottest regulatory issues we had to deal with had come up during my Senate hearing—registering and regulating hedge funds. These new investment entities had grown to be enormous, influential, and highly profitable. The SEC staff estimated that, as of 2003, there were some 6,000 to 7,000 hedge funds operating in the United States, managing over $600 billion in assets, as well as a growing number operating outside the U.S. And despite their name, many of these funds were not truly "hedged" but rather engaged in some highly risky forms of investment. Yet regardless of their size and power, hedge funds weren't required to register their securities offerings or register themselves as investment companies, mainly because they dealt only with "accredited investors" (very high-net-worth individuals and institutions).

There were signs that hedge funds represented a potential source of significant risk for the capital markets and for investors. In the previous five years, the SEC had brought fifty-one cases against hedge fund advisors, alleging frauds amounting to more than $1.1 billion in value. What's more, almost four hundred hedge funds and at least eighty-seven hedge fund advisors had been involved in mutual fund abuses involving market timing of trades and other self-serving practices. With hedge funds representing a significant percentage of the equity trading in the United States, many observers were concerned about the potential for damage to the integrity of the markets that these abuses revealed. I shared that concern.

Our knowledgeable SEC staff spelled out all these facts in a powerful report that they delivered in September 2003. They recommended that we require hedge funds to register, make specific disclosures to investors, and be subject to SEC inspections and examinations.

As with all significant policy changes, this proposal was brought before the commission itself for a vote. To understand what happened next, a bit of explanation as to how the SEC operates is in order.

In terms of the overall management of the staff and agencies of the SEC, the chairman acts as chief executive officer. The SEC commission itself, operating in its regulatory role, is governed by five members—the chairman and four other commissioners. By law, no more than three commissioners may be members of either of the major political parties. In practice, this means that at any given time the chairman and two other commissioners represent the party of the president, while the two remaining commissioners represent the other party.

During my chairmanship, the three Republicans on the commission were myself; Paul Atkins, an attorney who'd spent four years on the staff of former SEC chairman Richard C. Breeden; and Cynthia Glassman, an economist who had worked at Ernst & Young, Furash & Company, and the Federal Reserve. The two Democrats were Roel Campos, a Harvard-trained attorney who was a graduate of the U.S. Air Force Academy, and Harvey Goldschmid, a Columbia Law

School professor who had been an advisor and general counsel to former SEC chairman Arthur Levitt.

For the commission to act on any matter, a simple majority vote is required. In the great majority of cases involving routine enforcement rulings and sanctions, the vote is unanimous. But in cases involving policy change, votes are often along party lines—although this pattern is far from universal. In fact, the SEC has a history of pragmatism and bipartisanship that is laudable. Though commissioners naturally have varying philosophies and perspectives, they all generally share a commitment to the free enterprise system and the protection of the public that leads them to search together for consensus solutions that will benefit all parties.

When the question of requiring hedge funds to be registered and regulated by the SEC came to a vote, Campos and Goldschmid (the two Democrats) voted yes, while Atkins and Glassman (the two Republicans) voted no. I cast the deciding vote—voting yes, supporting the position taken by the Democrats and my staff that hedge funds should be registered and regulated.

This would prove to be one of several three-to-two votes that would help make the SEC under Donaldson into somewhat of a cause célèbre in certain financial and political circles.

Another was our vote on the so-called order protection rule—a rule that required traders and other intermediaries to fill orders for stock purchases at the best price then available anywhere in the U.S. national market system. The idea was straightforward. Rather than allowing traders to ignore a better price for the sake of making a quicker and potentially more lucrative trade, the rule would force them to act in the best interests of the investor. The rule had been under development for several years by the SEC staff; it was finally passed on my watch, as I added my vote to those of the two Democratic commissioners for a three-to-two margin.

Yet another split vote came on a proposed rule affecting the board of directors of mutual fund companies. Before and during my tenure at the SEC, the seven-trillion-dollar mutual fund industry, which held the responsibility for the retirement savings and other investments of tens of millions of Americans, had been roiled with scandals. Some of the biggest names in the business had been charged with front-running (that is, making self-serving investments just before larger transactions on behalf of clients that they knew would move the markets), conflicts of interest, and other improper or manipulative behaviors. *U.S. News & World Report* ran a screaming headline that spread across two pages of the newsmagazine: CAN YOU TRUST YOUR MUTUAL FUND? Even John Bogle, the widely admired head of Vanguard Funds and a founding father of the mutual fund industry, was questioning the integrity of many mutual fund organizations.

SEC staffers studied the problems in detail and came up with a series of proposals for remedying them. Some were straightforward and quickly implemented, including new disclosure rules and regulations governing improper practices. But one of the most controversial was a requirement that at least three-quarters of the members of a mutual fund's board be independent directors.

At the time, many of the directors were officers or shareholders of the mutual fund management companies themselves, which created a clear conflict of interest: How could these directors be expected to consistently vote in favor of policies that would benefit investors rather than the management companies themselves? Insisting on more independent directors would alleviate this problem. We passed the proposal, along with a number of others that mandated greater transparency and prohibited self-dealing actions on the part of mutual funds—and once again the vote was three to two, with Chairman Donaldson and the Democrats making up the majority.

I need to make it clear that the commission took hundreds of routine votes during my tenure. As I've noted, many were unanimous votes, and those that were split decisions were not always divided along partisan lines. Disagreements of this kind are natural when a team is made up of intelligent, experienced, and strong-minded individuals rather than people who merely rubber-stamp the chairman's decisions.

But inevitably, the cases in which major policy changes were approved when I voted with the two Democratic commissioners against the two Republicans captured media attention. It's the old principle of man-bites-dog: The spectacle of a Republican chairman appointed by a Republican president voting with the Democrats surprised many observers and conjured up the possibility of "civil war" among the members of the commission. Conflict, of course, is inherently newsworthy.

In this case, the conflict was not entirely fabricated by the media. There were some Republicans who were shocked and appalled to discover that Bill Donaldson—a Wall Street Republican and a friend of members of the Bush family who many had expected to serve as a mere caretaker at the SEC—was actually taking his responsibilities as the nation's chief financial regulator seriously, even when that meant voting with the Democrats to implement rules that some in business considered too intrusive.

One of those who was shocked by my stances and my votes was my fellow commissioner Paul Atkins. A self-styled libertarian, Atkins reflexively sided against practically every form of government regulation, and he found it hard to understand how any Republican could think otherwise. As soon as he realized that I intended to make my own decisions regarding appropriate SEC policies—and that my concern for the integrity of the markets and for protecting investors was just as great as my solicitude for the bankers and investment firms of Wall Street—Atkins began sniping at me.

It started with snide criticisms and condescending remarks during and after commission meetings. I recall Atkins commenting after one particularly heated debate, "Chairman Donaldson, you don't know *what* you think."

"On the contrary," I replied, "I know exactly what I think, and my decisions as chairman reflect that thinking." (In reality, of course, Atkins understood what I thought—he just couldn't abide it.)

At one point, when our once-collegial relationship had seriously deteriorated, Atkins even told me, very frankly, "Be careful, Chairman Donaldson. I'm going to get you. I'm going to bring you down."

At the time, I had no idea exactly what he meant. Only later did I learn through second- and third-hand reports that Atkins had gone out on the lecture circuit, giving speeches in which he bad-mouthed the SEC and me personally.

Atkins wasn't alone in regarding me as a traitor to free-market orthodoxy. Those on the far right—on Capitol Hill, in conservative think tanks, and in business lobbying groups—began to complain about my aggressive stand in favor of transparency. *Congressional Quarterly*, which covers government from the inside, reported on "the recurring whisper that Donaldson's approach to regulation is akin to 'Stalinist planning.'"[24]

The conservative *Wall Street Journal* launched a steady barrage of attacks on me once they realized I would be neither a compliant lapdog nor a passive caretaker. When the SEC voted to implement hedge fund registration, the *Journal*'s editorial page called it "one more example of the lack of understanding of the hedge fund industry and modern financial markets that Mr. Donaldson has exhibited throughout this entire debate."[25] (It's ironic how quickly my reputation as a consummate Wall Street insider seemed to evaporate the moment I took a stand that the *Journal*'s editors didn't approve of—now, it seemed,

I was an ignorant outsider unable to comprehend the damage that the SEC and I were causing.)

I was also increasingly subject to serious pushback from some business leaders and their lobbyists and spokesmen. *Business Week* observed:

> Silver-haired and soft-spoken, William H. Donaldson doesn't look like a wild-eyed radical. But to many corporate chiefs, the Securities & Exchange Commission chairman's agenda smacks of an extremist manifesto. Business is furious with his push to make it easier for shareholders to nominate directors to corporate boards, his plan to change the way mutual funds are governed, and his determination to oversee hedge funds. And Corporate America is going all out, lobbying Congress, the Administration, and other SEC commissioners to force the chairman to back down.[26]

In October 2004, the U.S. Chamber of Commerce for the first time in history sued the SEC, demanding that we back off our proposal to require independent members on the boards of mutual fund companies—just one of a series of criticisms from the Chamber concerning our tougher stance on regulation and rule enforcement. The Chamber's outspoken president, Thomas J. Donohue, angrily denied suggestions that his assault on the SEC might be linked to his seat on the board of Qwest Communications, which had paid $250 million to settle an SEC complaint about fraudulent accounting practices—though he admitted that the Qwest experience "has educated me as to how the system works." The Chamber also joined forces with another interest group, the Business Roundtable, to fight against our proposal to give shareholders greater freedom to nominate directors.

Many organizations, including investors' rights groups and consumer protection associations, hailed our efforts. So did many in the media. The *Business Week* article describing the corporate attacks on me was headlined, "Stick to Your Guns, Mr. Donaldson." I did.

Some observers speculated that President Bush must be taken aback to find his hand-picked SEC chairman behaving like a loose cannon. My only evidence points in the opposite direction. As the controversy about the SEC began to spread around Wall Street and Washington, the President took a few moments to pen a personal note of reassurance. It read:

> June 20, 2003
>
> Dear Bill,
>
> I read the *Business Week* article "SEC Cop Means Business." The article confirmed the wisdom of your selection.
>
> You are doing a great job. I hope your spirits are high because you are making a significant contribution to our nation.
>
> With respect and best wishes,
> George Bush

I never got a call from the White House or from anyone who purported to speak for the president warning me to back down on a regulatory issue or soften my position on any controversy. That said, I had occasional conversations with high-ranking Republicans who tried to influence me. Sometimes they would suggest that, as a member of the Bush team, I ought to be more careful about challenging business interests. My reaction was always the same: I would listen to the arguments being offered and then indicate that I would do what I thought was best. Which is exactly what I tried to do.

* * *

Perhaps the biggest assignment that the SEC had to undertake in the wake of the Enron and WorldCom scandals was implementing Sarbanes-Oxley, the complex, multifaceted law demanding greater financial transparency and accountability from big business. For political reasons, Sarbanes-Oxley had been quickly drafted, passed, and signed into law, then dumped into the lap of the SEC to interpret, clarify, and enforce. It was a huge job.

It was also highly controversial, like any new rule that makes the practice of management more complicated and costly. The law mandated independent audit committees and independent auditors, including work limitations designed to minimize conflicts of interest; created the PCAOB (as I've mentioned) to oversee auditors and their activities; and greatly expanded the disclosure requirements affecting corporate finance. It also required the chief executive officer and the chief financial officer of a corporation to personally guarantee, via their signatures, the accuracy of the firm's financial statements with huge penalties attached for noncompliance, a provision that some business executives considered draconian.

Somehow we made it all work. The SEC staff took the highly ambitious mandates of Sarbanes-Oxley and codified them through dozens of specific rules and regulations. Many business leaders complained bitterly about the complexity and cost of these newly mandated procedures, while outside accounting firms, law firms, and consultants benefited from lucrative contracts for their advisory and training services in helping companies modify their procedures to ensure compliance.

But in the end, the vast majority of American businesses adjusted to the new rules with minimal disruption. A 2007 survey of 168 large companies (with average revenues of $4.7

billion) found that their average cost of compliance with Sarbanes-Oxley was $1.7 million, the equivalent of 0.036 percent of revenue—not exactly the horrific drag on profit that many critics had predicted.[27] And a 2011 study by the SEC itself found that compliance costs had declined in subsequent years, as the new accounting and disclosure procedures became routine and as SEC guidelines continued to be clarified.

Other studies have quantified the benefits of Sarbanes-Oxley, finding that companies have responded to the law by improving their internal controls, increasing transparency, and producing more reliable financial statements. There's even evidence that companies that took full advantage of the law by using the information it disclosed to improve their accounting processes have enjoyed greater stock price increases than other firms. In the long run, being open and ethical is good business.

The positive results produced by Sarbanes-Oxley are largely due to the remarkable work of the SEC's professional staffers during my chairmanship. Far from the spotlight, they labored with enormous energy, intelligence, and integrity to create a practical system that has greatly benefited American businesses and those who invest in them.

In the midst of all this unglamorous but important work, yet another scandal materialized. The mismanagement of so many significant companies had led many observers—journalists, public interest groups, politicians, and ordinary citizens—to focus a spotlight on the issue of corporate governance. Who actually runs American businesses? How are they chosen? What powers do they have? How are they rewarded? And whose interests are they actually serving? Questions like these took on a new urgency in an era when it seemed increasingly difficult for Americans to trust the good intentions and the integrity of many at the helm of big companies. And these questions applied not only to industrial companies but to those in the financial sphere—banks, investment firms, and the exchanges themselves.

At the SEC, I believed that the financial services industry had to set an example of good governance and unexcelled transparency for all of American business—and that the SEC should lead the way. As one step toward this goal, in March 2003 we asked the leading financial exchanges in the United States (ten in all) to review their entire management structures and report back to the SEC with certain basic information, including details on how they determined the compensation of their top executives. As I noted in a public letter outlining this request, "It is now more important than ever that self-regulatory organizations be examples of good governance. . . . Bottom line, how do your governance practices reflect those expected of corporations traded on your market?"

Within a few weeks, all the exchanges but one had responded with clear, detailed explanations of their governance structures. The only exception was the New York Stock Exchange. Instead, they sent us an explanation and a request: They had appointed a series of committees to investigate and respond to our questions, but gathering and presenting the information was proving more difficult than expected. Could we grant an extension?

We agreed to the request. And then the bombshell exploded.

The newspapers on the morning of August 28, 2003, were filled with the news that Richard Grasso, chairman of the New York Stock Exchange, had just signed a new contract that included an unprecedented $139.5 million payday, structured as an advance against a huge, fully funded retirement package that the Exchange had crafted specifically and exclusively for Grasso.

This was a stunner. I couldn't help wondering about the timing. Had this highly questionable deal been rushed through in an attempt to short-circuit any potential SEC rulings in regard to executive compensation at the exchanges? But even aside from the timing, the whole deal had a foul smell. At a time when millions of Americans had lost much of their personal savings and company pensions due to corporate negligence or outright fraud, the idea of diverting such a vast sum to a single individual, however deserving, felt insensitive at best, felonious at worst. What's more, as Senator Richard Shelby noted at the start of a Senate hearing into the matter, it called into question the entire concept of self-regulation:

> Many have criticized the current structure of the Exchange's board of directors for being dominated by directors representing specialists and member firms and lacking sufficient independent directors. Many also contend that the Exchange's self-regulatory structure, in which the chairman is essentially paid by the industry that he oversees, calls into question the Exchange's role as an unbiased regulator.[28]

As a former CEO of the NYSE, I had a special interest and responsibility in this case. I decided I had to get personally involved in order to minimize the damage to the reputation of U.S. business and the financial markets in particular.

I responded strongly. I sent a letter to Carl McCall, chairman of the NYSE compensation committee and a rising star in the New York State Democratic Party. It read, in part:

> In my view, the approval of Mr. Grasso's pay package raises serious questions regarding the effectiveness of the NYSE's current governance structure. I am especially concerned that the pay package was awarded before the Exchange completed its governance review, which has been pending since March.[29]

I attached a list of nine fundamental questions about the Grasso deal and the process that had produced it, and I requested complete answers within a week. The fundamental message was, in effect, *What the hell are you doing, and what on earth were you thinking?*

The Exchange was profoundly embarrassed by the public outrage that followed. Within weeks, Grasso resigned. Eliot Spitzer subsequently sued him, seeking repayment of the $139.5 million Grasso had received. However, the suit was dismissed by the New York State Court of Appeals in 2008.

Just two months after Grasso's resignation, in December 2003, the SEC approved a new corporate governance structure for the NYSE. It included a new, truly independent board of directors, an independent regulatory oversight committee, and four new board committees composed only of independent directors, one of which was in charge of human resources and compensation. Less than a year later, in November 2004, we issued similar governance proposals for all of the U.S. exchanges.

Although the NYSE's governance issues had been swiftly addressed by the SEC, the news media couldn't get enough of the Grasso story. One angle that many journalists particularly relished was my direct involvement as SEC chairman. Many stories were written looking back on my own stint as chairman of the NYSE—an appointment that some people had felt should have gone to Dick Grasso rather than me. (I don't doubt that Dick Grasso himself felt that way.) Our personal traits were described in terms that made us sound like polar opposites: Grasso the street-smart, plebeian, college dropout who'd worked his way up from the trading floor; Donaldson the silver-haired, politically savvy son of the Ivy League.

Working with these elements, it was easy for an imaginative journalist to conjure up a soap opera tale of rivalry, betrayal, and revenge; to imagine that Grasso's supersized payday was his way of sticking it to the old-school types who'd previously thwarted his ambitions. And now here was the final, ironic twist—that the same Donaldson who'd stolen Grasso's chairmanship back in 1995 should now swoop in to deprive him of his belated reward.

It made for a great story, especially for a media that (again) can't resist the temptation to cast every controversy in purely personal terms. But I've found that, when a story seems almost too good to be true, it's usually false. And that's the case here. As I've explained, Dick Grasso and I worked amicably together during my years as chairman of the NYSE. If he was resentful of me for taking "his" job, he didn't show it.

As for the public relations disaster that grew from his overblown compensation package, I'm sorry it ever happened (as I'm sure Dick is). But the role I played as the chief government overseer of the exchanges wasn't a matter of personal animosity between Dick and me. If anything, the entire debacle was a reflection of the times—of the corporate and personal excesses of the late 1990s and early 2000s, and of the weakening of social and business mores that those excesses helped produce.

It wouldn't have happened, of course, without a serious misjudgment on the part of the NYSE board, and in particular its compensation committee. But I think it also reflected a bit of hubris on Grasso's part. Having dedicated his life to the Exchange—and having spent much of his life working with and rubbing elbows with corporate chieftains from some of the world's biggest companies, for whom seven-, eight-, and even nine-figure annual paydays were common—I imagine that Dick sincerely felt, "Let's face it, I've earned this money!" He did deserve to be handsomely rewarded for all he'd done for the Exchange. But I think his sense of bearings had become a bit eroded, with the result that he failed to recognize when the deal simply went a step—or several steps—beyond what common sense would support.

Throughout my tenure at the SEC, the issue of executive compensation was a hot-button issue in American business—as it still is today. Some commentators even wondered whether the SEC itself should get involved in setting some limits on the gilded pay packages that many CEOs were receiving. I didn't favor any such step. Salaries in private enterprise should be determined by market forces and the good judgment of business leaders. But basic principles of good governance dictate that corporate boards need to be much more diligent about the oversight that they provide and the limits they establish. The era of board cronyism, with well-connected members of compensation committees routinely rubber-stamping outrageous compensation packages for CEOs, needs to end.

Almost every corporation likes to claim that its top executives are rewarded purely on the basis of outstanding performance. But all too often, the definition of "outstanding performance" is notoriously slippery. Simply hitting your quarterly or annual earnings forecasts shouldn't merit a king's ransom in bonus moneys and stock options. The biggest rewards should be based on the company's long-term performance, which should extend several years beyond the CEO's tenure. We've all seen executives walk away with their hundreds of millions in retirement pay, only to have their companies falter within a year or two of their departure. A true leader is someone who builds a solid and long-lasting entity—not a house of cards.

* * *

In the world of government regulation, very little is carved in stone. There's a common pattern of two steps forward, one step back, as political leaders follow the pendulum of shifting public opinion. Perhaps after several tumultuous years during which the SEC was perceived as pushing an aggressive regulatory agenda, it was inevitable that the Bush administration would want to ease the pressure on Wall Street—or at least be seen as doing so.

So when I announced my departure from the SEC, President Bush appointed Christopher Cox, a conservative Republican congressman, as my replacement. The general reaction was summarized by the headline on a page-one story in the *Wall Street Journal* for June 3, 2005: "U.S. Business Breathes a Sigh of Relief as Head of SEC Ends His Tenure—Nomination of Cox Signals Departure from Donaldson's Active Regulation."

Thus the "Donaldson era" came to an end at the SEC. Looking back, I would like to be able to say that we accomplished everything we set out to do during my years as chairman. But that would be an overstatement. Like any regulatory agency, we were operating in a highly charged political environment. Our efforts were subject to intense pushback from many elements in the business community, members of Congress, and even some of my fellow commissioners.

Legal and legislative challenges to our proposals eventually thwarted some of them. For example, the SEC ultimately failed to adopt our plan to make it easier for long-term shareholders to nominate directors and offer other proxy challenges. And the Chamber of Commerce's lawsuit challenging our rule requiring that independent directors constitute 75 percent of the board of a mutual fund company was ultimately successful; in April 2006, the D.C. Court of Appeals ruled that the SEC hadn't sufficiently analyzed the costs associated with the rule before issuing it, rendering the rule inoperable—a spurious decision at best.

I'm proud of the fact that, during my chairmanship, we sent a strong message to Wall Street that government regulation and oversight of the markets were real and must be taken seriously. This included an unprecedented number of enforcement actions and significantly greater sanctions against those found responsible for misconduct. The numbers tell the tale: Between October 1, 2002, and September 30, 2004, the SEC brought a record total of more than 1,300 enforcement actions and obtained orders for penalties and fines totaling more than $5 billion. We didn't pad these numbers by taking on easy targets or "little guys." For example, between May 2003 and May 2004, when the mutual fund scandals were hitting the news, the SEC brought charges against twelve of the twenty-five largest mutual fund groups in the United States.[30]

More important, we strengthened the SEC as an institution. We expanded the agency, enhanced the quality of its personnel, modernized its management structure, and improved its morale. The ultimate result was at least a partial restoration of the sense of public confidence that had been so badly damaged by the scandals of the early 2000s.

Public confidence, of course, isn't something that can ever be established permanently—or taken for granted. Within just a few years, the biggest financial meltdown since the Great Depression would cast an even deeper shadow over the reputation of many on Wall Street. But that's another story.

CHAPTER 11

In Sum:
Entrepreneurial Leadership

In writing this book, I have had occasion to reflect deeply on my leadership role in three major sectors of our national life: the for-profit business arena, the nonprofit world of academia, and the government. Looking back on a career with a number of surprising twists and turns, some notable accomplishments and a handful of failures, I have come to believe that a unifying thread that runs through the many professional activities I have engaged in can be summarized by the two words *leader* and *entrepreneurial*. Interestingly, I have come to see this in retrospect; I am not sure I thought enough about it at the time to have characterized myself in this way.

What exactly is entrepreneurial leadership? There are leaders and there are entrepreneurs, but not all leaders are entrepreneurs, and not all entrepreneurs are leaders. Simply put, I believe that *entrepreneurial* is a mind-set—a way of thinking—and *leadership* is a way of acting. Entrepreneurial leadership, then, describes the way such a leader behaves.

In today's complex world, entrepreneurial leaders are

needed more than ever to navigate global, economic, and political uncertainty and competitive pressure—whether in the commercial, academic, nonprofit, or government sectors. Leaders can no longer be linear in their thinking and acting; they must lead in an innovative, inventive way, working with diverse groups of people and resources to achieve the goals of their company, division, department, or organization. They must be able to define systems rather than be defined by them; they must push the boundaries of what was once thought possible. And no matter what, they must execute. Effective leaders must be entrepreneurial—which means getting things done, regardless of the obstacles.

Entrepreneurial leadership encompasses some other important attributes. Entrepreneurial leaders must have the ability to learn fast in environments of ambiguity and change, while providing clarity and coherence for those around them. They must know how to manage risk and anticipate the unexpected. They must have an inner drive to envision, innovate, and take advantage of opportunities proactively, opportunities often hidden in not-so-obvious places.

Entrepreneurial leaders are by nature optimistic, energetic, and spirited. They must take personal responsibility—an ownership mentality, if you will—and always lead for the benefit of the organization. Entrepreneurs can act alone; entrepreneurial leaders cannot. A critical key to success is hiring people with drive, curiosity, creativity, resourcefulness, adaptability—basic values in common, coupled with a willingness to challenge the leader.

Based on my experiences, successful and otherwise, as a would-be change-maker in institutions as varied as the State Department, the New York Stock Exchange, Aetna, and the SEC, I would make just a few basic recommendations to the leader seeking to transform an organization:

- *Pick your shots.* Rather than trying to inaugurate wholesale change, identify a few key opportunities that will make a substantial difference and focus your attention on those.

- *Move quickly.* Once you've picked the departments and programs most in need of a major overhaul, introduce new systems, protocols, and processes as fast as you can, so that positive results can be swiftly produced, generating support of additional reforms.

- *Install the right people in key positions.* Find leaders with a track record of success in reforming organizations, and give them the power to institute transformational changes that embody the values and goals your administration stands for.

- *Spread your message of change.* Use every communication tool at your disposal to inform your colleagues about the reasons for the changes you are implementing and the benefits the entire organization will enjoy as a result. And when you think you have communicated about your program sufficiently, redouble your efforts! The most successful leaders are usually those who communicate the most.

This may all sound quite straightforward, but an understanding of the real skills of entrepreneurial leadership, and an ability to apply them successfully, are quite rare. What follows is my expanded take on what defines an entrepreneurial leader.

Entrepreneurial leaders have the ability to see the world a bit differently from everyone else. They have *the drive to innovate*—the willingness to continually experiment, to test new ways of organizing and deploying resources, to abandon outmoded approaches when circumstances change; in short, to "make all things new," whether building a brand-new organization (DLJ and the Yale School of Management), captaining a venerable institution through the storms of revolutionary change (the NYSE), or reforming a damaged organization in danger of failure and irrelevance (Aetna and the SEC). They then make a personal commitment to that unique vision and dedicate themselves to winning over allies and supporters who can join with them in making it a reality.

The ability to envision and innovate underlies most of the great business success stories we associate with the word "entrepreneurship." For example, my friend Fred Smith launched his career of entrepreneurial leadership when he imagined the possibility of making overnight package deliveries throughout the United States easier and more efficient by using a spoke-and-hub airline network. Based on this concept, Smith created Federal Express, which revolutionized the delivery industry.

My own career as an entrepreneurial leader began back in the 1950s, when Dan Lufkin, Dick Jenrette, and I looked at the investment scene and noticed something that no one else seemed to have observed—a paucity of research and information about fast-growing small-to-midsized companies. This was a significant gap in the market, since many institutional investors, as well as thousands of individuals, were eager to find ways to expand their horizons beyond the familiar giants of American industry—IBM, GE, General Motors, and the like—whose growth prospects seemed to be slowing in recent years. Dan, Dick, and I conceived a unique vision of an investment firm that would develop in-depth reports on rising young companies similar to the studies that a consulting firm like McKinsey & Company might produce. The result was Donaldson, Lufkin & Jenrette, a new type of investment firm that played a role in helping to jump-start a new era in U.S. financial history.

At any given moment, not every arena of human activity may be ripe for reimagining by an entrepreneurial leader. But today there are a number of major challenges facing our nation that are crying out for fresh thinking. They include health care, education, economic inequality, global climate change, race relations, and our dilapidated infrastructure. I'd like to see our political leaders drawing inspiration from the work of entrepreneurial leaders in every field and having the courage to think in innovative ways about these and other problems that we have been struggling for years to address.

Entrepreneurial leaders must know how to manage risk and anticipate the unexpected. An entrepreneurial leader develops a talent for thinking about the future, and a habit of doing so consistently. Closely related to this is a cautious attitude toward risk. Contrary to popular assumptions, entrepreneurial leaders are not mainly risk-takers—people who thrill at the idea of putting all the chips on red in hopes of a giant payoff. Instead, they are continually scanning the horizon for emerging risks that could jeopardize their vision and working on plans to minimize or eliminate them. Then, when necessary, they exercise the will to take calculated risks.

When my partners and I founded DLJ, virtually all of our acquaintances on Wall Street and others in the industry agreed that we had no chance of success: "How can three young guys with minimal business experiences compete with the giant investment firms that have ruled the industry for decades?" Even my own father thought I was taking a foolish gamble. But I never really thought we were taking an unrealistic risk. We based the idea for DLJ on our instincts, our general business knowledge, and our observations from a few years doing research, managing money, and working in investment banking on Wall Street. And before hanging out our shingle, we raised enough capital from friends, family, and colleagues so that we could operate for at least three years and make any necessary strategic shifts and course corrections. Under the circumstances, I felt that our leap into the future was a prudent and well-calculated step—and I was right.

The unexpected is always highly likely. During the early years of DLJ, we faced a dramatic change in circumstances when fixed brokerage commissions were eliminated. At a stroke, this regulatory change dramatically reduced one of our main sources of income. Fortunately, we'd anticipated the change and were prepared to deal with it. DLJ expanded into money management and other services, rapidly becoming one of the most diversified and successful firms in the financial industry, enjoying varied streams of income that were largely insulated from changes in the investment climate.

Again, there are clear parallels to be drawn between the private and public sectors. Government is often called upon to anticipate and respond to unexpected challenges, from terrorist attacks to natural disasters to economic downturns. Our political leaders can learn a great deal about the art of anticipation and fallback by studying the careers of entrepreneurial leaders.

I applied this philosophy to my own work in public service. For example, as chairman of the SEC, I worked with the leadership team to create a new division of risk analysis. Its mission: to anticipate problems in the financial industry that might arise from new trading technologies and innovative investment strategies, and to develop regulatory approaches that could prevent these problems from triggering a market collapse and potentially wiping out billions of dollars' worth of capital. I'd like to see the government take a similar approach to the entire gamut of future risks our country may face, from the rise of China to climate change.

Entrepreneurial leaders hire and build teams that can execute as well as contribute strategically and creatively. They show a readiness to subsume personal power and rewards in the interests of attracting, retaining, and motivating the best possible collection of talent, empowering people to make change and growth happen, and inspiring a strong esprit de corps that makes any organization an exciting, creative place to be.

It's a leadership formula I first experienced in the U.S. Marine Corps and later tried to embed in every organization I have served.

Of course, organizations in different sectors of society present different leadership challenges to the teams leading them. Some of the constraints that affect leaders in government are different than those faced by business and nonprofit leaders. A U.S. president making cabinet appointments must consider such characteristics as party affiliation, political ideology, and personal loyalty as well as intelligence, talent, and experience. Sometimes personnel choices are made in part to reward those who played important roles in the campaign that elevated the president to the White House; it is also necessary to appoint individuals who bring gender, ethnic, and geographic diversity to the administration. Entrepreneurial leaders learn how to work within such constraints while maximizing the potential of the team they are constructing.

But despite the unique challenges involved in government, entrepreneurial leadership can still be applied to make federal, state, and local agencies run more effectively than they typically do. Just like a for-profit company or a nonprofit organization, a cabinet department or an agency like the SEC needs leadership that can create a shared vision, promote a sense of cohesion, and inspire every employee with the feeling that he or she is serving an important cause.

This isn't easy to do. It takes time, patience, and commitment from the leader at the top—as well as the willingness to share power and influence with people at every level, so that a true team can be built and energized.

In the business arena, entrepreneurial leaders must think and behave as if they own the company—whether they do or not. Entrepreneurial leaders must define systems rather than be defined by them; they must adopt an ownership mentality. They understand that they must take ownership of their choices, including the smaller, day-to-day decisions they make. They must take full responsibility for them rather than attributing them to "the system" or "circumstances." Entrepreneurial leaders also think continually about the big picture—the broader goal that everyone in the organization is supposed to be working toward—and strive to be guided not by short-term gain or personal profit but by long-term objectives that help everyone. Furthermore, entrepreneurial leaders find ways to encourage everyone in the organization to think and behave in this way, and create circumstances that help them do this.

At DLJ, we encouraged our team members to think like owners, literally, by giving almost everyone an ownership stake in the business. When we went public—itself an unprecedented move for a Wall Street investment firm—we made sure that ownership stakes were spread to the widest possible network of employees. We made some other unusual decisions regarding compensation with the same goal in mind. For example, rather than relying on the typical cadre of salespeople to promote our services to customers, we eliminated the traditional commission-based sales system and instead rewarded our professional staff through their long-term ownership payoff. The result was a set of customer-company relationships that were unusually close, transparent, mutually respectful, and based on the principle of shared benefit. Over time, DLJ earned a reputation as being the Wall Street firm where everybody wanted to work, largely because of our practice of treating every member of the team as an owner, with all the responsibilities, rights, and benefits associated with that role.

In the world of nonprofit organizations and in the governmental arena, there is no "owner" for an organization—no individual whose personal financial success will be irrevocably impacted by decisions on the job. At times, this can result in a sense of drift, complacency, or disengagement, with employees shrugging their shoulders over unexpected problems and saying, in effect, "Fixing that isn't in my job description." One of the big challenges for entrepreneurial leaders in a nonprofit organization or a government agency is finding ways to create a strong sense of mission and commitment on the part of every team member—a substitute for the sense of ownership that will call forth their best creative efforts.

This is one of the things we strove to accomplish during my time at the SEC. Having been given the job of regulating an array of highly—even aggressively—entrepreneurial financial firms, we realized we had to become entrepreneurial ourselves, simply to keep up. Recognizing that circumstances and challenges in the financial industry had changed with innovations in technology, global competition, and business strategy, we rethought the structure of the agency and redesigned the tools it used to monitor, analyze, and govern the behavior of corporate players. As a result, we were able to identify and close loopholes that were enabling some financial firms to take needless risks with customers' money and to implement rules that ensured a level playing field for all categories of investors.

None of this would have been possible if we hadn't encouraged all of our team members to think in broad, creative terms, as if they were all "owners" of the SEC and its mission, rather than merely cogs in the wheel, playing predetermined roles in accordance with familiar systems. I'd like see the federal government try to apply a similar approach to the long list of regulatory and other challenges it faces, striving to create teams of public servants with the kind of ownership mentality needed to address these challenges effectively.

The entrepreneurial leader takes action with bifocal vision. Entrepreneurial leaders need to master the management skills needed either to launch an organization or to transform and rejuvenate an existing one—skills that can break up stodgy bureaucracies and get sluggish corporations, hidebound government agencies, and complacent nonprofits to be responsive to the demands of change.

They must constantly be thinking about the big picture while also paying close attention to the details that make the difference between success and failure as they move to implement their vision. To adapt the slogan that boxing legend Muhammad Ali made famous, the entrepreneur must be able to "float like a butterfly, sting like a bee"—"floating" above the minutiae that sometimes distract and confuse less broadly focused managers, while "stinging" in focused situations where seemingly small matters can be crucial.

Another way of describing the distinction is to say that the entrepreneurial leader knows how and when to micromanage, while also giving team members the freedom they need to express their own creativity, values, energy, and drive.

At DLJ, my partners and I worked hard to get the most crucial operational details right. As I recounted in the first chapter of this book, when planning to announce our intention of taking DLJ public—a groundbreaking step that would challenge a long-standing rule of the New York Stock Exchange—we mapped out our tactics down to the minute, ensuring that we would control exactly how, when, and where the big news would break. In today's political jargon, you could say we wanted to be certain that we would "win the news cycle," thereby increasing the odds that we would win support from others in the business community for our unorthodox move. That's exactly how it worked out.

At the same time, when it came to managing our partners at DLJ, we aimed at having a light touch. If someone came into our offices with a big idea they wanted to try, we'd generally say "Go do it!"—provided, of course, that it didn't violate any of our company's deeply held ethical values.

An entrepreneurial leader must manage a similar balancing act between being big-picture-focused and detail-oriented, no matter what kind of organization he or she runs. When launching the Yale School of Management, my central concern was working with top academics to develop a unique curriculum that blended examples and techniques from the for-profit, nonprofit, and public arenas—but at the same time I made sure I stayed informed about the details of our student recruitment efforts, our faculty hiring strategies, our financial practices, and other administrative matters. When I was asked to help turn around the foundering insurance giant Aetna, I devoted most of my energies to figuring out which of the many disparate businesses we'd acquired during a decade of ill-advised expansion ought to be sold and which ought to be retained. But I also made time to engage in the most crucial details affecting our employee morale, customer satisfaction, and other stakeholder issues—even participating in a one-on-one dialogue with Aetna's feistiest shareholder activist during our annual shareholder meeting.

Most effective political leaders on the national stage are probably accustomed to practicing this kind of bifocal leadership. They're expected to develop and promote strategies for tackling the biggest problems facing our nation—while on the campaign trail they encounter thousands of individual citizens who are eager to share the stories of their most personal concerns, from the closing of a local factory to the pollution of a neighborhood pond. The contrast between these two sets of demands reflects the difficult balance between both leadership lenses.

High energy, optimism, and, hopefully, a sense of fun define entrepreneurial leaders. They must be gifted with a high degree of mental and physical energy, and with a sense of fearlessness about employing that energy. I've never known a *lazy* entrepreneur—or at least, I've never known a successful one! As they say in the world of sports, an entrepreneurial leader "leaves it all on the field" rather than giving just a 50 percent effort.

An entrepreneurial leader must be an optimist—someone who can see and feel his or her way to a solution no matter how serious the problems faced may be. Entrepreneurial leaders must be able to inspire others with a sense of confidence that encourages them to devote their very best efforts to the future of the organization and its mission.

At the same time, the optimism of the entrepreneurial leader must be an informed, realistic optimism rather than a blind or irrational self-confidence. As I've already noted, contrary to popular opinion, entrepreneurial leaders are *not* lovers of risk. In reality, they are constantly looking for ways to reduce risk. They take calculated risks only where the reward and the possible loss have been carefully measured and weighed.

If "optimism" is unrealistic—akin to the addicted gambler's unwavering conviction that the next spin of the roulette wheel is *sure* to produce a winning number—people will quickly come to recognize that fact. They will gradually abandon such a leader rather than go down with the sinking ship.

When I was asked by the board of directors to take the helm at Aetna, it was clear to everyone involved that the company was in dire straits. Despite the fact that it had steadily expanded, adding many thousands of new insurance customers every year for the preceding decade, it was hemorrhaging money, registering substantial, continuing losses of close to a million dollars a day. Under the circumstances, projecting a sense of optimism wasn't easy. Many had come to assume that it was only a matter of time before Aetna was broken up and sold off in pieces to the highest bidders.

Fortunately, I tend to have an innately optimistic viewpoint on life. Perhaps that's one of the reasons I was asked by Aetna's board to step in as CEO at a time of extreme danger. I resisted the temptation to panic. I spent a weekend with board members and Aetna's executive team analyzing the takeover bids that had already begun to arrive. We compared the financial offers being made with the demonstrable economic value of Aetna's component parts. Coolheaded analysis made it clear that the firm was worth far more than the offers suggested. Rather than break up the company, we identified the pieces with the greatest value as well as those for which we had the largest reserve of managerial experience and expertise. We decided that Aetna's future lay in focusing on the profitable and rapidly growing arena of health insurance, and we drew up prudent plans to sell off certain businesses that didn't fit into that strategy. In time, we transformed Aetna into a somewhat smaller company but one that was profitable, well managed, and poised for decades of growth.

In today's era of unpredictable change, the conflict between optimists and pessimists concerning our nation's future has become particularly acute. Many naysayers in the media, in politics, and among ordinary citizens have concluded that government is simply incapable of solving some of the biggest problems our nation faces. History suggests otherwise. A nation that conquered a vast frontier, led an international technological revolution, and helped defeat the forces of Fascism and Communism is capable of tackling any difficulty. There's every reason for Americans to be optimistic about the future of our nation, particularly if we apply the entrepreneurial approach to the problems we face.

It may surprise you to find a sense of fun in the list of essential qualities for an entrepreneurial leader. But without the ability to simply *enjoy* the work, it will be almost impossible to attract the top-notch people needed to help turn the entrepreneurial leader's dreams into reality. For this reason, "having fun" was listed among the official corporate objectives in DLJ's annual reports. We wanted to experience the kind of fun that arises naturally when smart, dedicated people work together in pursuit of a mutual goal. We tried hard never to take ourselves too seriously. And every year, we rewarded and highlighted an employee that all agreed had made a major contribution to the company's success—with janitors just as eligible as members of the C-suite team. After all, fun isn't fun unless *everybody* can get in on the act.

Our most successful national leaders, from Kennedy and Reagan to Obama, have been known for their wit and humor. An interesting modern-day counterpoint are the Golden State Warriors of the NBA—a phenomenally successful basketball team that plays the game with a palpable sense of fun and enjoyment. In today's highly polarized political climate, national leaders must be able to use the gift of humor to defuse tense situations, to humanize the opposition, and to reaffirm the bonds that unite rather than divide us.

* * *

In addition to the characteristics defining successful entrepreneurial leaders, there are two critical challenges all such leaders must face and address: the balance between completing the entrepreneurial phase and wanting to move on, and staying long enough to solidify the changes or achievements so that they don't collapse when the entrepreneurial leader leaves; and the related task of developing a plan to preserve the legacy created.

I have made career choices designed to maintain and maximize my sense of being engaged with and energized by my work with an organization. DLJ was one of the most financially successful and widely admired firms of Wall Street when I decided to change direction completely, leaving the private sector for a chance to serve in the State Department under Henry Kissinger. The fact that I'd always wanted an opportunity to work in the public sector certainly helped to drive that decision. But so did the fact that I was, simply, more energized by the start-up than by the day-to-day operations of running a company. Perhaps this is the curse of the entrepreneurial leader.

My career since then has followed the same pattern: a few years at a particular organization helping to launch it (as I did at the Yale School of Management), to reshape it for a new era and a new set of challenges (as at the New York Stock Exchange and the SEC), or to rescue it from a near-death experience (as at Aetna). At most of the organizations, I could have held on for a few more years. In retrospect, I probably should have done so in several cases.

I have come to recognize that I am fully energized and motivated primarily by an entrepreneurial challenge—the chance to build or rebuild an organization. Other leaders are far better suited to the task of maintaining and nurturing a successful organization, keeping it on the glide path to success in a basically stable environment. But for the entrepreneurial leader, the question always remains: how long until you get it right enough for the organization to survive and flourish as you move on?

The second challenge is how to preserve the legacy. An entrepreneurial leader needs to create a team of people with the patience and commitment to carry on the good work and nurture the organization so it can continue producing great results for years to come, long after the original founder or change agent has departed.

* * *

One other essential quality of the entrepreneurial leader remains to be discussed. I believe there's no substitute for *personal integrity*—a reality that can sometimes force you to face extremely difficult, painful choices. In the end, life is about striving continually to do the right thing, and about being willing to offer, and accept, forgiveness for the times we fall short.

One element of integrity is the readiness to transcend merely personal, selfish goals. Some would-be leaders are driven mainly by ego—the desire to bask in the limelight of others' admiration and praise, or the love of power for its own sake. Entrepreneurial leadership in the sense I'm describing is about goals that are much greater than ego. If you want to achieve big things, you must be willing, even eager, to share both the credit for your accomplishments and the benefits they generate with the team members who played a role.

For an entrepreneurial leader, it's not all about money. The desire for wealth alone has never been enough to build a lasting organization. I've explained that entrepreneurial leadership begins with a powerful vision—an innovative view of the world that many people find eye-opening, believable, and alluring. Entrepreneurial leaders owe it to themselves and to their followers to remain true to that vision, and not to compromise or betray it for the sake of profit or other secondary goals.

Finally, the integrity of an entrepreneurial leader requires a profound commitment to the value of individuals. If an organization hopes to attract and retain the best people, it must treat everyone—employees, customers, partners, donors, grantees, regulators, even competitors—with respect, fairness, and honesty. When you behave in this way, people will recognize that you and your organization are trustworthy, and they will be drawn to doing business with you. By contrast, there's no quicker way to destroy an organization than to hire people who aren't quite trustworthy. When that happens, even the best-laid plans are unlikely to come to fruition.

The traits of the entrepreneurial leader are very personal, of course. It's probably easy to see how my list has been shaped by my own experiences as a leader, as well as by my own values. But I hope that the relevance of these traits to the challenges faced by any leader—whether in the business, nonprofit, or government sphere—is also apparent.

EPILOGUE

Where Are They Now?

Looking back over the varied experiences recounted in this book, it's startling to me to realize that my career began almost sixty years ago, in the fall of 1959, when Dan Lufkin, Dick Jenrette, and I first opened the doors of our fledgling investment firm. The years have truly flown by. And surveying that span of decades, I realize that this book would be incomplete without briefly bringing the story up to date with a few notes on the current state of the organizations I helped to shape. The enterprises I led have experienced very different fates in the years that followed, reflecting the turbulence and unpredictability of the world we live in and perhaps in some cases my inability to lock in the gains we made before I left.

When I departed Donaldson, Lufkin & Jenrette in 1973, the future of the company appeared to be bright. Our earlier moves toward diversification, all research-based, had helped make DLJ an innovative force on Wall Street, and for a time, the company continued on that path after my departure. DLJ became a leader in investment banking, merchant banking, venture capital (through a subsidiary called the Sprout Group), and correspondent brokerage (through Pershing LLC, a small independent clearinghouse that DLJ bought and built). DLJ also created one of the first online brokerage portals for its clients, way back in the mid-1990s, before most companies had even begun to think about such things. DLJ's technology in this area would ultimately be bought by E-Trade, which today is one of the world's biggest online trading companies, with more than 3.5 million brokerage accounts.

DLJ also became a leader in the origination of high-yield bonds—those corporate debt instruments often derisively termed "junk bonds" that are actually a very useful tool in raising capital for companies that don't enjoy the triple-A credit rating that the world's biggest and richest businesses command.

Once upon a time, high-yield bonds had a sketchy reputation on Wall Street and were a relatively tiny factor in the financial world. But in the 1980s, under the leadership of Fred Joseph and Michael Milken, the old-line investment bank of Drexel Burnham Lambert began using high-yield bonds to raise funds for fast-growing businesses. They also got into the mergers and acquisitions field, using high-yield bonds to create war chests for both friendly and hostile takeovers, perhaps most famously in the successful bid by Kohlberg Kravis Roberts to take over the consumer-goods conglomerate RJR Nabisco.

These were the kinds of innovative, entrepreneurial moves that would have been admirable and even in the spirit of DLJ if they had been guided by the same commitment to integrity that my partners and I insisted on. Unfortunately, that wasn't the case at Drexel Burnham. Beginning in 1986, charges of insider trading, stock manipulation, and fraud began swirling around the company, which found itself pursued by the zealous and ambitious Rudy Giuliani, then U.S. attorney for the Southern District of New York. By 1990, Drexel had filed for bankruptcy protection, and soon the once-proud company was no more.

Drexel's collapse was DLJ's gain. A number of the most talented people at Drexel—experts at using high-yield bonds as a tool for corporate growth, and untainted by the shady practices that had led to the downfall of Michael Milken—joined DLJ. Under the leadership of Bennett Goodman, a Drexel alumnus, a high-yield bond program was developed at DLJ, which assumed the mantle of leadership in that arena.

In December 1984, DLJ was purchased by Equitable Life Assurance, which kept Dick Jenrette on to run DLJ as an independent unit until 1986, when he was succeeded as CEO by John Chalsty. Three years later, in 1989, when the entire Equitable empire was floundering, they asked Dick to run Equitable itself, and he led a successful revival of the company before finally retiring in 1996. Dick subsequently became well known and deeply respected in the world of historic preservation for his work in restoring old homes, a story he told in his 2000 book *Adventures with Old Houses*. Dick was appointed chairman of the Advisory Council on Historic Preservation by President Jimmy Carter. Dick passed away on April 22, 2018.

Meanwhile, Dan Lufkin continued to pursue the passion for environmental protection that originally led him to leave DLJ. He served as Connecticut's environmental commissioner and helped draft the state's groundbreaking environmental legislation. Later he was asked by Pete McCloskey, the well-known Republican congressman from California, to help launch the first celebration of Earth Day, which is now recognized annually around the world.

Unfortunately, Donaldson, Lufkin & Jenrette itself is longer in existence. DLJ was purchased by the Credit Suisse Group in 2000 for $11.5 billion, which merged it into Credit Suisse First Boston. It was a deal that had some superficial plausibility at the time but that was doomed to failure in the long run.

One of the problems was that DLJ's biggest business at the

time—the high-yield bond business—was in a period of long-term decline. That meant that the single largest asset that Credit Suisse was buying had significantly less value than they anticipated. And when many of the best managers in the high-yield bond department took their leave soon after the Credit Suisse acquisition, the value of the business shrank even further.

Another problem was the huge cultural gap between DLJ and Credit Suisse. Earlier in this book, I described the unique blend of policies and personalities that made DLJ such an attractive place for talented people to work. Credit Suisse didn't have the same kind of entrepreneurial, human-centered atmosphere. They imposed on DLJ a European, bureaucratic, nonentrepreneurial style of management. As a result, people began leaving in droves soon after the acquisition occurred. Within a short time, the DLJ community had scattered to dozens of companies all over Wall Street and beyond, and the special bond we'd created and nurtured over many years basically died.

Some of the specific innovations that DLJ brought to Wall Street have also faded from the scene. Today the kind of research we pioneered at DLJ is rare. Dick Jenrette talked about the problem in a 2001 interview. "When we were starting out, we rebelled against statistical, simplistic research reports. And now all you read is that a company's profit margin declined by so much, that it's at 120 percent of the S&P average. It's all statistical. I read research and I can't even find out what a company does half the time. There's no effort to explain what its competitive edge is. It's not qualitative, it's all computer models."[31] Sadly, I don't think the situation has improved since then.

One reason is changes in SEC rules that restrict the flow of information from inside companies to the general public. In our early days, we wouldn't recommend a company until we'd had the chance to meet with the CEO and the leadership group, discuss the company's plans with them, and evaluate the strength of the firm's management. Today, a CEO can't conduct such a meeting because of SEC regulations that require that all material information about a firm be communicated at the same time to everyone who may be interested in investing. The motive behind such rules is understandable, even laudable: The idea is to level the playing field and make it impossible for a few insiders to reap big profits from leaks of secret information. But the rules also reduce transparency and make it harder for investors to understand what's really going on inside a business.

Another problem is conflicts of interest. Since most investment firms make the bulk of their incomes from investment banking fees, there's pressure on analysts to provide happy-talk research reports that simply parrot the positive news that the company managers themselves provide. There are even stories about researchers being internally reprimanded or punished for giving honest evaluations of companies their firms are doing business with. Needless to say, that would not have happened at DLJ.

For these and other reasons, there's less time and effort being invested today in the kind of in-depth, analytical research we excelled at.

Fortunately, the soul of DLJ is being kept alive through the many DLJ alumni all over the world, many of them still accomplishing great things through the entrepreneurial spirit they nurtured at DLJ. The list is long and impressive. I previously mentioned Joe Reich and Oscar Tang, who founded Reich & Tang, as well as Bennett Goodman, who built DLJ's high-yield bond business and today is a partner of the Blackstone Group. Others on the list include Stephen A. Schwarzman, founder of that same Blackstone Group, and Hamilton E. "Tony" James, formerly its president and COO, and now its vice-chair; Safra A. Catz, CEO of Oracle Corporation; David Einhorn, founder and president of Greenlight Capital; Jamie Dinan, founder and president of York Capital Management; Susan Decker, former president of Yahoo!; Ken Moelis, former director at UBS Investment Bank and founder of Moelis & Company; Paul Singer, founder and CEO of Elliott Management Corporation, and many others.

To this day, when I run into an old DLJ hand at a conference, at a party, or just on the street, he or she almost invariably says, "You know, DLJ was the best place I ever worked." They loved the firm because of its ethos of fairness and teamwork, the excitement of building it, and above all its entrepreneurial spirit. And today, although I went on to experience many other challenges and successes in the business arena and beyond, I still look back on my years at DLJ as a high-water mark of my career.

* * *

The second major institution that I helped to create was the Yale School of Management (SOM), where I served as founding dean from 1975 to 1980. As I explained earlier in this book, it was an exciting and very rewarding experience. I had the chance to learn about a leadership arena that was new to me—the world of academia—and to build an important new organization with roots in one of the world's greatest educational institutions—my own alma mater, Yale University.

Today, it's profoundly gratifying to me that the school we built over forty years ago remains very successful. The unique approach to leadership that we pioneered, which focuses on the commonalities and interrelationships among for-profit, non-profit, and government organizations, has become even more relevant and important in the intervening years. And SOM has continued to be an innovator in the world of management education. Although it looks quite different today, it has continued to innovate with the times, while keeping its initial core values and mission intact. In 2006, it introduced a team-taught "integrated curriculum" for all MBA students, which moves beyond the traditional siloed approach to business education by focusing on the crucial interconnections among various aspects of leadership. SOM also now requires MBA students to fulfill a global studies requirement, reflecting the ever-deepening ties among businesses, governments, cultures, and peoples around the world. In these and other ways, SOM remains a leader in creating educational programs that are timely, relevant, and reflective of the dynamic, complex world in which today's managers must operate.

Thanks to this progressive approach to education—as well as a stellar roster of faculty members—Yale has consistently ranked among the best business schools, though it is better termed a "management school" and has never conformed to the traditional curricular expectations of a business school. Applications for admission have been increasing steadily—a 46 percent jump between 2011 and 2017, greater than that enjoyed by any peer school.

Thanks to the high-quality training they receive, SOM alumni have thrived. The more than four thousand men and women who have graduated with Yale management degrees work in every sector of industry, government, and the nonprofit arena. Many have spent time in multiple sectors, or pioneering unique new niches where two or more sectors overlap— illustrating precisely the kind of interdisciplinary approach we knew today's leaders would need, and that we designed SOM to inculcate. Notable SOM alumni reflecting this include Indra Nooyi, class of 1980, CEO of PepsiCo; Jack Griffin '88, former CEO of Time Inc.; David Warren '88, CFO of the London Stock Exchange and former CFO of Nasdaq; Donald Gips '89, former U.S. Ambassador to South Africa; Daniel Weiss '85, president of the Metropolitan Museum of Art and former president of Haverford College; Jaime Gonzalez Aguadé '96, former president of the National Banking and Securities Commission of Mexico; Neal Keny-Guyer '82, CEO of Mercy Corps; Laszlo Bock '99, CEO and cofounder of Humu, and former vice president of people operations at Google; Gail Harrity '82, president and COO of the Philadelphia Museum of Art; and Kenneth Ofori-Atta '88, minister of finance of Ghana.

What's more, our alumni contribute their time, talent, and treasure at unusually high levels. In 2016, SOM received donations from a record-high 51.9 percent of alumni, marking the third straight year of greater than 50 percent participation. The loyalty and support of SOM's alumni speaks volumes about the value of the education the School is offering.

By every measure, the Yale School of Management is playing an important role in helping to create new generations of leaders for an increasingly complex world. The fact that I played a part in bringing this remarkable institution into being is one of the proudest achievements of my career.

* * *

During the early 1990s, I served as chairman and CEO of the New York Stock Exchange (NYSE) during a particularly difficult time in its history. Unlike at DLJ or the Yale School of Management, I wasn't helping to launch a brand-new institution but rather helping to shepherd a venerable one through a series of tough challenges. I had to push hard for changes that would modernize the Exchange, prepare it for a rising avalanche of technological changes, and equip it for intense competition from around the world. In some ways, I was able to foster a spirit of innovation and modernization that paved the way for a nimbler stock exchange, better equipped to survive and thrive in the twenty-first century.

Recognizing the need for increased capitalization to finance technological improvements, the NYSE merged with the electronic trading firm Archipelago in 2005. The merged companies became a for-profit, publicly traded business, known as NYSE Arca, the following year. In 2007, another merger, this one with the European stock market Euronext, further increased the scope and scale of the company, creating the first transatlantic stock exchange. Known as NYSE Euronext, the business is now owned by Intercontinental Exchange.

Access to the NYSE is now overwhelmingly via electronic order delivery. The traditional system whereby ownership of a seat was required for anyone seeking to trade directly on the Exchange has been eliminated. Now, one-year licenses are available to would-be floor traders for $40,000—a fraction of the price once demanded for the coveted seats, which rose as high as $4 million in the late 1990s. All of these changes were essential adjustments for the Exchange to keep up with the times.

However, still other reforms that have not occurred would be desirable. For example, the most powerful investment firms have never embraced the degree of transparency that might have prevented the subsequent rise of "dark pools" of money, with an undue influence of the movement of stock and commodity prices. The transition to electronic trading, with all the complicated technological shifts involved, has not always gone smoothly. Episodes like the so-called Flash Crash of May 6, 2010, when the Dow Jones Industrial Average suffered a then-unprecedented 998-point drop in its value, have raised questions regarding the excessive power of high-frequency traders using complex computer algorithms to execute transactions. It's clear that exchange leaders, national and international financial regulators, and the heads of the world's biggest investment firms need to work together to guard against practices that produce extreme volatility and the possibility of manipulation, leading to needless economic uncertainty and public distrust of markets.

Despite these challenges, the NYSE today remains by far the world's largest stock exchange, whether measured by total market capitalization of its listed companies, average daily trading volume, or any other relevant measure. It seems clear that the NYSE, even as it continues to evolve for changing times, is here to stay.

* * *

Another organization that I helped lead during a period of turmoil was the insurance giant Aetna. Probably my biggest contributions to the turnaround that Aetna enjoyed in the early 2000s were setting a sound strategic direction and managing the executive team that brought order, focus, and stability to the company's complicated business lines after eliminating those that didn't fit with Aetna's mission. Also high on the list was my role in recruiting and hiring Jack Rowe and Ron Williams, who led the company as it moved out of several unprofitable lines of business in the health care area in 2002, decreasing its membership count from 19 million to 13 million. Aetna then launched a new period of expansion based on organic growth through introducing innovative new health care products and attracting new customers rather than through company acquisitions. Revenues and profitability grew accordingly.

In response, Aetna's share price also rose dramatically; it reached one peak in December 2007, after seven years of steady improvement, took a hit (along with the rest of the market) in the Great Recession of 2008–2009, and then resumed its steady upward march, which has basically continued to this day.

Even more important, Jack and Ron continued the process of improving relations with the health care community and rebuilding damaged employee morale. In October 2003, a federal judge in Florida approved a settlement between Aetna and approximately one million physicians who had accused the company of cheating them on payments and interfering with patient care. The settlement included direct payments to physicians and improvements in both the transparency and the fairness of Aetna's claims-payment processes, and bore a price tag of around $470 million. A lot of money, yes—but a reasonable investment in winning over some of Aetna's most important stakeholders, and a big step toward achieving a new status as the best-respected company in the health insurance business. Doctors, nurses, and patients began talking about how Aetna had been transformed from a skinflint insurer into a caring, responsible partner. By 2008, Aetna had begun a multi-year run as number one in the *Fortune* magazine ranking of most admired companies in "Health Care: Insurance and Managed Care" category.

The new Aetna also played a positive role in the national effort to reform our dysfunctional health care system. Aetna led the industry in helping to shape the legislation that ultimately became the Affordable Care Act (ACA) of 2010—sometimes called Obamacare. Ron's position as a leading expert on health care reform helped Aetna to become a top provider of coverage to millions of newly insured customers through the state exchanges created under ACA.

However, as everyone knows, U.S. health care continues to be an arena of economic, social, and political turmoil. Today, the future of Obamacare is uncertain. The 2017 repeal, by a Republican-led Congress, of the individual mandate to purchase health insurance—one of the linchpins of the insurance exchange system established by Obamacare—has called into question the long-term stability of the private health insurance market.

As a result, many companies in the American health care industry are struggling to reposition themselves for survival in an unpredictable future. Aetna is no exception. In 2015, Aetna announced a plan to acquire rival insurer Humana for some $34 billion—only to have the deal thwarted by a federal judge's ruling, in January 2017, that the merger would reduce the choices available to senior citizens. Then, in December 2017, an even more dramatic merger was proposed, this time with Aetna as the target company. CVS Health, owners of one of the country's biggest drug store chains, sought to purchase Aetna for $69 billion.

In the years to come, it will be fascinating to see the kinds of new synergies that health care executives will strive to develop based on combinations like the CVS-Aetna merger. Hopefully, American citizens will find that their access to high-quality, affordable health care will be enhanced by the new corporate giants that are emerging in this volatile business arena.

* * *

Finally, let's take a look back at my leadership role at the Securities and Exchange Commission, from 2003 to 2005.

In retrospect, it's clear that my efforts to embed a proactive approach to financial regulation achieved mixed success. Many departments and individual staffers within the SEC grasped the value of the philosophy I sought to instill; many of them eagerly embraced the concept of "risk intelligence gathering" as a crucial role of the agency. As a result, the SEC began doing a better job of "looking around corners and over hills" than it once did. During 2016, one agency staffer told my old deputy Peter Derby, "We used to see the financial markets in a black-and-white snapshot. Now we're getting an image of them in full color—and we're gradually moving toward high-definition video."

However, some of the specific tools that my leadership team created are no longer being used by the SEC in the same way. In September 2009, the Office of Risk Assessment that we launched was reorganized and renamed the Division of Economic and Risk Analysis. Under the new name, it ceased conducting ear-to-the-ground investigations of issues in the financial markets and instead basically restricted itself to large-scale data analysis. This is a valuable activity, but it's no substitute for the kind of personal networking with industry insiders we hoped to make the norm.

Even more frustrating, the public tip line for reporting potential financial fraud we launched was shut down soon after my departure in August 2005. Fortunately, under the impetus of the 2010 Dodd-Frank reforms, the SEC subsequently launched a new tip line that soon began to uncover cases of fraud and other misdoings.

Despite the vagaries of Washington, the overwhelming majority of the reforms instituted on my watch remained in force after my departure from the SEC, including the various rules and regulations promulgated under Sarbanes-Oxley. (And to the credit of my successor Christopher Cox, the SEC under his chairmanship was generally strongly supportive of those rules and enforced them fairly and appropriately.)

However, ensuring that financial markets operate with fairness and integrity is a never-ending battle. In the years since I left the SEC, that battle has raged on, reflecting a continual series of political and economic shifts.

In 2008–2009, the bursting of a giant housing bubble helped lead to one of the biggest financial collapses in history, which in turn helped generate the worst economic crisis since the Great Depression.

One response to what some have called the Great Recession was the establishment by President Barack Obama of the Economic Recovery Advisory Board. This was an informal group of experts charged with providing feedback and guidance on economic policy from "beyond the echo chamber of Washington, D.C.," as the president put it when announcing the board's formation in February 2009. The board was led by Paul Volcker, the distinguished former chairman of the Federal Reserve Board, and I was one of fifteen other members, drawn from business, academia, and the nonprofit sector, as well as from both political parties. It was an honor for me to be named to the board, and a number of the ideas we proposed were sensible ones, focused on topics like tax reform, simplification of corporate regulations, and employment-boosting initiatives. Unfortunately, as often happens in Washington, the board's recommendations went largely ignored by the administration and Congress, and it ceased to exist early in 2012.

A more substantial response to the financial crisis was the 2010 Dodd-Frank reforms, mentioned in Chapter 10. These new accounting regulations were driven by the desire to prevent Wall Street firms from engaging in excesses like those that helped to precipitate the collapse of 2008–2009, thereby ensuring greater transparency and trust throughout the business and financial communities.

Now, as of early 2018, a political battle is taking shape in Washington over the future of Dodd-Frank. Conservative Republicans, who dominate Congress and control the White House, are looking for opportunities to eliminate some of the 2010 law's provisions, perhaps making it easier for financial firms to go back to some of the abusive practices that helped cause the crash. We'll see what happens next.

* * *

After a lifetime of leadership roles in organizations from different sectors—for-profit business, a prestigious university, and two governmental agencies—it's not surprising that a look back at the long-term outcomes I achieved reveals a mixed bag of successes and disappointments. No individual can control the future of any institution once he or she departs. All you can hope is that, during your time as an entrepreneurial leader, you helped to develop a culture of integrity, achievement, and camaraderie, hired people with the right skills and values, and built organizational structures designed to foster lasting success.

If you've done all those things, you can glance back at history with a sense of inner satisfaction, knowing you did your best to create circumstances in which those who followed in your footsteps would have an opportunity to build on your work. It gives me some sense of satisfaction that I can do that.

Image Credits (continued from copyright page)

Page 7, Gerald Ford and Nelson Rockefeller: Official White House photos.

Page 8, Yale Corporation: Yale University Corporation and University Advisory Groups Photographs (RU 751). Manuscripts and Archives, Yale University Library.

Page 8, Dean of Yale SOM: Copyright Yale University, reprinted by permission.

Page 9, Kingman Brewster: Copyright Yale University, reprinted by permission.

Page 9, opening ceremony: Copyright Yale University, reprinted by permission.

Page 10, George H. W. Bush: Official White House photo.

Page 10, Reagan and Gorbachev: © 1992 NYSE Group, Inc. Used with permission of NYSE Group, Inc.

Page 12, *Institutional Investor* magazine: Reprinted by permission of PARS International Corp.

Page 12, George W. Bush: Official White House photo.

Page 13, HBS Alumni Bulletin: Reprinted by permission of Alumni Marketing and Communications, Harvard Business School.

Page 13, *Institutional Investor* magazine: Reprinted by permission of PARS International Corp.

Page 13, SEC staffers: Courtesy of the Securities and Exchange Commission Historical Society.

Page 14, SEC triumvirate: Courtesy of the Securities and Exchange Commission Historical Society.

Page 14, *Wall Street Journal* cartoon: Reprinted by permission of The Wall Street Journal.

Page 15, Barack Obama: Official White House photo.

Source Notes

1. Jerome Karabel, *The Chosen: The Hidden History of Admission and Exclusion at Harvard, Yale, and Princeton* (Houghton Mifflin, 2005); quoted in "In and Out" [book review] by John Silber, *Boston Globe*, October 30, 2005.

2. "Richard Jenrette," interview, Harvard Business School *Entrepreneurs* series, http://www.hbs.edu/xentrepreneurs /richardjenrette.html.

3. "Dan Lufkin," interview, Harvard Business School *Entrepreneurs* series, http://www.hbs.edu/xentrepreneurs/danlufkin.html.

4. "Richard Jenrette," interview, Harvard Business School *Entrepreneurs* series, *op. cit.*

5. Jeffrey Schmalz, "Ford Heirs Fight, and Entertain, in Seeking Estate," *New York Times,* October 1, 1988.

6. Robert J. McCartney, "William Donaldson, Seeking to Reform the Stock Market," *Washington Post,* March 2, 1991.

7. Kurt Eichenwald, "A Leaner but Not So Mean Wall St." *New York Times*, October 19, 1992.

8. Justin Schack, "Can Bill Donaldson Save Aetna?" *Institutional Investor,* July 1, 2000.

9. Milt Freudenheim, "Aetna Plans a Recovery: H.M.O.'s May Not Make It," *New York Times,* March 19, 2000.

10. Aetna Annual Report 1999.

11. Schack, *op. cit.*

12. Schack, *op. cit.*

13. Johanna Bennett, "Aetna Told to 'Take Steps Now' to Boost Value— Activist," *Wall Street Journal,* April 7, 2000.

14. Laurie Ledgard, "While Aetna's Not for Sale, Word Is It's Hot to Split," *Hartford Business Journal,* May 8, 2000.

15. Diane Levick, "Lid Stays On at Aetna Meeting," *Hartford Courant,* April 29, 2000.

16. Johanna Bennett, "Aetna Eases Rules in Connecticut as It Mends Managed-Care Fences," *Wall Sreet Journal*, May 11, 2000.

17. Diane Levick, Andrew Julien, and Hilary Waldman, "Aetna to Loosen Controls," *Hartford Courant*, May 11, 2000,

18. Diane Levick, "New Health for Ailing Aetna," *Hartford Courant*, July 9, 2000.

19. 1080 News, WTIC-AM Radio, Hartford/New Haven Conn., July 20, 2000.

20. Pamela L. Moore, "The Right Doctor for Aetna?" *Business Week,* May 1, 2000.

21. Bill Brubaker, "Insurer's Makeover Has Come Up Short on Promise of Change, Long on Lawsuits," *Wall Street Journal,* February 25, 2001.

22. James J. Cramer, "Lies My Broker Told Me," *New York Magazine,* January 6, 2003.

23. Greg Farrell, "Donaldson Shifts from Manager to Marine as Chairman of SEC," *USA Today,* September 11, 2003.

24. John Cranford, "Lightning Rod on Wall Street," *Congressional Quarterly Weekly,* May 30, 2005.

25. "Hedge Fund Hubris," *Wall Street Journal,* October 2004.

26. Amy Borrus, "Stick to Your Guns, Mr. Donaldson," *Business Week,* May 24, 2004.

27. "FEI Survey: Average 2007 SOX Compliance Cost $1.7 Million," *DSS Resources,* http://dssresources.com/news/2490.php.

28. "Panel 1 of a Hearing of the Senate Banking, Housing, and Urban Affairs Committee," November 30, 2003, https://votesmart.org/public-statement/26413/panel-i-of-a-hearing-of-the-senate-banking-housing-and-urban-affairs-committee#.WCXCczLMyqA.

29. Letter from William H. Donaldson, Chairman, Securities and Exchange Commission, to The Honorable H. Carl McCall, Chairman, Human Resources and Compensation Committee, New York Stock Exchange, Inc., September 2, 2003.

30. Christopher Hilbert and Joseph McLaughlin, *The Donaldson Years at the SEC,* paper presented at the 12th Queen's Annual Business Law Symposium (Kingston, Ontario), October 14, 2005.

31. Justin Schack, "The Pioneers," *Institutional Investor,* October 1, 2001, https://www.institutionalinvestor.com/article/b15134m9hgz5mt/the-pioneers.

Acknowledgments

When I first conceived of writing a memoir, I had no real idea what it would entail. My wife, Jane, and my children had been suggesting to me over the years that I should do it. I had resisted for quite a while, perhaps having an intuition about how much time, effort, blood, and sweat it would take.

But here I am. Hopefully the book will be interesting and helpful to the people who will read it, quiet my family, and give me the satisfaction of having examined my life and told my story.

I will start by thanking my family for pushing me. I'm especially grateful to Jane, who has been a true partner throughout the project, reminding me about things to include, keeping me honest, and periodically suggesting what to omit. She also dusted off her copyediting skills from long ago to tighten up the manuscript.

Karl Weber has been a true collaborator, overseeing the research and the writing, and managing me! His style and mine meshed well, and his content and organizational suggestions have made this a better book. And through a long and complex process, he has exhibited the patience of Job!

Although they are too numerous to thank individually, I also want to acknowledge all the people who worked with me over time, helped me achieve what I did in moving institutions forward, and hopefully benefited from my entrepreneurial leadership style. In particular, I would like to thank Dick Jenrette, Patrick Von Bargen, and Peter Derby, who gave of their time to be interviewed by Karl during the course of developing the book.

Marisa Parascandola, my assistant, was invaluable at the logistics level, especially handling all the scheduling, pictures, and permissions.

I'm grateful to my daughter, Kim Donaldson, who devoted time and talent to suggest additions that were very helpful to me. My friend Tina Weiner drew upon her impressive background in the publishing industry to provide advice and guidance as I navigated the unfamiliar journey of authorship. Also, SOM alumni Jed Bernstein, Henry and Cathy Lanier, my sister-in-law Nancy Phillips, and Jeff Yudkoff helped to make that chapter come alive.

And, of course, I want to thank the people at Greenleaf, an entrepreneurial publishing house itself that represents the best of this new, increasingly popular breed of hybrid publishing. Their staff members, including project manager Tyler LeBleu, editor April Murphy, designer Neil Gonzalez, distribution lead Kristine Peyre-Ferry, marketing lead Chelsea Richards, and consultant Justin Branch, were a pleasure to work with and helped ensure that this book would be published with a high degree of professionalism.

It goes without saying that any misrepresentations or errors that have found their way past us all are my responsibility.

Now I can finally relax!

About the Authors

William H. Donaldson

William H. Donaldson is currently chairman of Donaldson Enterprises. Earlier in his career, Mr. Donaldson served as the 27th chairman of the Securities and Exchange Commission. The cofounder of the financial firm Donaldson, Lufkin & Jenrette; he was also chairman, president, and CEO of Aetna Inc.; chairman and CEO of the New York Stock Exchange; and founding dean of the Yale Graduate School of Management. Previously, he was undersecretary of state to Henry Kissinger and counsel to Vice President Nelson Rockefeller. Mr. Donaldson has been a director of numerous publicly held corporations and privately owned businesses and was selected as Businessman of the Year by the Associated Press in 1970.

Currently, Mr. Donaldson serves as chairman of the Financial Services Volunteer Corps, is a director of the Volcker Alliance, and is a member of the FDIC Systemic Resolution Advisory Committee. He was also a member of President Obama's original Economic Recovery Advisory Board. Over the years, Mr.

Donaldson has served on boards of many philanthropic, art, and educational institutions, including the Ford Foundation, Lincoln Center for the Performing Arts, Yale University, and the Aspen Institute.

He holds a BA from Yale University, an MBA with distinction from the Harvard Business School, and is a Chartered Financial Analyst. He served as a first lieutenant in the U.S. Marine Corps in the Far Eastern theater (Japan-Korea). Mr. Donaldson, the father of three and the grandfather of three, lives with his wife Jane in New York City and Waccabuc, New York.

Karl Weber

Karl Weber is a writer and editor who specializes in topics relating to business, politics, current affairs, history, and social issues.

Among other works, Weber has coauthored three books with Muhammad Yunus, founder of Grameen Bank and winner of the 2006 Nobel Peace Prize, including the *New York Times* best seller *Creating a World Without Poverty*. Weber also edited three best-selling books by former President Jimmy Carter, as well as the number one best seller *What Happened: Inside the Bush White House and Washington's Culture of Deception* by former White House Press Secretary Scott McClellan.